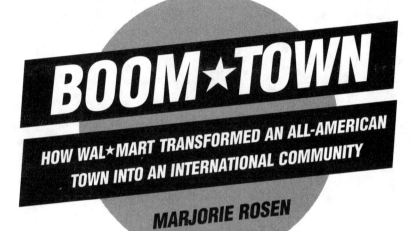

BOOM★TOWN

HOW WAL★MART TRANSFORMED AN ALL-AMERICAN TOWN INTO AN INTERNATIONAL COMMUNITY

MARJORIE ROSEN

CHICAGO
REVIEW
PRESS

Library of Congress Cataloging-in-Publication Data
Rosen, Marjorie.
  Boom town : how Wal-Mart transformed an all-American town into an
international community / Marjorie Rosen.
     p. cm.
  Includes bibliographical references and index.
  ISBN 978-1-55652-948-1 (hbk.)
  1. Wal-Mart (Firm) 2. Diversity in the workplace—Social aspects—Arkansas—
Bentonville. 3. Multiculturalism—Arkansas—Bentonville. 4. Bentonville (Ark.)—
Commerce—Social aspects. 5. Bentonville (Ark.)—Social conditions. I. Title.

  HF5429.219.U6R67 2009
  305.8009767′13—dc22

                              2009023528

Interior design: Sarah Olson
Map: Chris Erichsen

© 2009 by Marjorie Rosen
Published by Chicago Review Press, Incorporated
814 North Franklin Street
Chicago, Illinois 60610
ISBN 978-1-55652-948-1
Printed in the United States of America
5 4 3 2 1

In memory of my father

And for my own spirited multicultural family

Contents

DIVERSITY COMES TO NORTHWEST ARKANSAS

TOWNS AND TOWNIES, THEN AND NOW

THE HISPANIC EXPLOSION

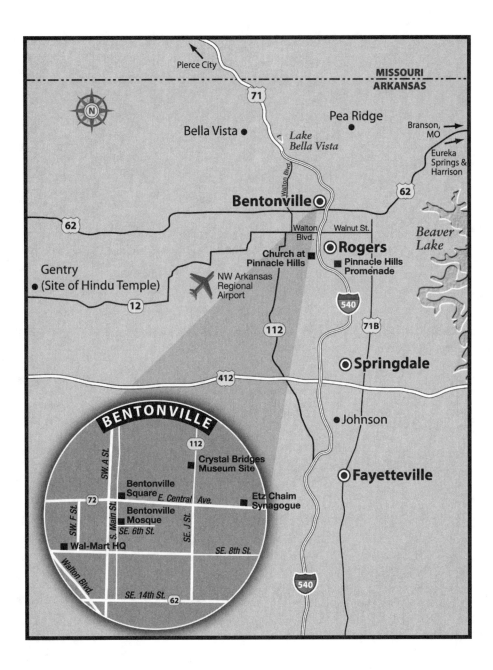

A Note from the Author

. . . .

Boom Town: How Wal-Mart Transformed an All-American Town into an International Community is a major departure and challenge for me in terms of subject matter and scope, since throughout most of my career I have been a working journalist specializing in movies, women's issues, and popular culture. What initially attracted me to Bentonville as a microcosm for social and cultural change in the United States was an article in the New York Times on June 20, 2006, with the headline "In Wal-Mart's Home, Synagogue Signals Growth," about a small group of Jews, most of whom had migrated south to work for Wal-Mart in its Bentonville, Arkansas, office. I thought the struggles of these Jews in a rural and almost totally Baptist community might be an interesting departure point for a book, and so I contacted Etz Chaim, the new synagogue, and six months later traveled down to Bentonville to spend Hanukkah with its congregation.

Yet once I started learning about Bentonville and Northwest Arkansas, I decided that that story—the saga of its budding multiculturalism—was much bigger and more compelling than that of the Jewish community alone. Much to my surprise, I discovered that there were also growing pockets of Hindus, Muslims, and Laotians who had settled in the town that Sam Walton and Wal-Mart had put on the map. What's more, the area boasted burgeoning communities of Hispanics and Marshall Islanders. And so I started to investigate, to read, and most of all to talk to people in the community.

During the past two and a half years I have made numerous trips to Northwest Arkansas and interviewed more than 150 residents who live there, both longtime locals and transplants, speaking with many of them a number of times in the course of my research. I thank them all for being so forthcoming. Still, for reasons that are sometimes apparent and sometimes private, I have used pseudonyms to protect certain people's identities.

It is my good fortune to have made friends among these men and women who have shared their Hanukkahs, Passovers, Easter Sundays, and Yom Kippurs with me, as well as their searing hot summer afternoons and fiercely bitter winter nights, their sudden ice storms and Northwest Arkansas power outages. Like Bentonville itself, which is responsive to and reflective of so many events—the roller-coaster global economy and the deepening recession, as well as various elections, community issues, and newly forged immigration laws—the lives of the area's people are in constant passage. Studying a town, I have found, is very much like watching a living organism morph and grow. Sometimes changes are imperceptible; occasionally, they are dramatic; and often, they are surprising. And in the end, I believe that this journalistic study captures the tapestry of a world in transition and underscores the changing nature of rural America as a land of increasing multiculturalism, diversity, and opportunity.

Introduction

. . . .

This is the story of an American town and the people who live there—a town that was once rural, snow white, and emphatically Christian. Like so many other small towns across our nation, it is in the process of undergoing dramatic and once-unimaginable changes that are affecting its workforce and religious life and completely redefining its sense of community.

Bentonville, Arkansas, is known primarily as the town that Sam Walton built and the world headquarters of Wal-Mart, until April 2009 the largest and most controversial U.S. corporation.[1] Owing to the gradual urbanization of this tiny Bible Belt community over the past decade—the way it is changing from an all-white, largely Baptist world and one-time "sundown town" into a diverse society like that which we find in our big cities—Bentonville might just represent the new face of small-town America.

Bentonville is located in Benton County in the northwest corner of Arkansas, the second-poorest state in the nation. Yet in the past seven years, its population has exploded to thirty thousand, growing by 40 percent; and, along with neighboring communities that make up Northwest Arkansas, it has become a major boom town, dotted with fancy malls, ethnic restaurants, and plastic surgery centers. This is thanks, in part, to the fact that not only Wal-Mart but also two other major employers, Tyson Foods and J. B. Hunt Trucking, have headquarters in the area.

But the primary reason for the area's growth is that in recent years Wal-Mart executives and suppliers have immigrated here from such big cities as Chicago, New York, and L.A., and from countries as far-flung as India, Mexico, and Peru. Some of these men and women are Jews (they recently founded the first synagogue in the area in fifty years); others are Hindus, Muslims, and Mormons. Still others are minorities, including Hispanic immigrants, Laotians, Marshallese, and African Americans. In fact, Springdale has the largest population of Marshallese in the country. And Northwest Arkansas's Hispanic population, which has grown by 51 percent in the past five years, is, according to a 2007 Winthrop Rockefeller Foundation study, the fastest growing in the nation.

Because Bentonville has always been so emphatically Christian (at last count there were more than 261 churches in the area), with much of its population not just worshipping on Sunday mornings but also spending weekday nights at Bible study and church get-togethers, the trajectory of its recent evolution is that much more remarkable. For the story of this community, and its men and women, is, in a sense, that of this country's national, religious, and cultural identities in flux. It is the story of cultures clashing and cultures embracing and enriching one another. And almost all propelled by Wal-Mart.

When Sam Walton arrived in Bentonville in 1950, it suited him fine that the town was a nondescript Ozark backwater—the kind that cartoonist Al Capp poked fun at when he created the hillbilly outpost Dogpatch for his comic strip *Li'l Abner*. Bentonville, in fact, suited Sam's wife, Helen, even better. The couple had moved sixteen times during their first two years of marriage, and as they searched for a new locale to raise a family and create a business, she warned him, "I'll go any place you want so long as you don't ask me to live in a big city. Ten thousand people is enough for me."

With a population of a mere twenty-nine hundred, this town, which Helen called "sad looking," had plenty of room to grow before the young couple might feel the need to push on, and room, too, for a retail store right on the bustling Bentonville Square—Walton's 5 & 10.[2] What's more, it was rural and well situated, with enough good quail hunting in neighboring Oklahoma, Missouri, and Kansas, as well as Arkansas itself, for Walton to indulge his passion year-round.

For most of the latter half of the twentieth century, Bentonville sprouted by small increments, even if Walton's business, which he named Wal-Mart in 1962, expanded wildly. In October 1970, Walton took his company public, selling 300,000 shares of stock at $16.50 apiece. By 1979 the company was doing a billion dollars' worth of business a year. As for its population, tiny Bentonville had almost tripled, numbering 8,756 by then, although it was still well under Helen's magic no-no of 10,000. More to the point, it remained Bible Belt Christian and white as grits.

Today miles of strip malls featuring fast-food restaurants and chain stores are replacing the farms and fields that stippled the landscape as recently as five years ago. Motels and gasoline stations stand guard, like soldiers, along the recently widened Interstate 540, the major artery connecting Bentonville to communities like Bella Vista in the north and Rogers, Springdale, and Fayetteville to the south. At almost every turn there are new housing subdivisions advertising sprawling five-thousand-square-foot homes with cathedral ceilings, clerestory windows, and double living rooms—a far cry from the small Craftsman stone bungalows and Victorian cottages lining Central Avenue, the street that runs into Bentonville Square, the former center. Rush hour traffic now bottlenecks the way to Pinnacle Hills, where the garish Church at Pinnacle Hills, with its trio of crosses towering over the highway, stops traffic on its own.

Bulging at the seams, Bentonville seems like a small town on steroids. The population now spills randomly into Rogers, Springdale, and Fayetteville, so that it is difficult even to define Bentonville—Greater Bentonville basically encompasses most of Northwest Arkansas, with a population of three hundred thousand.

The major fact of Bentonville-proper is that the Wal-Mart home office, at the intersection of South Walton Boulevard and Southwest Eighth Street, anchors the town and the county. Wherever people have chosen to live, they work here, hold twice-a-week meetings with vendors here, and, until recently, attended mandatory 7:00 A.M. Saturday cheerleading sessions here (now the army of company cheerleaders is so large that the home office has had to move the meetings to the huge auditorium at Bentonville High School to accommodate them).

This was not the normal progression of small-town America. The seeds of the boom go back to 1987, when Sam Walton decided to partner with Wal-Mart's suppliers, sharing computer information with them for a more effective relationship. His decision immediately created a need for a larger and more sophisticated IT department. Then, sometime in the early 1990s, as relationships grew closer, Wal-Mart made it known, although never in writing, that it expected its vendors to have a presence in the area. Suddenly, Schlitz, Procter & Gamble, IBM, and other major companies were sending teams of their best sales, marketing, and technology people to live in Bentonville to accommodate Wal-Mart, which was, by then, everyone's number-one sales outlet.

By 1994, Wal-Mart employed more than four hundred thousand people worldwide. The company hired the African American human resources ace Coleman Peterson to head up what management liked to call the People Division. His mandates were to keep the company's top employees in the fold and to diversify, diversify, diversify. Which he did. Slowly, Bentonville, the tight-knit, white Christian community, started to change. This meant that a variety of well-educated urban types of all ethnicities and religions, often with MBAs or advanced engineering degrees, began migrating to the area.

Before long, kaleidoscopic change was overwhelming the town. People who arrived even five years ago cannot believe how it has simply mushroomed from a small, unsophisticated area into a boom town. As more people arrived, more construction was necessary. And so more people arrived.

Certainly, we have all heard of company towns. Hollywood is one. Silicon Valley, while not precisely a town, qualifies. Detroit and Rochester, as well. Bentonville, home of the world's largest retail corporation, which these days brings in revenues of more than $400 billion annually, is indisputably another.

And in many ways Wal-Mart has turned out to be a surprisingly good neighbor. Never mind, for now, the well-publicized outcries against the corporation for its poor insurance coverage of its more than two million employees; never mind the landmark class action suit charging institutional discrimination on behalf of its female employees; never mind the secrecy, petty firings, and spying on reporters (which Wal-Mart, by the way, denies having had anything to do with). And, for the time being, take no notice of the company's remorselessly antiunion stance. Despite all that, Wal-Mart has set a forward-thinking tone in its own backyard.

Granted, the goal has self-evident rewards: the better the schools, roads, and law enforcement, the higher the quality of employees that the company and its vendor partners can lure here and keep happy. And so, Wal-

Mart has made grants to the schools; to local summer camps for disadvantaged children; to the high school's football field, Tiger Stadium; and to help build a stunning new public library.

"Wal-Mart is a good corporate partner, and we have an excellent relationship," says Bentonville's police chief, James Allen. "If we were going to put on a program for the kids at the Youth Police Academy and were running short of funds, we might call them and say, 'We need $1,500 to do this,' and they'd write a check for it. It's a good relationship. But we're not a company police department. We're here for everybody."

Undeniably, the presence of Tyson Foods and J. B. Hunt, the area's two other billion-dollar companies, also contributes to its prosperity and diversity. The growth and suppleness of these three industries have conspired to create, from this one-time economically deprived farming community, an economy to be reckoned with. Up until this point, the plenitude of jobs for unskilled workers combined with inexpensive living conditions has also attracted the area's burgeoning Hispanic population, which has increased by 51 percent since 2000.

The consequences? Cold stark fear—at least, among a segment of the white Christian majority, which sees its comfortable, all-white way of life fading. "Now there are traffic jams and gang activity, and just go into the emergency room," says Doris Lewis, who like her husband, William, has lived in Fayetteville her entire life, "and it's full of 'those people' getting free health care."[3]

Certainly, Northwest Arkansas is trying, for better or worse, to address this population explosion. The school systems have had to gear up to teach English to Hispanic students, and law enforcement officials are suddenly, and some say, hysterically, worried about gang violence. Even though there has been little proof of such activity, they have sent teams of police officers for federal training in gang detection, just as they have enrolled others in a program with the Immigration and Customs Enforcement agency (ICE). Known as 287(g), this program allows them to detain immigrants who do not have proper documentation.

Yet the dominant culture has accepted new groups such as the Muslims, Hindus, Jews, Laotians, and Mormons, in part because their numbers are smaller and a substantial number of them tend to be better educated and more middle class.

And how exactly has Wal-Mart helped to shape its suddenly multicultural community? Go into a Wal-Mart, and you find good value, which Sam Walton always insisted on passing to his customers, often at the expense of his "associates," the term used to describe all Wal-Mart employees, from the checkout cashier in a small store to the CEO. By giving good value, Wal-Mart swallowed up the small stores in Walton's own town. Today while local strip malls thrive, as do Wal-Mart Supercenters and Sam's Clubs, the one-time center of town, situated around Bentonville Square, where Walton opened his first variety store, is struggling to survive.

Wal-Mart's fingerprints are everywhere in Bentonville and Northwest Arkansas. Even the look of the new boom town resembles that of a Wal-Mart store: it is nothing if not functional. Take the Wal-Mart home office, an efficient one-story red brick shell on the outside with functional battleship-gray walls and floors inside. No lamps are permitted to offset the brutal fluorescent lighting. Not a penny extra has been spent to make the environment pleasing. Work space is cramped, bathrooms, untidy. In the home office, almost every associate works in this utilitarian atmosphere, redolent of those Soviet apartment blocs built to dampen the spirit of individualism. Wal-Mart Supercenters, designed like oversized military Quonset huts, are not much better.

Similarly, the public landscape, to a visitor driving down Walton Boulevard or along Interstate 540, reflects the same just-built, boom town pragmatism. No town planning here, and no personality—no visual appeal, no gesture of elegance or even whimsy. Just miles of one- and two-story office parks (also called business campuses) and strip malls. Oh, look, there's Wendy's, McDonald's, The Olive Garden—fill in the blank. Oh, look, the Marriott, the Comfort Inn, La Quinta. Oh, look, the police station—or is it a public school? Not even the churches, which look alike, save for the slavishly modern Pinnacle, have personality. The cumulative effect is one of congenial blandness.

Only Fayetteville, the southernmost town in Northwest Arkansas, escapes this unimaginative sameness, in part because it is older, bigger, and more established. Besides, as home to the University of Arkansas, the town has a history of its own going back to the nineteenth century. It has also nurtured such well-known architects as Edward Durrell Stone and E. Fay Jones, who designed Sam Walton's home. Fayetteville even has a landmark commission, which has helped to retain its character.

And yet Bentonville may be in the process of learning. Perhaps the bland will be transformed into the stylish when the Crystal Bridges Museum of

American Art, within walking distance of Bentonville Square, opens in 2011. Built as a $60 million valentine from Sam's daughter, Alice Walton, to her hometown, it has been designed by Israeli-born artist Moshe Safdie as a showcase for world-class American art. So far Walton has been buying up important works by Winslow Homer, John Singer Sargent, and Gilbert Stuart, among others.

The debut of Crystal Bridges will be something of a coming-out party for Bentonville, one more step in its transformation from shy country bumpkin into strutting, nouveau-riche debutante and pseudo-urban arriviste.

However, there is one current wrinkle in prosperity that has yet to be fully played out—the national recession and subprime mortgage crisis, both of which are creeping dampers on the local economy. With cheap immigrant labor fleeing because of the freeze in construction and the aggressive enactment of the harsh federal 287(g) program, who will build the houses and malls, and who will eviscerate the chickens on the lines? Will the boom go bust? And what kind of impact will it have on individual lives?

The saga of Bentonville resonates for another reason as well. In post-9/11 America, bitter differences of political opinion and religious conviction exist at home and abroad. Public animosity and intolerance divides Muslims and Jews in the Middle East; and here at home, despite President Barack Obama's emphatic victory and the critical tasks that faced him immediately on assuming office, rancor and hostility still define Republican and Democratic politics. This makes it all the more important for us to be able to read about a place in this country where people of different faiths and ethnic backgrounds have come together, attempting to live harmoniously for the common good. In Bentonville, Christians, Muslims, Jews, African Americans, Hindus, Latinos, Mormons, Laotians, Marshallese, and Hispanics are living and working side by side and, for the most part, prospering. Occasionally they stumble, but together they are creating a world far more diverse, rich, and exciting than when the town existed simply as a whites-only stopover between Joplin, Missouri, and Little Rock.

After all, the town that Sam Walton built has relevance for these precarious times, with our overriding concerns about money, religion, immigration, and ethnicity. The story of how this rural Ozark community became urbanized and diversified is also the story of our evolving American society, showing us that what unites us, when given a chance, is far stronger than what divides us.

Part I

. . . .

DIVERSITY COMES TO
NORTHWEST ARKANSAS

1

A Black Man Redefines
a White Company

··········

When Wal-Mart decided that it was necessary to create diversity in its home office, the company hired a black man from St. Louis and brought him to white-bread Bentonville to take on the job as head of human resources.

And so Coleman Peterson, a tall, elegant, and immaculately tailored African American, arrived in town in April 1994, a few weeks before his pretty, light-skinned wife, Shirley, and their two children. What Peterson and his family found was a world that was profoundly different from the diverse urban environment they had just left. "Bentonville was not only white, but it was also rural," he observes. "The environment here was everything *but* urban. So were the types of homes, the availability of restaurants, art, entertainment, and music. What I did find, however, were honest, kind, hard-working people. Also, the Wal-Mart culture was a terrific place to be."

Peterson readily admits that it was difficult to uproot his family, in part because of reasons such as the one above. "We had a lovely home in St. Louis. The kids were in great schools, and we really didn't want to move,"

11

he says. "But I could see that Wal-Mart was going to be larger and more successful, and from a career point of view, it was a good move for me. Also, I could see Wal-Mart's future and how it was going to influence the global economy. It was a fantastic opportunity for someone who cared about people. I told my wife that I was going to commit to ten years and then retire and do other things I wanted to do. So I started on April 30, 1994, and retired on April 30, 2004, although I still do independent consulting for the company."

As head of Wal-Mart's human resources (HR)—the People Division— Peterson had a goal to hold on to the company's top employees by offering perks and opportunities and to cast a wide net in an effort to bring diversity to the company's four hundred thousand employees worldwide.

Although he grew up in the inner city of Chicago during the late 1950s and 1960s, Coleman Peterson learned important diversity lessons early on. The son of a corrections officer and a clerk who worked in a retail warehouse, he was a gifted student who won a place at Lane Technical High, one of the best schools in the city at the time.

"Out of fifty-five hundred students, all males, there were only six or seven African American boys," he says. "And here I got my first sense of diversity. Before that, my world was simple—you were either black or white. Yet here students referred to themselves in different ways. You were German or Irish or Polish or Swedish, Catholic or Jewish. And I was like, 'I don't understand these differentials. You're all *white!*' But then I began to understand that the world makes differences—they're not intended to be bad or negative, it's just that we like to put people into categories. That's how we define and process things. And so because of that, I developed a nondefensive approach to race and ethnicity. And since I was naturally curious about other people's backgrounds, I thought it was fair turnabout for them to be equally curious about mine."

Peterson, who holds a bachelor's degree in English literature and a master's degree in industrial relations, both from Loyola University in Chicago, understood, on joining Wal-Mart, not only that he had to diversify, but that it was even more important to modernize the company's thinking regarding hiring.

"For me, the challenge was to bring the human resources group into the twentieth century," he says, explaining that Wal-Mart's HR organization back then was as unsophisticated as Bentonville itself. It was structured neither traditionally nor with people who had HR experience. "Most of the company's HR people at that time had been promoted out of the operating side of the business," he explains. "So they were experienced operators and had good people skills and values. They also understood the Wal-Mart culture. But they weren't necessarily trained in the basics of recruitment compensation or in organizational and training development. My challenge was to begin to try to professionalize the HR group.'"

Peterson also intuited that in this unpolished, simple, old-boy environment, he could not just stroll in, take charge, and start throwing the current HR buzzwords at his more rural colleagues. "I understood that in order to be effective, you couldn't come in using all these highfalutin terms," he says. "You had to reduce things to the lowest common denominator because you were trying to drive an understanding and various initiatives through the organization. So I came up with something that I called 'Get, Keep, and Grow.' It was basic-speak for focusing on three areas that made the company better."

For Peterson, *Get* meant, obviously, "recruiting." "We began to pay more attention to whom we hired and how we hired them, and so we began to professionalize the recruiting process," he says.

The second part of his equation was *Keep*. In 1994, Wal-Mart's turnover rates were going through the roof. "Wal-Mart was like a leaky boat, and even if we got good people, we were losing them," he said. "So we had to focus on the second bucket, *Keep*, or 'retention.' And the subheads under retention were the following: improving our orientation program so that people could be successful in their jobs; improving the medical plan; and improving pay. We also needed to improve the feedback processes for which we said not only, 'We want you,' but, 'We want you to stay.'"

Finally, Peterson explained, there was the *Grow* section of the equation. "As the company expanded, we needed people to assume greater responsibilities," he says. "So this third part, or bucket, focused on training programs for entry-level people and development programs for leaders in order to make them more effective. In the end, I was focusing on everybody, from entry-level associates [employees] to executives."

Under his aegis, the company also developed a senior-level training process in which top-level vice presidents actually train officer-level management. "Rather than sending them to Harvard or Stanford for training," says Peterson, "if it was a finance topic, the chief operating officer taught it; if it was a human resources topic, I taught it; and if it was an operations topic, literally, the president of the company taught it. So it was a very high-level program which raised the level of senior managers." He also put into effect a process for succession planning. "What happens if the CEO gets hit by a bus?" he asks. "We have put into place a way of assessing talent once or twice a year, looking at available slots, and anticipating who is in the pipeline and what their potential is. That is part of senior-level develop-ment, too."

. . . .

Remarkably, in the ten years that Peterson presided over the Wal-Mart Peo-ple Division, the company almost tripled in size—to 1.1 million employees. What's more, in 1994, when Peterson arrived at Wal-Mart, the company, which had already reached more than a billion dollars in sales, employed fewer than 40 African American employees at its home office. Today, there are more than 1,000. (And the corporate Web site claims that the company employs more than 237,000 blacks around the globe.)

As for Wal-Mart's use of *associates* in place of *employees*, historian and Wal-Mart critic Nelson Lichtenstein aptly describes the term as an effort at "faux classlessness" and discusses the unspoken religiosity of Wal-Mart culture, citing *The Wal-Mart Way*, a 2005 book by Don Soderquist, the retired chief operating officer and senior vice chairman of Wal-Mart, Inc. Here, Soderquist, who now runs his own Soderquist Center for Leadership and Ethics, writes, "I'm not saying that Wal-Mart is a Christian company, but I can unequivocally say that Sam founded the company on the Judeo-Christian principles found in the Bible."[1]

Questioning some of Soderquist's assertions, Lichtenstein observes, "Actually, Walton took his Presbyterian identity rather lightly, and unlike Soderquist, who was a graduate of evangelical Wheaton College and has contributed heavily to like-minded Arkansas churches, the company founder thought profit sharing schemes and Ozark picnics more central to the Wal-Mart ethos than do contemporary executives. But Soderquist is right in emphasizing the extent to which Wal-Mart exists within a cultural universe that is Protestant even if corporate officers refrain from declaring this evangelical sensibility an overt component of the Wal-Mart culture."[2]

So it is all the more remarkable, then, that Coleman Peterson was hired to broaden that market. "I think a lot of people at Wal-Mart would give me credit for raising the profile of the diversity issue," he says. "There are a couple of aspects I concentrated on. The first was getting the dialogue on the table with the leaders about how important the issue of diversity is, and then defining it. And the second aspect was the whole issue of keeping score. In other words, how reflective are we of our communities? That is, what is our actual statistical performance in comparison to where we 'should' be?"

When Peterson came to Wal-Mart, it was with the understanding that he would reach out to minority and women's organizations in order to improve the company's diversity representation. In short order he began traveling to top-rated African American colleges like Howard University and to universities that were training young MBAs of all creeds and faiths. He began hiring middle- and upper-level managers for the home office, men and women who were from big cities such as New York, Chicago, Minneapolis, and Dallas and who were of different backgrounds and faiths—Jewish, Hindu, Muslim, and Mormon—coming from as far away as Pakistan, Bangladesh, Brazil, and Indonesia. Clearly he made a real difference among minorities, since today the organization is the nation's leading employer of Hispanics and African Americans.

And to answer criticism that minorities are brought in simply to fill low-wage positions, Peterson replies, "The entire U.S. Wal-Mart operation is run by a Hispanic, Ecuador-born Eduardo Castro-Wright; our external diversity operation is run by an African American woman, Charlyn Jarrells Porter; and our Asian operation by a Hispanic, Vicente Trius. One of our operational groups is run by an African American man, another by an African American woman."

Some in Bentonville also say that Peterson, because of his focus on bringing smart, diverse upper and middle managers into the fold, was more responsible than anyone else at the company for transforming the area into what locals call "Vendorville"—that is, a town where the major companies that sell to Wal-Mart have also established permanent offices and staffs. The arrival of these vendors and suppliers may account for two things: first, the fact that the population of Bentonville itself, between the years 2000 and 2007, grew by almost 40 percent, to 30,000, and second, the fact that the surrounding area has become so multiethnic and multiracial.

Peterson insists that, contrary to rumor, Wal-Mart has never had a policy in place that insists on the supplier's on-site presence. "Sometimes things that people have attributed to Wal-Mart have never been mandated by Wal-Mart," he says, adding that it is the third parties who are making decisions that they believe are in their best interest as it relates to Wal-Mart. "Walk a mile in a vendor's shoes," he adds. "You've got a business outlet that represents 20 percent of your company. Where are you going to be located? Does the majority interest have to tell you that it wants you there? Of course not."

Still, the difference between the ways companies now do business with Wal-Mart and the way they used to do it is striking. In 1994, says Peterson, Procter & Gamble sent 15 people to Bentonville to do the company's business with Wal-Mart; at the time P&G worked out of leased office space in Fayetteville. Now more than 250 P&G employees and their families live here, and the company has its own two-story office building. What's more, there are daily nonstop flights between Bentonville and Cincinnati, where P&G's home office is located.

The new and expanding vendor population contributed to the growing need for office parks, more and better housing, and more sophisticated support services in Northwest Arkansas. And the recruitment of Wal-Mart personnel—especially systems analysts and technology workers—from the finest MBA programs across the nation, from big U.S. cities, and from distant foreign countries has spawned an increasing diversity in the population, even though it remains heavily white, Baptist, and churchgoing. As it turns out, some of these men and women who have come to the area for the tremendous working opportunities, especially the women, choose to wear native garb to work and are encouraged to do so. In fact, so many people from various cultures are now working at the Bentonville office that Wal-Mart has instituted a local Diversity Committee, which meets monthly to help families better assimilate into both the corporate and local cultures.

"A lot of these diverse people that you see here are the results of Coleman's work," says Peterson's wife, whose nickname is Peaches. "I take a lot of pride in that." She is also proud, she says, that some people in the company call her husband "the culture keeper" because he preserves the culture of Sam Walton. "You should always be able to say what you think and be honest with people," she explains. "When Cole worked at Wal-Mart, he instituted what was called the open-door policy, where you did that with no repercussions."

Bad Press—or Bad Policies?

It is difficult to reconcile Peterson's push to diversify with the fact that Wal-Mart has been hammered in recent years by various groups claiming discrimination as a result of lack of diversity. Peterson has also had to deflect a barrage of negative press directed toward the corporation concerning its poor health insurance coverage, exploitation of illegal immigrants, and refusal to promote women. *Dukes v. Wal-Mart Stores, Inc.,* an $11 billion class action lawsuit, originally filed in 2001 by six women and representing more than two million women who have charged Wal-Mart with discrimination, is still pending. (On February 13, 2009, Wal-Mart won a small temporary victory in its attempt to nullify the class action aspect of the case when the Ninth Circuit court in San Francisco granted the corporation's petition to rehear it en banc, in full court.)

Yet if anyone at Wal-Mart can emerge from the battle over women's rights at the company unscathed, it is probably Peterson. In the book *Selling Women Short: The Landmark Battle for Workers' Rights at Wal-Mart,* author Liza Featherstone, while critical of the company, noted that behind the scenes, Peterson "repeatedly let his colleagues know that women were underrepresented in company management and offered suggestions on remedying the problem, including the idea of hiring a point person to oversee diversity initiatives."[3]

Publicly, however, Peterson defends Wal-Mart against what he perceives as unjustified slights. "I want to respond to [some of] these charges in two ways," he says. "Let's take California, where the newspapers said, 'Wal-Mart had five hundred instances of people working off the clock.' By the way, I was a witness in that case in California. Now here's the reality, here's what is being missed: Companies C, D, E, F, and G have fifty instances of people working off the clock. But with Wal-Mart, those five hundred instances represent one one-hundredth of a percent of what could have happened, whereas with the other five companies, the number represents 20 percent. The difficulty is that most people don't understand the scale. Everything that Wal-Mart does looks big on the scale, but if you look at how efficiently we operate in terms of the percentage of occurrences, we're outperforming many other organizations. I have literally had our competitors' human resources people say to us, 'We're glad you guys are there because you get bumped for everything, and we just travel right under the radar.' And that's real."

Peterson brushes off both bad press and occasional stories of employee mistreatment. "It's like anything else," he says. "On any given day in any company, something is going to go bump in the night. Stuff happens and people do things stupidly, sometimes on purpose. What seems to have happened with Wal-Mart, because of its size, is that people try to draw this image that its leaders wake up in the morning trying to figure out how we can screw the employee. That's just not true. The people who run Wal-Mart are people of high integrity. They have very strong value systems."

Wal-Mart, in fact, has attempted to answer some of its harshest critics by splashily making diversity one of its top priorities. In 2004 then-CEO Lee Scott pledged to promote women and minorities in the same percentages that they applied for promotion, or else he would forfeit 15 percent of his bonus. (There is no indication that he actually did either.) What's more, the company Web site (www.walmartstores.com) devotes an impressive amount of space to diversity initiatives, issues, and information, and tells us: "Diversity is a way of life at Wal-Mart. And our commitment to diversity is not just something we talk about, it's who we are. Our dedication to diversity extends from our board of directors to our associates; from our suppliers to our customers; and to every aspect of our business."

Which suggests in no uncertain terms that diversity has emerged as the zeitgeist of our times.

Moving into a Snow-White Land

The Peterson family's move from a comfortable, integrated St. Louis neighborhood was momentous but also a little disconcerting. During her first weeks here, Peaches actually witnessed a KKK rally in Bentonville Square. "I went because my philosophy is 'Know your enemies and look them in the face,'" she says. "When I showed up, I wasn't afraid, although I should have been."

As a dozen or so men in white robes marched across the square shouting racist slogans, embarrassed bystanders literally apologized to her. "It's really not like this here," one said. "This has never happened here," another offered.

In the end, says Peaches, "I was relieved and comforted by their reactions."

Still, with such a welcome, the Petersons decided that it would be safer to live in a secure, gated community. So, while renting a condo in nearby Bella Vista, a few miles north of Bentonville, they built a lovely, rambling, pale brick home on a rolling piece of property off the golf course at the elite and mostly white Pinnacle Hills Country Club and Estates in Rogers, a few miles south, where they still live.

On Easter weekend in 2007, Peaches, who acknowledges amicably that "with that name, everybody thinks I'm an airhead," eases into the plush sofa of her elegant beige and white living room, whose wide windows look out over the backyard, the pool, and the Pinnacle Hills golf course, and talks frankly about the difficulties of moving into this area. First, she worried about the lack of blacks in the community. When the Petersons first came to town, she says, there were so few that she started a group for local black families to get to know one another.[4] They brought in a black Santa every Christmas and invited black playmates over for their son, Collin, who was six at the time, and friends for their daughter, Rana, then fifteen. And Peaches discovered an interesting dynamic: those black families who had moved here from the northern states were well traveled and sophisticated, while those who had been born and raised in the South still "live on the plantation. They were always talking about white-versus-black issues. But blacks from the North don't really see the world like that, so there's a divide."

Peaches was concerned as well with the lack of diversity. "My kids had never been raised in an all-black world. I just don't believe in that," she says. Still, when Rana came of dating age and asked her parents if they would be comfortable with her dating outside her race, Peaches found her beliefs being tested: "I thought I was wise to say, 'I'd like you to marry someone like your father.' And my daughter, being who she is, asked, 'Is that a call for me to marry a black man?' I couldn't say anything, so she called me a hypocrite."

In the end, Peaches explained to her daughter that despite the changes in society over the years, a person still had to be strong to marry out of her race. "In my heart of hearts, I don't care," she says. "I come from that margin because as a very light-skinned black person I've experienced prejudice both from whites and from dark-skinned black people who didn't like me because I had Caucasian features. Sometimes people couldn't tell whether I was Mexican or Asian, especially when I was younger and wore my hair long and straight. And how ridiculous that people who would lie in the sun to get a tan and become my color would also be racists against people who *are* my color. That's why racism seems so silly to me. But I worry about how you deal with the negative things that people can do."

And yet racism seemed part and parcel of growing up black, whether in the North or the South. Peaches' own grandfather had been a slave who worked for a sharecropper in Alabama, and her father, one of thirteen children, also worked for that sharecropper. "Sharecropping was another form of slavery," she says. "This sharecropper would not allow any of the children to be educated, so my father's older brothers and sisters smuggled him out of town." He migrated to Chicago where he worked in the steel mills, all the while managing to educate his younger siblings. "Some of them had college degrees he denied himself," she says.

From the time she learned to read, Peaches was a bookworm. Yet on starting school, her teachers told her parents that they shouldn't expect more than C work from their daughter "because basically that was good for a black person." When she was twelve, her family moved into an all-white neighborhood. "And people threw bricks at our house," she says.

What was remarkable, Peaches observes, is that neither of her parents ever harbored any kind of racism, "which they really should have. And somehow they instilled in me a mind-set that you judge people by the content of their character and the way they live their lives."

Her words, echoing perhaps the most famous line in Dr. Martin Luther King's "I have a dream" speech, are no coincidence. Peaches followed Dr. King's philosophy and was active in civil rights in high school. Still, with firsthand knowledge of how difficult it was for whites to get beyond skin color, she worried about moving to Arkansas. As concerned as she was because there was no culture in Bentonville at the time, not even ballet classes for her daughter, she was even more worried for the family's safety. "My husband traveled out of the country for Wal-Mart. He was in China one day and Paris another," Peaches explains. "And I wanted to be in this gated community because I was scared."

It was on a trip to Argentina with Peterson that Peaches realized he had his own plane and personal security, as do most top personnel at multinational corporations who travel internationally, and she, too, had been given a bodyguard for the duration of the visit. "Well, I never liked it," she says, "so I never asked him a lot of questions."

Settling in Bentonville, Peaches immediately decided to learn about the local schools. From the beginning, she had been concerned about their quality. "After all, Arkansas was ranked the forty-ninth state for education. *Number forty-nine*," she says. "So I was shocked that the schools were good. I should have guessed that because Wal-Mart was already bringing in executives from around the world. And the company poured a lot of money into the schools to make sure they were keeping up with technology. If you leave Northwest Arkansas, schools are horrible. But in this little corner of the state, they are something else."

Working as a scholarship counselor at the high school, which today has a mere 74 black students in a population of 3,103, and running twice-a-year diversity seminars for the student body was part of her effort. "I wanted to know where I had brought my kids," she says. "I wanted to know the ugly, and I wanted to know the good. I saw more good than ugly, but there was definitely ugly, too."

Keeping the Ozarks White

There's no getting away from the fact that the history of the Ozarks with respect to its African American population has not been pretty. This is one reason why their numbers here in Northwest Arkansas have always been strikingly small. Seeds for the region's marked absence of blacks were sown way back in the pre–Civil War era—with racial divisions that have at various points created fear, lingering tensions, and violence.

Another reason for the small number of African Americans is that the area's infertile soil made it difficult to grow the normal array of plantation crops such as cotton, beans, and corn. Consequently, pre–Civil War era farmers rarely owned slaves the way they did in the Delta, along the eastern border of the state, where plantation owners depended on them.

Other, more political factors contributed to this demographic as well. By 1843 ordinances were in place to deny free blacks entrance to the state. In 1859, on the cusp of the Civil War, the state legislature passed a law requiring blacks to leave Arkansas by the beginning of the New Year or be sold into slavery. Although the law was suspended a year later, by then most free blacks had already fled.

Yet during the Civil War parts of Northwest Arkansas sided with their Missouri neighbors and the Union army rather than the Confederacy. What's more, after the 1862 Battle of Pea Ridge, the Confederate army virtually abandoned the area.[5] In the years immediately following the Civil War, a small number of free African Americans returned to the state, settling in the Ozarks along the Missouri-Arkansas border. They built their own churches, bought their own farms, and opened their own shops.

It did not take long for the white population of the South to respond to these thriving communities of free blacks. In 1866, two years after the end of the Civil War, six Confederate army veterans in Pulaski, Tennessee, founded an organization that they called Ku Klux Klan, a reworking of the Greek word *kuklos* for "circle." One among the founders, James R., or Jim, Crowe noted that the Klan's significance was neither political nor social; it existed, at first, simply for the men to play practical jokes on the public while riding through the countryside, frequently wearing white robes and tall, silly hats that obscured their identities. Soon the riders began to wreak havoc on local African American communities, some of whose members whispered that these pale marauders were really the ghosts of Confederate soldiers killed in the war. Most blacks, however, understood that the masked white riders were both very much alive and committed to terrorizing and massacring them. Very slowly the Klan gained appeal throughout the South and along the Mason-Dixon line. The Black Codes, or Jim Crow laws, took effect, first informally and then, with *Plessy v. Ferguson* in 1896, officially. Although many attribute the name, Jim Crow, to a minstrel show character, it is more than likely that this character was originally inspired by Crowe himself. By the 1920s the Ku Klux Klan would claim more than four million members, many of whom were doctors, lawyers, lawmakers, and some of the wealthiest and most upstanding people in their communities.

Little wonder, then, that in 1891, twenty-eight years after Abraham Lincoln issued his Emancipation Proclamation, Arkansas passed the first of its Jim Crow laws, ordering the separation of white and black passengers in railroad cars and at train station waiting rooms.

Then in 1900 Arkansas elected as its governor Democrat Jeff Davis, a racist and segregationist who later served as a U.S. senator as well. When President Theodore Roosevelt visited Arkansas in 1905, Governor Davis greeted him with a speech defending the practice of lynching; Roosevelt, long held in contempt by certain Southerners because he had entertained Booker T. Washington, the noted African American educator, at a White House lunch, reportedly came back with a speech pointedly underscoring the importance of upholding the letter of the law.

At the same time a strong countermovement began to take hold in the virtually all-white counties bordering the Mason-Dixon line. Cox Newspapers recently did an extensive computer analysis of thousands of U.S. Census records dating back to the Civil War, documenting two hundred counties "where black populations of 75 people or more seemed to vanish from one decade to the next," wrote Elliot Jaspin of the Cox News Service. The analysis also identified "13 countywide expulsions in eight states between 1864 and 1923, in which more than 4,000 blacks were driven out. These are only the most extreme examples of a widespread pattern." In only three of these incidents were any whites arrested or convicted of illegal behavior.

"A series of at least six race riots in the Ozarks, along with smaller undocumented expulsions, led to the almost total whiteness of most Ozark counties, which continues to this day," James W. Loewen wrote in his book *Sundown Towns: A Hidden Dimension of American Racism*.[6] Loewen points out that between 1890 and the 1930s whites chased African Americans from town after town by violent means, just as those in the western states had banished the Chinese a few years earlier, and he claims that an 1894 lynching of a black man who was dragged from police custody in Monett, Missouri, right across the border from Pea Ridge and Bentonville, set the violence in motion.

Benton County sits at the northernmost corner of Arkansas, not far from Powell, Joplin, and Pierce City, Missouri, the latter then a town of three thousand people. Here, in 1901, another of the above-mentioned race riots, or purges, took place. At the time a local newspaper reported that a mob of armed and angry whites lynched a "Negro" named William Godley and that in the fifteen hours that followed, they rampaged through Pierce, "determined to drive every negro from its precincts." In the process the mob incinerated an elderly black man in his home with the aid of state militia rifles "and drove dozens of negroes from town."

Similar occurrences played out in Harrison in Boone County, Arkansas, about thirty miles due east of Benton County. In the 1890s it was a biracial county where the black population, probably 300 to 400 people out of 1,438, coexisted peacefully with the whites.[7] But two incidents spelled an end to Harrison's blacks. During the first, in 1905, white mobs whipped African Americans, bound them to trees, and torched their homes. With the second, in 1909, a mob tried to lynch a mentally challenged black prisoner who had injured a twelve-year-old girl. (Harrison, known for many years as a haven for white supremacists, has recently made strides at turning around its reputation.)

Individual crimes like these, attributed rightly or wrongly to African Americans in the area, often sparked pogroms. They usually began with lynchings, which the tabloid press of the day detailed, gory incident by gory incident. Local blacks got the message and fled. Word traveled, and blacks in neighboring towns also dispersed.

Such "bleachings," or ethnic cleansings, served, according to University of Missouri historian Dr. Patrick Huber, as "defining events in the history of their communities."[8] They also turned a number of Ozark towns, among them Rogers and Springdale, into sundown towns, so named because if blacks were traveling through or working in any of them, they were required to be gone by nightfall or risk being lynched. Bold signage posted on the roads leading into and out of both towns unsparingly warned of such a fate.

Although few in the North have even heard of sundown towns, those who have usually believe that these towns were an invention of the Deep South. However, the truth is that they were, rather, creations wrought from a melding of fear, intolerance, and violence that spread throughout the Ozarks deep into the midwestern and northern states, and even as far west as California.

Often the sundown communities bragged about their whiteness. As far back as 1907, Rogers, six miles from Bentonville, advertised in its *Guide and Directory* that it had "no Negroes or saloons." Nearby Siloam Springs boasted about its clear mountain springs, its public library, and the fact that it had "No Malaria, No Mosquitoes, and No Negroes." In a marketing brochure from the 1920s, the neighboring Boone County Chamber of Commerce advertised, too, that it did not have "mosquitoes or Negroes."

Given the antiblack political climate in Northwest Arkansas, the Ku Klux Klan soon showed up to try to enlist members in tiny Bentonville. On July 13, 1923, a crowd of more than two thousand—larger than the population of the town—gathered to hear the KKK lecturer Dr. J. H. Moore. The organization, according to the *Morning News's* "Millennial Moment," "used electric bulbs to light up a cross, gave lectures from the back of a truck and played music."

By September 1923, the Rogers KKK was actively courting the town and the county, hoping that the national organization would secure a number of local charters. As a lure, it bequeathed to Rogers a deed to four lots "just east of the Maple Grove school in the fourth ward" to be used for a park and school playground—an investment of $1,300 or so, quite an impressive sum at the time. Nathan Bright, another KKK lecturer and Louisiana college professor, spoke at the Campus Park, making the point that "America must be made safe for Americans."

The organization's attempts to win the hearts and minds of Benton County did not work. Despite the property gift to Rogers, neither Rogers nor Bentonville allowed local Klan charters.

....

Considering the region's long-standing history of ethnic cleansing, it is remarkable that Bentonville, from the beginning, resisted becoming a sundown town. Indeed, it was able, for a while, to coddle and preserve a small black population. There is evidence of this in a compelling portrait of six black baseball players from a local Bentonville team, circa 1912, which was featured in the Springdale Shiloh Museum's Play Ball! exhibit during the spring of 2008. The young men in the photo, posing in slapdash fashion, were part of a regional Negro league that extended from Fort Smith to Joplin, Missouri. Yet, the players' names aside, no other information was available. Did these young men hold other jobs? Who came to see them play—just blacks? Whites? Both? How long did the league survive, and why did it eventually disband?

These men may have been from the area known as the Clique, just north of Bentonville, where a small group of former Benton County slaves settled toward the end of the nineteenth century. Within a few years, they had built three black churches here. One, the Colored Baptist Church, also housed the Bentonville Colored School, which offered a curriculum through the eighth grade. In "Benton County Schools That Were, Volume 1," Billie Jines, a Pea Ridge journalist, recounted the recollections of Elizabeth Gilbert Dishmon, who "remembers . . . a two-story structure a block east of the old Post Office, which is now owned by the county. That building was also used for the Colored Baptist Church and for lodges for both the men and the women. These were the United Brothers of Friendship (UBF) for the men, and the Sisters of Mysterious Tens (SMT) for the women. Both school and church used the first floor, while the lodges met upstairs. When Mrs. Dishmon reached the age of 18, she, too, joined the SMT lodge."

Jines went on to describe how Dishmon recalled "the singings and programs held at the school, to which many white residents of Bentonville came. . . . Sometimes these programs and dances were held in the Opera House up over the bank." Dishmon also told of how the children would carry water for the school from a spring a block down the slope from today's courthouse on Central Avenue.

A photograph snapped circa 1909 of students and their teacher in front of the wood building that served as the Bentonville Colored School accompanied Jines's description. On the left side of the picture and across the entire second row stand thirteen girls who look to be from ages nine to sixteen, all scrubbed and immaculately dressed, their skirts extended to midknees, their hair pulled back from their faces. On the right are seven boys of about the same age in long pants, white shirts, and slightly wrinkled cotton suit jackets. Many have on high boots; all wear serious, intense expressions, as does the teacher at the center of her brood, her hair piled neatly atop her head in a Gibson Girl–like knot. The photo holds many mysteries: Were the children's families middle class, or were the boys and girls wearing their Sunday best? Were they told *not* to smile, or was their reserve related to their privileged but uncertain positions in a mostly white world? And who took the photo—a white or a black—and what was its purpose? Nobody knows.

A Small Black Community

Bentonville's small, intact black community thrived during the 1920s. One of the few surviving African Americans born in town during that era, Leatrice Gloria Robinson Stewart remembers growing up with her four brothers and three sisters—eight Robinson kids in all. "We lived down the hill, where Lynne and Jim Walton live now," she says, referring to Sam and Helen Walton's billionaire son and his wife. "We had a little garden, where my father, who I think worked on the WPA, had planted cherry and apple trees, and we had a cow, chickens, and a hog. And we grew potatoes and vegetables. And the only things we had to go to town for were flour and corn and stuff like that. All we had to do was come up the hill, and the school was right there."

In those days schools and restaurants were segregated, a reality that Stewart accepted placidly. "I never did care about going to white restaurants. We just ate our food at home," she said. "But there was a little place that colored people would go to, run by a black man called Bill Levi. And we'd get hamburgers and soda pop and ice cream." On Saturday nights she and friends would head for Bentonville Square. "And we'd sit on the corner and watch people go by. Stores would stay open till 11 or 12 P.M. every Saturday night."

Although schools and restaurants were segregated, Stewart says that the community itself was not. "I had all kinds of white friends," she explained. Considering that Bentonville abutted the sundown towns of Rogers and Springdale, the informal integration of the Bentonville children was fairly remarkable.

Young Gloria, as she is known, attended the Bentonville Colored School and graduated after eighth grade. After getting her diploma, she married and had three sons. When her husband decided to move to Pennsylvania, Stewart had no interest in leaving her hometown. "So I would say that *I* left him," she says. Raising her boys without help, she made ends meet by cleaning houses. Occasionally, when the woman who cleaned Helen Walton's home was on vacation, Stewart stepped in.

Although recently hampered by a laundry list of ailments such as bursitis, arthritis, heart disease, high cholesterol, and diabetes, Stewart still leads a vital life. "I just cannot sit down," she says. "Even though I cannot walk as much as I used to because my hips hurt quite a bit, whenever I think that I want to go to town, I will go anyway."

Indeed, three or four mornings a week for years, she has walked the half-mile or so from her home to Harp's, the supermarket in the Midtown Shopping Center, right above the square, to buy food. Sometimes she stops by the Peter Pan Dry Cleaners to catch her breath and say hello to Perry Stamps, who used to own the enterprise and now works there every morning. Once a month or so, he takes her out for a catfish dinner, one of her favorites.

Stewart prides herself on the fact that her eldest son, Carl, who was born in 1946, integrated Bentonville's school system. For years, black students who wanted to continue their education and attend high school had to move to larger towns such as Fayetteville if they could afford it; others simply graduated from elementary school and left the area to find work. Yet the Depression and World War II played havoc with the area's agricultural economy, and the black population in town dropped so drastically that the Bentonville Colored School closed permanently.

By the time Carl came of school age, few educational opportunities existed for African Americans. One young girl, he recalls, traveled by Greyhound bus line into Fayetteville every day, forty-five minutes down and forty-five minutes back, to the closest black school in the area. But from first to third grade, he attended what he calls "private school." He was the only student of Cinco Crawley Dickerson, a woman who had moved to town in 1920 from Fort Smith and taught for twenty years in the Benton-ville Colored School until it shut its doors. During the time it flourished, she was responsible for forming a PTA and campaigning to raise money for a new school and playground. Now, with the school closed down and the black population diminished, she would come by the Stewart house-hold each morning, pick up young Carl, and bring him back to her home for his lessons. Around dinnertime, Gloria would come by for him; or if she was at work, Dickerson would drop him off. Carl says that Dickerson tutored him well; by age five, he could read from the Bible, and in the third grade he was working at seventh-grade level.

And then, he says, "I do not know what happened, but they decided to change some things."

What happened, in fact, was that a year earlier, in 1954, the United States Supreme Court, by a vote of 9–0, had passed *Brown v. Board of Education*, overruling the long-standing *Plessy v. Ferguson* (1896) decision that upheld "separate but equal" facilities. The court, in its landmark decision, now ruled that schools *must* desegregate. The following year, in *Brown II*, it ordered desegregation "with all deliberate speed."

On one day like no other, Cinco Dickerson brought Carl, then eight, to the white folks' school on Central Avenue and Second Street for a chat with the principal. "I guess he kind of sized me up to see what I was going to be like," Carl says. "And after a while, he asked me, 'How would you like to go to school here?'"

Having been taught privately and isolated from other children during the school week, this small boy, on hearing the laughter and animated chat-ter of children rising up from the playground outside the principal's office, immediately felt a sense of anticipation, even delight. "So they integrated me into the Bentonville school system—the only black. It was 1955," he says.

What he does *not* say, but which is true nevertheless, is that this momen-tous desegregation was done quietly, with little fanfare, and with great dignity.

And Carl Stewart never again had to study alone.

Black but Blending In . . .

Looking back, Carl mainly regrets that "Mrs. Dickerson," as he still calls his former teacher, had not been offered a job at the high school. "I knew she would have liked that," he observes. "But they had no black teachers. That would have been a landmark for her, too." Among Carl's white classmates were the former Bentonville mayor, Terry Coberly, and Sam Walton's four children.

Did Stewart's mother give him any advice about how to negotiate his way in an all-white school? No, says Carl. "You see, I was raised with the white kids. I played with them all the time. I didn't just go to school with them."

School integration in other parts of the state did not go quite so well, so quietly, or so quickly. During the summer of 1957, Little Rock made plans to integrate its public schools. But on September 2, Arkansas's governor, Orval Faubus, called out the Arkansas National Guard to prevent nine black students from integrating the city's two-thousand-student Central High School. After a three-week standoff, Mayor Woodrow Mann and U.S. congressman Brooks Hays asked President Dwight Eisenhower for help. He federalized the Arkansas National Guard, effectively taking the troops away from the governor, and brought in members of the 101st Airborne Division to help maintain order. Under the protection of the U.S. Army, on September 25, 1957, the nine black students finally entered Central High. Still, in 1958 Governor Faubus closed Little Rock's schools for a year rather than going forward with integration.

The world of Bentonville reflected little of the hostility and racism that shook Little Rock. Like his mother, Carl recalls his youth in halcyon terms and with no antagonism toward the dominant white community. "I could go just about anywhere I wanted in town without being hassled or bothered," he says. "People treated my family with great respect, and they treated me with respect." Sometimes, as a small boy, he would visit Crow's Drugstore on the south side of Bentonville Square. "There was a white woman who worked behind the counter and really liked me," he says, "and she would always give me an ice-cream cone."

From early on, Carl was taught how to behave, in part because his mother was a stern believer in discipline: "She had a switch, and if necessary, she did not hesitate to pull that baby out and use it on me."

The family assimilated, to some small degree, within the white community. They went to the all-white Nazarene Church in Bentonville, and Carl recalls having had plenty of white friends, including Sam Walton's two younger sons, Jim and John, the latter of whom died in a plane crash in 2005. (The Walton offspring also included Rob, the eldest boy, and Alice, the baby of the family.) "I played football with John and basketball with Jim," he says.

Even so, a sufficient number of whites in school—kids he had *never* played with—had never seen or known blacks, and they were curious. "When I got to the fifth grade, people always touched me and looked at me and were amazed by the way I looked," he says. "They were thinking, 'He has different hair or different skin color.' They looked at me as a novelty."

Still, by high school, he says, "There were a few little racial slurs, but most of the time there was no problem at all."

A natural athlete known as Flash in grade school, Carl also became strong working after school for Bentonville Hardware and Furniture, delivering beds, chests of drawers, oak tables, and other heavy items. Looking back, he says, "I played basketball and football, boxed, and ran track and field. I guess you would say I'm a powerhouse. I was highly athletic."

But in his junior year he developed asthma and stopped playing football. In 1966, two years after graduating from Bentonville High, Carl was drafted; he was deployed to Vietnam in 1967, where he served for a year. There, he says, "I contracted Agent Orange, and it has beaten on me." A host of chronic ailments followed, but Carl soldiered on. For more than thirty-eight years, in fact, he has been working at Glad Manufacturing Company, the makers of trash bags. "In fact, I was probably the first black person to work in Rogers," he says.

Stewart's athletic prowess served him well, if not professionally, then as a social instrument. After getting out of the service, he says, "I played basketball with Sam [Walton] every Sunday. He'd walk up to my house so that I could drive him down to the high school to play on its basketball court. Sam was pretty good. He wasn't a real good shooter, but he had enough muscle to get in there and get the other guy's ball away from the hoop. And if you passed him the ball and he was in the clear, Sam would make the shot.

"But he was as tight as the bark on a tree. He never said, 'Let me fill your car up one of these days,' although he once offered me a job at Wal-Mart. However, what he offered me was piddling compared to what I was already making. Also, I knew what kind of man he was, and I didn't want to work eighty or ninety hours a week, or anything like that—and he was mighty hard on his workers."

It was 1971, Carl remembers, and Glad Manufacturing, then part of Union Carbide, was paying him $3.20 an hour, more than double what Walton had offered. "So I could not take the job," he says. "I know now that he probably would have promoted me, but I do not kiss nobody's backside to get any job or favors."

Carl regards his childhood as "very unique. All my life things have been different from what most people would expect. They would expect a lot of anger from me," he says. But his faith has helped him all along. "I had a comforter," he explains. "God Almighty was my comforter. And I do not carry anger around in me about something that might have happened or did happen. I know without a doubt that everything that happens is not because of man—it's because of God's will."

These days, married (to his second wife) and the father of two grown sons (one of whom is earning a graduate degree in education at Le Moyne College in Syracuse, New York), Carl still lives in the area. His most enduring bond continues to be with Gloria Stewart. Mother and son eat breakfast together every morning, and she prepares dinner for him almost every evening. "We share a special relationship," he says. "She's hard to beat."

Honoring a Token Black

A bronze plaque on the side of the Arvest Bank building, formerly a hotel on the north side of Bentonville Square, pays tribute to the town's most enterprising black shoeshine man. It reads:

> Arthur "Rabbit" Dickerson (1897–1978): A Shining Star. Arvest Bank honors a legendary community leader, Rabbit Dickerson, who enriched the lives of decades of Bentonville families. His friendship, integrity, and dedication to his shoe shine business located on this spot provided generations with lively discussion and exceptional customer service.

Rabbit, a local man who had attended the Bentonville Colored School, ran a successful shoeshine business right off the square for more than fifty years. Known for his engaging personality, he married Cinco Crawley, Carl's teacher, in 1922.

Gloria Stewart knew Rabbit well and recalls him as a decent, nice man. "They called him Rabbit because he looked like a rabbit, I think," she says with a small, spry laugh. "He was little and had big ears. He was really good—a good person. And he was even real good at making money. Everybody would go to his shine parlor to get their shoes shined."

The Bentonville/Bella Vista Chamber of Commerce eventually awarded Dickerson its first annual Arthur "Rabbit" Dickerson Award, given to those with outstanding service to the community. (Helen Walton and Mayor Terry Coberly would become future recipients as well.)

· · · · · · · · · ·

As for the sundown towns, it is striking that no "sundown" signage exists today, although a few in Washington and Benton counties say they can recollect its existence. "I'd seen the sign," Carl Stewart told me. "Yes, it was said that at night blacks in Rogers should not let the sun set on them, but back in high school I did not give it much thought. When I played football against Rogers, my team protected me."

A retired Springdale truck driver, Homer Smith, in his mid-eighties, is another one who bears witness. "Yep, I saw the sign when I first come here in '42," he says. "The sign was on 71, both north and south of Springdale. 'Nigger, don't let the sun set on you,' it said, maybe not in those exact words, although the average people didn't believe in it, just the leaders. And Rogers had the same thing."

These days curators at the Rogers Historical Society and the Shiloh Museum in Springdale believe that local communities, embarrassed by their own histories, may have gone to great lengths to destroy the signage and other physical evidence of Northwest Arkansas's shameful past.

A Corporate Wife

Peaches Peterson began her journey as a corporate wife back in St. Louis when she was barely twenty-two. As the partner of an executive officer who was clearly bounding up the corporate ladder, she befriended a Jewish woman whose husband was also an executive. "She became my mentor," Peaches explains, "and I watched her. I was smart enough to know I needed to learn. I needed to be Coleman's helpmeet and, as a corporate wife, to understand how to help him do whatever he wants to do."

Peaches says that she felt a special need for discretion here in Bentonville because her husband was heading Wal-Mart's People Division. After all, Coleman Peterson was privy to so much sensitive information about the company, its lawsuits, and its employees, and Bentonville was not just a small town but a company town; Wal-Mart was central to everyone's economic and social life. "It's a job where you know so many things about the organization. And people gossip," Peaches says. "But I could not because it could be misconstrued. And I couldn't go out with curlers in my hair because somebody was always watching me. So I could never be myself."

Her own constant watchfulness, combined with the fact that there were so few African American families in town, created a sense of isolation. As a consequence, Peaches says that during her early years in Bentonville, "I was very lonely. I'm still lonely here."

But her free time was limited. She was mentoring other women, helping her husband recruit families to the area, and taking care of her children. In 2006 she became the director of scholarships for Bentonville High School. Little time was left to make friends—especially good friends.

. . . .

In a town as white as Bentonville, where a welcome mat of good-ol'-boy southern racism—that local KKK rally on the square—greeted the Petersons when they first settled here, it might be reasonable to expect Peaches and her children to have experienced more of the same both at school and in the community. That was rarely the case. From the beginning, she says, her white neighbors extended kindness.

"They reached out to us in many ways that they didn't really have to," she says. "And in ways that have endeared this place to me."

On the family's first night in town, before Rana had even attended one day of high school, a teenager came by and took her to dinner. Yet another family picked up Collin and took him fishing. By the time school began a week later, the Peterson kids had already made friends.

Cynics could argue that the family received preferential treatment because of Coleman Peterson's important position at Wal-Mart. Whatever the reason, there was an outpouring of hospitality.

Still, occasional problems did crop up. "I call it the dark side of Bentonville," Peaches adds. When Collin was eight, she received a call from his school principal, telling her that one of the children had thrown a racial insult at him and was going to be suspended for a few days. "Instead we called the parents and told them that they needed to talk to their son," says Peaches. "And that was it. Collin, in all his school years, has only had about three incidents that I know of, and we handled them like that. But he is a big kid, so nobody messes with him. And the school was good and very proactive."

Primarily, the students that Peaches dealt with were neither racist nor unwelcoming; they were simply curious. They had never in their lives had conversations with black people; they had never been to the home of a black family. "I had kids at school who as late as last year said, 'Shirley, what's the deal about black hair?' Or, 'Shirley, do you like rap music?' And I would say, 'No, I hate rap music. I like jazz and classical music.' And they would say, 'We thought all black people like rap.'"

Peaches recalls a young black girl who could speak perfectly good English but instead spoke black English, or Ebonics, at school because she felt that was the way she would be accepted by whites. "And we had an hour-long conversation about her diction, and I said, 'Let me tell you something, I've never spoken Ebonics. And if I heard my son speaking Ebonics, he'd be in serious trouble.'"

Peaches suggests that children who want to assimilate are often their own worst enemies. "They don't understand much," she says. "They are just balls of hormones." She describes the Bentonville High School cafeteria during lunchtime as a place where all the Hispanic students sit at one table and the black kids at another. "And with the Hispanics talking and laughing in Spanish, the white kids think they are being talked about. Actually, everybody thinks you're talking about them. So if you *are* Hispanic, why wouldn't you just share the joke with somebody who is *not*?" she asks. Perhaps because that would be the adult thing to do—and yet not even adults manage to do it.

Bentonville High's black students are not guilt-free either, she says, and recalls receiving a phone call from the principal after one black teenager became indignant when a white teacher read a poem using the word *nigger*. "The boy got the teacher in a tizzy," says Peaches. "He claimed he was offended because he wanted to be called *tinted*. He was a troublemaker, first of all, and was getting to this teacher, who was overly sensitive about not wanting to offend. She had never heard of the word *tinted* in that context."

And for good reason. During the meeting with the teacher, the parents, the principal, and the troublemaker himself, Peaches demanded to know where the word *tinted* came from. "And the boy started cracking up. He knew he was being a jerk," she says. "And I told him, 'Your parents need to bawl you out. You did this to play on this teacher, and that's not right.' Kids of every culture play the race card at school."

· · · · · · · · · ·

The situation for Rana was more fraught with peril than for most children—and certainly more than for Collin, now a lanky and quiet young college student, who grew up in the Bentonville school system. Teenage Rana, a second-semester junior when she first enrolled at Bentonville High School, was not just the new girl in town; she was also the school's only black female student (she had one black male classmate, Carl Stewart's son Ron). Under any circumstances, it would have been difficult for the new girl in town, but her situation was underscored by her age and race. Peaches acknowledges that her daughter survived some painful experiences, saying, "I don't think she told me about a lot of the things. But she told me some."

On this Easter weekend in 2007, Rana, twenty-eight, and visiting from Chicago with her boyfriend, who happens to be white, is anxious to be part of the conversation. It is to her credit that she made friends easily back then, because she is, and was, an intimidating young woman—African American, yes; beautiful, yes; but also an accomplished concert pianist, track star, and cheerleader. Still, whether or not Bentonville had ever seen such an urbane youngster, she figured out how to fit in with her white classmates and win a place on both Homecoming Court and Student Council.

Race-related dangers rarely cropped up. Mostly, students were curious. "They had questions like, 'Can I touch your hair?'" says Rana. "The racism that I saw, rather than being directed toward me, was usually directed toward Mexicans. And it was 80 percent about economics."

Yet every once in a while this vivacious young woman was forced to confront certain racial realities. When the Tigers, Bentonville's football team, played in nearby Harrison, back then a haven for white supremacists, the Petersons wanted Rana to stay home and not cheerlead that night. But her coach and various parents promised to look out for her. "People wouldn't let me walk places by myself," she says. "They didn't make a huge deal of it, but it was an unspoken comfort that they gave me. One dad was a big former football player who took his Hummer up to the game, and he sat by the cheerleaders the whole time, wearing his cowboy hat. And he kept saying, 'Have you had any problems yet?' And I'd say, 'No.'"

Integrating the school was one thing, but integrating teen society in a small southern town was quite another, even for a girl as popular as Rana. She had an abundance of friends, but no dates—not for her senior prom and not for any Saturday night. Everybody's pal, she was nobody's girlfriend. "No one even tried to make out with me—that's how I'd term it," she says.

For her junior prom, everyone just assumed that Rana would be going with the other black student at the school. "'Whoa,' I thought, 'who said I was going to the prom with him?'" she now observes. "But since we were the only black students within a fifty-mile radius, they thought we had to go together."

In her senior year, a different problem arose. Again, Rana had no date. She did have a close white friend, a football player named Darryl, whom everyone thought would ask her to the prom.[9] She waited and waited: "And then my best guy friend told me that Darryl *wasn't* going to ask me. He said, 'Darryl's dad told him that if Darryl asks you to the prom, he'll kick him out of the house.'"

"And by the way," Peaches intervenes, "Darryl's parents went to church with us every Sunday."

Rana eventually forgave Darryl but says, "It was weird. After that, I felt that there would always be a rift between us."

As for her senior prom, that critical rite of passage, she did not go. Instead, she spent the night "dancing on a tabletop" at a fraternity house at the University of Illinois, her mother's alma mater, which Rana would also attend the following September, majoring in advertising. Yet memories surrounding her prom still smart. "I felt bad that things like this happened and made me angry," she says. "And because I didn't want my parents to feel guilt about me."

Outsiders Who Are Insiders

Embodying the essence of achievement, the Petersons have provided Bentonville with the pivotal image, like TV's Cosbys, of blacks as successful middle-class citizens.

Ask Rana Peterson, and she will tell you that her mother contributes to the diversity and multiculturalism of the community as effectively as her dad does. "Every time I come home, I discover that my mom has influenced a lot of people here. She does not give herself credit, but that influence is like nothing I've seen before," says Rana. "Every time there's a racial issue at the high school, they call her. People just respect her opinion. Mom is not like my father or me; she has a more subdued style and a quiet sophistication, a wisdom and warmth. I think that's what draws people to her." Moreover, says Rana, her mother is a rational force who understands racism and how to deal with it.

Often the white population here does things out of ignorance, not out of racism, Peaches says. She wants young people to be able to empathize—to understand what it feels to be the only one, or one among the few, whether the context is racial or cultural. She brings up the example of a fifteen-year-old Sikh boy from India who entered Bentonville High wearing a scarf wrapped tightly around his head. "At first the school wanted to suspend him," she says, explaining that school regulations forbade wearing hats. Yet the boy insisted on wearing what looked like a do-rag, which covered a knot of hair on top of his head. "And I said, 'Guys, you can't suspend him. That scarf is part of his culture. He's *required* to wear that.'" And eventually the school backed off.

Indeed, Peaches Peterson has, over the years, evolved into a de facto community ambassador. "I always tell people I'm Wal-Mart's secret weapon because the company often calls me, especially when they are trying to recruit a minority family, and asks, 'Will you talk to these people?' And, of course, I do."

In the end, she says, "My approach to this issue of race and bias is that basically we're all responsible for growing where we're planted. There are lessons to be learned for those in both majority and minority situations, and if we're wise, we'll learn them well and share them. Ultimately, if we don't dialogue about the race thing, we'll never be all that we can be."

The Petersons, it seems, have already won a crucial victory. In Bentonville, at least, they are known not just for the color of their skins but for the content of their character.

A Muslim Philanthropist
Champions the Jews

· · · · · · · · · ·

Imagine this: a Palestinian contractor living in Arkansas who has studied the Torah, speaks Hebrew, and donates his time and expertise to help a tiny Jewish community build its first synagogue. That's the stuff that movies, and perhaps Israeli dreams, are made of. But real life?

"Well, this really goes to the core of my beliefs. I believe we should all live and let live," says the contractor, Fadil Bayyari, a Muslim who lives in Springdale, part of the Northwest Arkansas community that experienced a great economic boom between 1994 and 2007. "Palestinians and Jews are so much alike it's not even funny. We think alike, we have the same ambitions and backgrounds. If you read the Bible, the Torah, and the Koran, you'll see that our forefather is Abraham, whether we want it or not. And we are all children of God. I believe in reaching out to people and getting along."

Bayyari is something of a local hero because of his generous if flamboyant gesture to work with the Fayetteville Jews on their first permanent home. His office, on a slip of narrow country road a few miles from the Johnson exit off Interstate 540, occupies the first floor of a small, single-story building in the Bayyari Business Center, a makeshift-looking enclave he owns that includes a convenience store and auto transmission shop on land he also owns.

It is inside this utilitarian-gray, corrugated steel–sided box that Bayyari runs his multimillion-dollar business. Today he is president of Bayyari Construction and Properties, serves as chairman of the board of the Jones Center for Families and is a member of the Northwest Arkansas Community Foundations and several other local boards of directors.

But what is striking about him, early on this gray and icy winter morning, is his Zen-like air of calm and the unpretentious nature of his enterprise. In fact, Bayyari's mother-in-law runs the small office. And Bayyari himself usually sits behind a shiny but modest wooden desk in a comfortable room right off the reception area.

A small, compact man in his late fifties, he is wearing blue jeans, a jeans jacket, and a white baseball cap with a Rotary Club insignia. His beard is graying, and his eyes are a warm brown. But it is Bayyari's accent—a southern drawl peppered with a slightly guttural Middle Eastern edge—that is most appealing.

"Hiya," he says, holding out his hand. "How are you?"

This self-made man has emerged from a world that hardly promised wealth or success. Fadil Hasan Bayyari grew up in the Palestinian city of Tulkarem on the West Bank, the son of a middle-class produce and chicken farmer. "I worked for my dad since I was eight, and we always dealt with the Israelis," he says. In fact, after 1967 the Bayyaris bought poultry from and traded with them, "and it was okay." Young Fadil recalls his childhood in a land far more peaceful than today. "I was six or seven, and I'd go by the railroad tracks and watch the Israeli crop dusters in the fields. And I always wanted to go across. Once, in fact, I did, and United Nations security guards brought me and another kid home that night. But it was a nice, peaceful time, and I had a great childhood running in the fields."

Bayyari attended Birzeit College, in the West Bank, where he met a number of American students. Perhaps as a consequence, the United States figured vividly in the future he imagined for himself. After graduating, he decided that he had three basic choices: working in the family business, joining the PLO, fighting the Israelis, "or just basically leaving," he said. "You know, get the hell out of Dodge, so to speak."

In 1971 he came to the United States, a package of his mother's falafels under his arm, and right off the bat was identified as a foreign greenhorn by a Chicago cabbie, who took him into the city for a price equal to a month's spending money. There he enrolled at Roosevelt University and found a job as a dishwasher at a Chicago restaurant for $1.25 an hour. But soon he abandoned both dishwashing and school for McDonald's, quickly rising first to the position of cook, then eventually manager. Along the way, he acquired an American wife and a reputation for being smart and reliable. McDonald's transferred him to Los Angeles and then to Hawaii, but Bayyari left when A. A. Zayani & Sons, the company that owns Rolls-Royce and other business investments throughout the Gulf, hired him to work in the Middle East, primarily Bahrain.

The job was terrific, but when his boss, a close friend, was killed in a car accident, a grieving Bayyari and his wife decided to return to the States.

This time they headed for Eureka Springs, Arkansas, where his wife had vacationed as a child. But as pretty as the town was, in only a few days Bayyari intuited that it was no wellspring of opportunity. So once again the couple picked up, driving west to the Bentonville area. "And we realized that the University of Arkansas was in Fayetteville," he said. "My wife could get her Ph.D. in microbiology, while I could find myself something to do. That is how it all started."

Appropriately enough, a Wal-Mart connection became the catalyst for future success. Bayyari, who got a foothold first by renting, then buying, a series of local fast-food shops called Waffle Hut—he has long since sold them—says that he had always wanted to get into the building business. In Chicago he had taken courses in preengineering, and in Bahrain much of his work taught him the nuts and bolts of building. Then, he says, he got lucky: "And I met a man, Willard Walker, who became my friend."

Walker, a local legend, had run the first Wal-Mart store in Rogers. "And he had done really well, holding on to company stock and investing in real estate," says Bayyari. "He was about thirty years older than I, and when I told him how much I liked the building business, he showed me a commercial subdivision in Springdale—this was probably 1983—and asked if I'd want to build there. I said, 'Willard, I do not have the funds,' and he said, 'Who's talking about funds? Come into the house, and let's have coffee.'"

The next day Walker offered him the deed to one of his lots. "And he said, 'Don't worry about money. When you have it, pay me.' That was my first break."

Bayyari built a warehouse on that property and leased it to a coffee company. Within six months he was able to pay Walker back. So, Walker gave him another lot in a similar deal. "He never charged me interest, and I'll never forget that," says Bayyari, who began to build the blocks of his construction business just as Wal-Mart was expanding its footprint abroad and also, more importantly, at home.

The two men developed what Bayyari calls "a strong personal relationship." Walker, who died in 2003, gave his young disciple another gift as well—he taught him the principle of giving. "He is my hero," Bayyari says, adding that Walker's widow, Pat, still runs the couple's charitable trust and is one of the state's major philanthropists.

. . . .

An extraordinary characteristic of Northwest Arkansas is its philanthropic bent, made all the more remarkable because the area's population, encompassing the Wal-Mart bedroom communities from Bella Vista south through Bentonville, Rogers, Springdale, and Fayetteville, tops out at little more than three hundred thousand, and because these local philanthropists—unlike, say, the Rockefellers—started out dirt-poor and with no family history of charitable giving.

And though Wal-Mart deserves some credit as a benefactor, the truth is that in his day Sam Walton was actually known as a tightwad who had to be spurred on to charitable giving by his wife, Helen. Even today, Wal-Mart's philanthropic impulse, while sizable, seems paltry considering its gargantuan hold on the retail economy and its astonishing revenues, which now top out at more than $400 billion a year. Still, Walton from the beginning encouraged his employees to be community minded, understanding that it was good publicity for the corporation and, even better, cost him nothing. He also helped to make multimillionaires out of a number of men who worked with him, men who had more charitable natures than he.

Most of these men and their wives, Bible Belt churchgoers down to their fingertips, put their faith-based values to work in their philanthropic endeavors. It is striking that their celebration of these values so perfectly recapitulates the argument that Max Weber, considered by many to be the father of sociology, first made in *The Protestant Ethic and the Spirit of Capitalism*, initially published in Germany in 1904. He posited that capitalism grew in the West because Protestants, unlike Catholics, held a basic uncertainty about salvation. They devoted their lives to hard work, saved their pennies, and, like Sam Walton, reinvested primarily in their businesses, viewing frugal living and worldly success as a sign of God's grace.

This was key to Willard Walker, whose generosity helped jump-start Bayyari's career. Walker's sense of community responsibility eventually emerged as one of the most striking stories of Northwest Arkansas. He was managing a Tulsa variety store when Sam Walton, with an eye for talented workaholics, recruited him to come to Arkansas and be the first manager of his 5 & 10 on Fayetteville Square. "I had to move myself there, work half days for free until the store opened, and I remember sleeping on a cot in the storeroom," Walker would recollect.[1] "But he said I would get a percentage of the profits, and that appealed to me."

Later, Walker opened Springdale's Wal-Mart No. 3 and managed it until he retired in 1972. But he was a risk taker as well and borrowed from everyone he could to buy Wal-Mart stock. "Bud [Walton's brother] and Sam came down to the store one day, and Bud said: 'Willard, I sure hope you know what you're doing.' He told me I had more faith than he did," Walker observed. "I always knew it was going to be successful."[2]

In fact, in 1992, Sam Walton observed, "I don't believe we ever had one who bought more stock than Willard. And of course he feels pretty good about it today."[3]

That's because Walker turned a modest stake into a large fortune. He and Pat, who lived modestly, eventually established the Pat and Willard Walker Charitable Foundation, which as of 2005 had assets of more than $20 million. Over the years the Walkers gave many millions to establish the Pat and Willard Walker Family Memory Research Center, the University of Arkansas for Medical Sciences cancer research center, and the Willard J. Walker Graduate Business Building at the Sam M. Walton College of Business. They also helped to build Springdale High School's Performing Arts Center, which houses the Pat Walker Theater, and its Willard Walker Fieldhouse for Bulldog football. "Our entire state has been made a better place to live, work, and educate our kids because he lived and gave so generously," Springdale's then-mayor, Jerre Van Hoose, said in 2003 when Walker died of congestive heart failure at eighty-one.

Any discussion of the humanitarian impulse of Northwest Arkansas would be incomplete without also acknowledging Harvey Jones, who made his fortune by establishing Jones Truck Lines (JTL) in Springdale, one of the largest trucking businesses in the country. Jones also left an impressive endowment to the area, the Harvey and Bernice Jones Center for Families, with $71 million in assets, and the Jones Charitable Trust, with $4.8 million more. Even as a young man, Jones proved himself to be community minded, developing the area's first hospital, Springdale Memorial. His wife, Bernice, a teacher, shared his passion for service, supporting the Baptist Youth Ranch and many local ministries.

It was Bernice who had the vision to create a community center dedicated, as the mission statement for the Jones Center for Families explains, "to serve families, strengthen community, and glorify God." The Joneses built this singularly well-designed modern facility, which includes a natatorium; a 185-foot-long ice rink that is home to the Arkansas Figure Skating Association and the Ozark Hockey League; a gymnasium; an indoor track; a computer room; and a wedding chapel, all free to anyone who drops by. The Center, open since 1996, offers free English and Spanish lessons and a wealth of fitness and wellness classes. An Adventure Center teaches climbing and rappelling, and a Family Resource Center provides free office space to more than forty nonprofit organizations.

Such public-spirited couples as the Joneses and Walkers might well have been channeling the philanthropic philosophy of the late steel magnate Andrew Carnegie. Before dispersing his own massive fortune, he noted in a brief essay, "The Gospel of Wealth," published in the *North American Review* in 1889, that the responsibility of a wealthy man was "to consider all surplus revenues which come to him simply as trust funds, which he is called to administer . . . to produce the most beneficial result for the community . . . [and] doing for them better than they would or could do for themselves."

Bayyari, too, carries on the tradition. He donated twenty-five acres of land valued at around $600,000 for the construction of a Springdale elementary school (it is named after him), he built a seven-acre park in Fayetteville, and he has contributed to homeless shelters and built, for the cost of materials alone, the first mosque in the area, a number of churches, and now the synagogue Temple Shalom in Fayetteville. All this seems a natural consequence of his own broad sense of acculturation and goodwill toward other people.

Old Lives for New

How did Bayyari become interested in building the synagogue in Fayetteville—and building it gratis, at that? The Palestinian credits his friend Ralph Nesson, a Jew, with steering him in that direction. "In fact, I'm meeting Ralph for lunch today," he tells me. "Why don't you come with me?"

In a matter of minutes, Bayyari is steering his gray Range Rover down winding roads and through wooded farmland. At one point, no more than five minutes from his office, he points to a stately red brick home set way back on twenty acres and surrounded by a wrought iron gate. Unlike any other in the neighborhood, it resembles a European manor house. "That's my home," he says. Bayyari lives there with his wife, Lori; their teenage children, Sophia and Joseph; and, in her own guest cottage behind the main house, his mother-in-law and secretary, Pat Cope. His daughter from his first marriage, Sara Boelkins, in her thirties, works as the chief pilot for Wal-Mart's aviation division.

Bayyari's family life has been tested a number of times. In 1990 his oldest child, David Lyall, also a pilot, was killed in a plane crash while studying at flight school, sending Bayyari's twenty-three-year first marriage into a tailspin from which it could not recover. "That's the toughest thing that ever happened to me," he says. "The loss was devastating to our relationship. She was doing her Ph.D. in microbiology and got busy with her research. And I got busy with my work, and we drifted apart. My son's death really broke my marriage, just broke it."

But Bayyari, a survivor, soon met Lori. Perhaps because he was still mourning David, the relationship stumbled. The pair, with two small children, split up. And almost as if he were trying to recapture his past, Bayyari, on a trip to the Middle East, met a Muslim woman from the West Bank, married her, and brought her back to Arkansas. "But she couldn't adjust," he says. "Basically, she was jealous of my kids, and every time I went to meet them and my former wife, she'd throw fits. I couldn't put up with it, so I took her back [to the West Bank] and we got divorced."

During this turbulent period of what he calls "my rebounds," which lasted about four years, Bayyari then met a Jordanian woman. Once again he relocated her to Arkansas, and once again the relationship did not work out. How much did that marriage, too, reek of nostalgia for his West Bank homeland and the culture of his birth? "In the back of my mind, yes, it did," he admits. "And I thought maybe I'll be happier. But I discovered pretty quickly that no, no, I'm so different after thirty-seven years of living in this country that I couldn't adjust to their way of life and their thinking, and they couldn't adjust to mine—both wives, as a matter of fact. So we each have to be blamed for it."

Proving to himself that he was more American than even he had realized, Bayyari kept being drawn back to Lori, who worked as his office manager, and their children. "And we've fallen in love again," he explains. "I guess we had to kill that first relationship to make things come alive a second time. And, I admit, I was immature; I shouldn't have married those two other women. I rushed into it. You know, when I came here as a boy, I was nineteen and had no experience, especially with the other gender. I was very green. But recently I have done a lot of growing up."

As a sign of his new maturity, Bayyari says, he remarried Lori in February 2007. "We've worked out our differences, we're back in the same big house we'd built for the kids," he says, "and we're happy."

. . . .

On a sunless January day, Lori Bayyari greets me at the door of their home, wearing jeans and a black T-shirt. With blond hair spilling around her long neck and a mischievous smile, she looks more like a teenager than the mother of two and mistress of this elegant estate, with its kidney-shaped pool, stable, six horses, and meadow.

When I express surprise to find such a magnificent manor house in working-class Springdale, she herself admits that, at first, she did not want her husband to build here. The area's racist history had preceded it, and she says, "People thought of it as a dirty, racist town. I don't remember the sundown signs, but I've heard so much about them." In fact, when her son was in first grade, she invited one of his teachers, an African American man, to a party at their home, and, she says, "When he learned I was living in Springdale, he said he wasn't going to come." She finally persuaded him to do so and says, "I like it now. The town is trying to outlive its past, trying to change. Still, there's a large Hispanic community here that feels it is being picked on, and I can see why they feel that way."

An easygoing and patient type who met her husband almost twenty years ago at the bar of the Springdale Holiday Inn, Lori, this morning, is allowing young Joseph, who has stayed home from school with a cold, to skateboard around her shiny kitchen and living room, with its cathedral ceiling and beautifully upholstered floral armchairs. She has managed to survive Bayyari's two interludes with Middle Eastern brides without bitterness and speaks openly about their tough times.

"Fadil is *much* better at business than he is in his personal life," she says deftly. "I knew he always loved me. He just had no sense at the time. But he never turned his back on us. And I realized what a good man he was."

· · · · · · · · · ·

Marriage aside, Bayyari's personal life mirrors his eclectic worldview in numerous ways. Although the beats of his daily routine are quintessentially southern, he still holds on to many of his Muslim traditions. He prays five times a day, beginning at 4:00 A.M., when he gets up. Then he goes to the gym, where he and a group of friends walk briskly for five miles around an indoor track. By 7:00 A.M. Bayyari is in his office working. Fridays, he leaves early for midday prayers either at home or, when he can, at the Masjid Hamzha, the Islamic Center of Northwest Arkansas in Fayetteville—the mosque he himself built.

While he holds his own religion sacred, Bayyari has deliberately sought to blend in. "To do well in this country, you have to reach out, you have to assimilate," he explains. "I raised my kids from day one to be Americans first. Yes, their daddy comes from the Middle East, but that is second. I celebrate my background, and I try to take the best of that culture, along with the best that this culture gives me."

No doubt, marriage has also figured in his Americanization, and Bayyari's nondogmatic way of raising his kids has developed in relationship to the Christian women with whom he has shared his life. (His first wife was Catholic, and Lori is Baptist.) And the kids? "I was born to Muslims, and I practice Islam. I had no alternative," he explains. "Well, my wife and I thought that we were going to give the kids the opportunity to pick. If she wants to take the kids to church, I have no problem. I practice my faith in my way, and I don't want to force it down anybody's throat."

His approach has led relatives in the West Bank to think he is "weird." "They believe I should make my kids become Muslim," he says. "But, no! 'Be *anything*,' I think. 'This is Islam; this, Christianity; and this, Judaism. You pick.' That is the way it is in my household."

Resurrecting a Controversial Tradition

It is noteworthy that from 1990 to 2000, the decade prior to 9/11, the Muslim population of the United States exploded, increasing by more than 169 percent. As of 2007, 2.35 million Muslims lived in the United States, 65 percent of whom are foreign-born, the Pew Research Center reported in a recent study. After interviewing 1,050 Muslims living here, the study concluded that many of them, even though newly arrived, are, like Bayyari, "highly assimilated into American society."[4]

Mason Hiba is one. The Syrian native, forty-four, owns two upscale clothing stores called Mason's in Fayetteville and is planning a third in Rogers. He originally came here from Damascus in 1983 to study electrical engineering at the University of Arkansas and says that since 9/11 he has become suspicious of the fundamentalist aspects of Islam, as has his Muslim wife, who does not wear the traditional headscarf. "I think Islam is going through a revolution right now, and there's a lot of conflict about ideas and thoughts, a lot of instability," he explains. "And I just don't want to be part of it. The radicals have the microphones right now, and I hate that. If you listen to them, they win. I'm not about listening to them at all."

This conflict within the American Islamic community is something that the Pew study reports, perhaps inadvertently: "On balance, [Muslims] believe that Muslims coming to the U.S. should try and adopt American customs, rather than trying to remain distinct from the larger society. And by nearly two-to-one, Muslim Americans do not see a conflict between being a devout Muslim and living in a modern society."[5]

What is striking about so many Muslim women in Northwest Arkansas is their adamancy about wearing the *hijab* (headscarf that identifies them as Muslim) in order to obey the Koranic command to "cover up" as a gesture of modesty and respect for God.

· · · · · · · · · ·

On a Sunday afternoon so humid that beads of perspiration glisten across her brow, Mahfuza Akhtar greets me at her door. An administrative assistant in the University of Arkansas's Middle Eastern studies department, which was established in 1994 through a $21.5 million gift from the Kingdom of Saudi Arabia, she lives with her two sons and husband in this small, immaculately kept home in a treeless, almost entirely white Christian suburb of Fayetteville. Attractive with thick, dark curly hair, Akhtar wears a bright green robe and yellow pants, called a *kamiz* and *shalawar* respectively, which is the customary dress among Bangladeshi Muslims. Showing me around her living room, she points out the family's prayer mats, small, multicolored rugs that are carefully folded in a corner near the mantel, and picks up a small jar from the mantelpiece. "This contains soil from Mecca," she says. "It is from one of the grad students in our department. He recently converted to Islam and gave this to me."

Mahfuza, who came to the United States with her husband and sons in 1996, grew up in an upper-middle-class family in Dhaka, Bangladesh—one of seven girls and two boys—which ultimately produced four college teachers, two executives, and two sisters who are doctors. "I got a master's in biology, then taught for twelve years in a woman's college," she says, her words tumbling out at breakneck speed. "People say, 'How come all you girls are highly educated?' It's a blessing from God. My dad was a government official who raised us with a good attitude. 'Being a Muslim, you have your identity. But you also have to be educated to stay in society,' he told us. That's his motto."

A matchmaker friend introduced her to her husband, Dr. Ibrahim Ali, an entomologist. Ali had received his doctorate from the University of Arkansas and returned to Dhaka to find a bride. First, their parents spoke and, as Mahfuza puts it, "settled," or arranged, the marriage. Both she and Ali were scientists, intelligent, well educated, and good looking. It was also important to Mahfuza that her groom did not drink, smoke, or have a history of serious relationships. "We have the same thinking and the same ideas," she says. "That brings us closer to each other.

"We are the only dark people in the neighborhood," she declares, but she does not mind at all. In fact, everyone on the block has been welcoming, especially the pharmacist next door, who recently became a church pastor and who, soon after Akhtar moved in, stopped by to share his harvest of fruits and vegetables; in return, Akhtar divvies up her summer blackberry crop with him. "I never think, 'Oh, they are Christians. We do not need to mix,'" she says. "We are very close. And they are interested in our religion. They always want to know what we are doing."

Although Akhtar and Ali socialize with Hindus and Christians, Mahfuza expresses puzzlement that whenever the Christians invite them to dinner, it is always at a restaurant. "We eat together, and we sometimes invite my husband's colleagues to dinner at our home, occasionally for our holidays of Ramadan and Eids. But during Christmas break they invite us to a hotel and never to their homes," she says, as if to suggest that Christian hospitality at home may be reserved only for other Christians. Still, she feels lucky to be in Fayetteville. A Muslim acquaintance in Wichita complains that Christians there do not accept Muslims. And a friend in California finally took her *hijab* off "because," says Mahfuza, "she got a lot of social pressure."

Mahfuza herself did not wear a *hijab* when she first came to the United States. Then, sometime before 9/11, she found herself out of a job and for the first time had time to read the Koran. "And like a magnet, it had conduction," she says. "It was midnight, but I was still studying. And since we believe the Koran is from Allah, we have to follow it."

One of the Koran's teachings, which Mahfuza had never previously understood, was modesty. Wearing the *hijab* would mean that she was modest, or fully covered, with only her face and feet exposed. When she began putting on the *hijab* regularly, she was surprised to discover that people behaved more respectfully. "After 9/11, they paid more attention and asked a lot of questions," she says. Sometimes, these stymied her. "I thought, 'I don't know what my religion is.' And then I studied it."

More than a hundred years ago, Qasim Amin, an Egyptian attorney, noted in his landmark 1901 book *The Liberation of Women* that the status of women was ineluctably bound to the status of nations. Men, he wrote, treated women like slaves devoid of any intellect or moral compass. "This is the secret behind the imposition of the veil upon women for its continued existence," he said. "The first step for women's liberation is to tear off the veil and totally wipe out its existence."

Did Mahfuza ever consider the *hijab* as antifeminist or reactionary? "No," she insists. "I'm a very strong person for women's rights. Islam never says that those who wear *hijabs* are cut off from mainstream society. And since I started to wear the *hijab* in 1996, I never feel constricted. My husband is not asking me to do it. It's my decision."

She and Ali may be intellectually forward-thinking, but their religious convictions inform their conversation and define their moral universe. "We communicate about film and society and what is going on," Akhtar says, then immediately returns to the subject of modesty. "We recently studied how the students dress on the campus here. We cannot look at them. Their dress is too tiny, tiny, tiny. Unprofessional."

Mahfuza explains that the word *jihad* means "self-control," although the generally accepted definition is that it means a "fight" or "struggle." In the West, *jihad* has a military connotation, referring to a holy war or a crusade, but the word is often used in a more spiritual or individual context.

"Men and ladies should both control their desire," Mahfuza says. "Showing your boob will automatically bring some attraction. That's why we have a dress code—to cover your boob parts and head in public. But at home you can take off everything. It is our belief that the beauty of the lady should be preserved for the husband."

Unalloyed romantics might celebrate such notions of modesty and concealment, but many Western women would find them, if not unpalatable, then, at the very least, absurdly old-fashioned and a misplaced gesture of obeisance.

When Ahktar first came to Fayetteville, she and her husband rented an apartment with a communal swimming pool. One hot summer day, Mahfuza's two sons, then quite young, were splashing around in the pool and begged her to join them. As was her custom back home, she waded in to her knees, wearing a long, cream-colored *kamiz*. The building manager ran over and insisted she leave the pool, saying that she could not wear a dress, because she would sink. "'I can swim,' I told her," she says, but her protest was to no avail.

Since Islamic custom dictates that women cannot publicly show their legs, arms, or midriffs, they usually do not swim at all. "I'm careful not to get wet, since I'm shy to show my boob in public," she explains.

Asked how religious she considers herself to be, Mahfuza describes herself as neither extremist nor fundamentalist but "in the mainstream of Islam." Still, she prays five times a day and talks a great deal about being a good Muslim, which, she says, "means submission to the will of God."

Once a month the family attends a potluck dinner at the two-story Islamic Center in Fayetteville, which Bayyari helped to build and which is already too small to accommodate all its members comfortably. At these events the women pray and eat upstairs and the men, downstairs. "This is because of space problems," she says. "It's so small we sit on the floor. So when I cook, I bring two dishes—one for upstairs, one for down. Here, the men won't have a fascination for the women."

No matter the size of the space, however, Islamic men and women always pray separately. Usually, women kneel in lines behind the men. "We pray, shoulder-to-shoulder, to show that we are all equal, rich and poor," she says. "Also, we believe in Satan, and when we are shoulder-to-shoulder, the devil cannot come between us."

Mahfuza claims that such segregation is primarily for the benefit of women. If a woman is pregnant or ill, she says, she can easily leave without interrupting the men's prayers. "Also, if a huge fat lady prays, and the men are behind her, they will be distracted by her butt," she offers, adding that men, more easily tempted by women, also need to pray more often. "Ladies are blessed. They get extra benefits for taking care of their husbands and children. Some people say Muslim women are deprived, but it is written that we all are equal. This was the last sermon of the Prophet before he died."

. . . .

Since the spring of 2006, the Bentonville Muslims have rented, for $600 a month, a tiny single-story house on a side street off North Walton Boulevard, about three minutes by car from Wal-Mart's home office, where so many of them work, and they have created an impromptu mini-mosque. For the corporation's Muslim employees, it is easier to pray here than to drive the forty or so minutes to Fayetteville's Islamic Center. Many IT workers visit this quiet, tree-lined residential street for afternoon or early evening prayers. And women from the community teach Sunday school here to a handful of children.

One sweltering Sunday morning in August, three Indian Muslim women wrapped in colorful embroidered *shalawars* and *hijabs* ignore the broken air conditioning in the small room as they read a Muslim version of Adam and Eve to five small children who are sitting, barefoot, on Oriental prayer mats. Another older group of kids sits in a circle, learning Arabic characters. The girls, too young to put on *hijabs*, nevertheless wear traditional Indian garb. Like the children's attention spans, the session is short, and after forty-five minutes or so, including a juice break, school is adjourned.

Afterward, the teachers introduce themselves to me. Bilquis Khod, a physician specializing in geriatric medicine, grew up in Kuwait and did her internship and residency in New York City before the Northwest Medical Center in Rogers recruited her to move to Northwest Arkansas. She says she has never experienced any prejudice, either in New York or the Ozarks.

Humera Khan is originally from India, but she earned her undergraduate degree in computer technology and business administration from the University of Wisconsin–Green Bay, which, she says, had a much larger Muslim population than that of Northwest Arkansas. She and her husband, both computer programmers, work at Wal-Mart's home office. "It's a wonderful community," she says. "And I personally don't care what religion you are. All my friends here are white Christian Americans."

Life for Khan was not so homogeneous in the days following 9/11, when she was living in Wisconsin. Occasionally, she says, locals "asked my daughter if her parents made bombs in the basement of their home. These stereotypes hurt. But I feel that if you're always good to everybody, people will realize it. Maybe not now, but later."

Khan wears a headscarf at all times, even at Wal-Mart, where she works forty-four hours a week. The rest of her attire, she says, is "business formal—that is, pantsuits."

Clearly the *hijab* seems to have emerged as a marker of Muslim women's post-9/11 social identity as well as a simple sign of religious obedience and modesty. Mohja Kahf, a Muslim professor at the University of Arkansas and the author of the 2006 novel *The Girl in the Tangerine Scarf,* has suggested that "for some young women, the veil in America works a bit like the Afro during the black power era."

Others, however, see it as something more sinister—that is, as a way for Islamist governments to retain control over their female populations. The controversial Syrian American psychologist and Islamic critic Wafa Sultan, a nonpracticing Muslim, told the *Jerusalem Post* that when she first moved to the United States, the Saudi government offered her a stipend of $1,500 a month to wear the *hijab* and attend a mosque.

Many American women, especially feminists who fought—and are still fighting—for equal pay, abortion rights, and a way to permanently shatter the corporate glass ceiling, regard the *hijab* as a gesture of subordination and submission. They read Muslim women's insistence on wearing the veil as both a setback to feminism and an act that defies assimilation and embraces separatism. Mahfuza Akhtar, for one, passionately rebuts this. "Those who think the *hijab* is antifeminist are lacking in knowledge," she says. "I'm an American citizen. I'm driving, shopping, swimming. I'm wearing *hijab* and doing the same things that white ladies without *hijab* do." As proof, Mahfuza recalls going out to a farm in nearby Prairie Grove with her two sons shortly before preparing food for the Islamic Center's monthly potluck dinner. Wearing jeans and her *hijab,* she slaughtered a lamb according to Halal guidelines, which means, she says, "We uttered Allah's name while we cut its throat." Then she skinned the animal and cut it into pieces. "I am a biologist, so I am good at cutting the skin," she explains her somewhat offbeat and, some would say, misguided interpretation of feminism. "Better than my husband."

Mahfuza vehemently insists that she never feels separated from the mainstream of America. "I cook American food at home. I wear pants. I'm American in my heart, and I have a responsibility to this society," she says.

"But I'm Bengali—always. And I want to blend these two cultures in my own way. *That* is what is comfortable for me."

Sticky Wickets?

On any warm weekend afternoon, thirty men, primarily Indians and Pakistanis, can be seen carrying kneepads, flat bats, and other exotic equipment toward the baseball field at Memorial Park, a forty-acre complex off Southwest J Street, right next to Bentonville High School. Sometimes as many as one hundred friends, fans, and family members, many of them women adorned in brilliantly colored native dresses and *hijabs*, accompany them. They are here to root for their favorite local cricket team.

Cricket? If anything proves the growing international nature of Northwest Arkansas, it is the regular matches that take place here on weekend afternoons or, from time to time, at a park in Rogers. Sometimes it is simply one Wal-Mart team against another. But when Wal-Mart challenges J. B. Hunt or Tyson, things can get competitive.

Zakir Syed, a direct import systems manager at Wal-Mart, plays occasionally on one of the company's three teams, although he says, "This year I wasn't that involved. But I'm thinking of having my group at work challenge a neighboring department as a team-building exercise."

A Muslim from India whose family moved to Jefferson, Indiana, when he was in high school, Syed studied computer graphics at Purdue, where, he says, "One of my professors told us that Wal-Mart's overall database was second only to the Pentagon's."

Syed has been working on that Wal-Mart database since October 2004 and is also treasurer of the Bentonville mosque. Only a few years ago, he says, local Muslims prayed in one another's apartments. Now a half dozen men show up at this one-room house for prayers each evening. On Friday nights, thirty or so attend. With such a tiny space, a mere curtain, and a flimsy one at that, separates the men and women. "I'm not a fan of that curtain thing," he says, "but you have to go by what the majority thinks is right."

The small congregation intends to build a real mosque in Bentonville in the near future. "We're trying to collect from within the community at this moment," he says.

Syed, who says that he has never gotten hassled in Bentonville because of his religion, chairs one of Wal-Mart's numerous diversity committees—

the one for Asians and Pacific Islanders. He oversees what the company calls "retention and recruitment" and says, "My responsibility is how to retain our internal associates. It's a challenge because when people get recruited from big cities, they might not like it here because it's a small town and there's not much to do. So with Asians, for instance, we help them to find Asian food stores. With Muslims, we tell them about the mosque or about Indian movies that play sometimes in Springdale. Whatever their needs are, we help them." Bentonville Muslims have not yet shown the same buying power that Grand Rapids, Michigan, Muslims have—a reality that inspired the Wal-Mart there to install an entire section during the winter of 2008 in order to cater to Muslims' food and clothing needs, everything from dates and hummus to *hijabs*. Still, Wal-Mart's gesture is an unabashed nod to the growing diversity across the United States.

For the past three years Syed has also been on the planning committee for the annual Multicultural Fair, which takes place on Bentonville Square. Many local sponsors participate, he says, but Wal-Mart remains the major force, having donated five thousand dollars every year. At the Muslim booth, locals can pick up pamphlets explaining Islam. "It's the second-largest religion in the world," he says, "but people know very little about it."

Syed is a strong proponent of diversity. "We who come from other countries look at things with fresh eyes," he explains. "I believe that the increasing diversity in this area also encourages people to have a much broader perspective about life. You know, Northwest Arkansas is growing so rapidly. And exposing people to new cultures is very important to help drive this change—and also to help everyone embrace it."

A True Assimilationist

Bayyari guides his Range-Rover vehicle into the parking lot of the eight-story Springdale Holiday Inn, right off the 540 and 412 intersections. As it turns out, his lunch with Nesson is also a lunch with 150 or so others—it is, more precisely, the weekly Springdale Rotary Club meeting in one of the hotel ballrooms, with its de rigueur buffet table heaped with warmed-over chicken. Here Bayyari goes into supersocial mode, oozing charm as he drawls hellos to an array of businesspeople at his table, waving or smiling to others.

The program begins when the Rotarians stand to recite the Pledge of Allegiance and sing "God Bless America." Bayyari joins in with gusto. Then a local woman makes a long-winded PowerPoint presentation about how to avoid stress through massage and yoga, the kind of stuff that regularly appears in women's magazines. At its merciful conclusion, the Rotarians applaud, then disperse to network. Yet the meeting has served its purpose; like a church, it offers a sense of community and civic engagement, but here the context is pure business.

Moments later, Bayyari, back in the parking lot, finally locates Nesson. Of middle height and middle weight, he is a year or two north of sixty, wears an open-collared white shirt and a thoughtful expression, and looks as if he might have just flown in from Manhattan's Garment Center. There is a lot of backslapping and warm banter between the men.

Nesson later recalls that he and Bayyari first met eleven years ago when Nesson joined the Rotary Club. "And I was very interested in learning more about him," he says, "because we stood out—a Jewish guy and an Arab Muslim guy in a sea of Baptists."

At that time, there were no African Americans in the Rotary Club (now there is one) and only one Hispanic (today there are eight). And Nesson decided that this was his opportunity to get to know someone who, he was pretty certain, had led a fascinating life. So the two men made a lunch date. "And," he says, "we became good friends."

Then the Jewish community of Fayetteville hit a snag in its attempt to buy a historical building and convert it into a synagogue—and that's when Bayyari came to the rescue. Temple Shalom, which operates out of the University of Arkansas Hillel, planned to pay $1.2 million for the Butterfly House, a unique glass structure built in 1959 by E. Fay Jones, a protégé of Frank Lloyd Wright, and transform it into its first permanent house of worship. This striking modern building, empty for years, sits atop a steep road on Rockwood Trail, an upscale area of the city. But homeowners and planning commission members alike vigorously opposed the conversion, balking at potential traffic hazards and complaining that a house of worship in their residential community would be a distraction.

While the Jews withdrew their bid rather than taking legal action, the Becket Fund for Religious Liberty, a Washington, D.C.–based organization, wrote a scathing note to the Fayetteville City Council and mayor: "To deny this congregation's application to be the first Jewish synagogue in Fayetteville . . . when Christian churches are located in other residential zones within the city would legitimately give rise to serious concerns" under federal antidiscrimination laws.

Yet Nesson himself defends Fayetteville's decision. "You have to know a little bit about how this community operates to judge whether it was anti-Semitism," he explains. "There are people who don't want their roads widened. They don't want more traffic, more apartment buildings, commercial buildings, or duplexes. They just want things the way they are." As proof, he points out that one of the most vociferous in the fight against the synagogue was a man whose own late wife had been Jewish.

Bayyari saw things differently. "To me, it's God's house," he later told the *Chicago Tribune*. "You don't resist having a house of worship in your neighborhood."

And so during a Rotary lunch, Bayyari approached Nesson. "And he said to me, 'I've been reading about what's happening, and it sounds like anti-Semitism to me. I want you to let your congregation know that if they decide to build a synagogue, I will build it for them at my cost for materials and labor,'" said Nesson. "For Fadil to have made an offer like that to us is just unbelievable."

Unsurprisingly, the Jews of Temple Shalom jumped at it. So did the local press.

Nesson believes that Bayyari's gesture is no public relations ploy. "Fadil is a person of conscience," he explains. "He cares deeply about what is going on around him. It brought tears to my eyes that someone who left a land of great conflict would come to the U.S., become successful, and want to give back the way he has. It is phenomenal."

Bayyari turns out to be one of those optimists who seriously believe that people can get along, no matter their color or faith. That being said, after his October 2008 trip to the West Bank, his first in ten years, he expressed uncharacteristic frustration and disgust. He had been held at a checkpoint by Israeli Uzis after a nine-hour trip from Amman, Jordan, to his hometown. "If the border was open and there was peace, I could have driven that distance in two hours flat," he says. But he was most disheartened by the West Bank itself—by the Israelis who keep building settlements there and by the Palestinians themselves. "Unemployment is high, the people are poor, the towns are filthy," he complains. "I was so disappointed in my people. But I could tell from their demeanor that they are mad and upset about the Occupation, no more and no less. They are in bondage to the Israelis. The Israelis need to get out of there and conclude a peace treaty with them. They all need to figure a way out of this standoff."

Cautiously critical of his fellow Palestinian Muslims as well, Bayyari blames them, and their late leader, Arafat, for having created their own desperate situation in the Middle East. And he seems more interested in understanding the big picture than in defending any specific politics. "I found out pretty quick that, hey, we are all children of God," he reiterates. "There is no difference among Jews, Arabs, and Christians, except in the way they worship."

Perhaps because he usually sees the world with such equanimity, he has had little difficulty assimilating into the larger Christian community. "Nobody in this town has ever said a bad word to me," he insists. "Never."

But according to Nesson, it has not been quite that easy for Bayyari. Shortly after 9/11, he says, Bayyari accompanied his wife to Springdale's huge First Baptist Church, where the pastor gave a hellfire-and-brimstone speech attacking Muslims. While it wasn't directed toward Bayyari, the speech disturbed him. "He felt insecure in that environment," says Nesson. "But he didn't want to draw attention to himself and felt helpless to correct this person's vituperation."

So Nesson suggested that the two of them—the Jew and the Arab—visit the pastor together. "I said, 'We ought to tell him Christians are not the only people around here, and if you stand at a pulpit and lecture about hatred and revenge, then you're endangering people's lives,'" said Nesson. "'And that is certainly not the Christian way.'" But, in fact, the two outsiders never did pay that visit.

It is characteristic of Bayyari that he does not dust off such a discomforting story for public consumption. One of his gifts, according to his friend Mason Hiba, is that he always chooses the honorable road. "Fadil is very generous. When something noble comes across his table, he feels responsible to take charge of it," he says. "For example, his kids go to a school that needed another classroom. And its director, who told me this, says he was just asking Fadil what he thought about how the work should be done. And Fadil said, 'This is how. And we can do it if you get me the paperwork by such-and-such a date.' He basically said, 'I can build it for you, and I will.'"

In April 2007, Bayyari, in a gesture of goodwill, brought his family to a Passover Seder at the Hilton Hotel, along with one hundred Jews from the

Fayetteville Hillel. "My kids liked it," he said. "We're building relationships with the Jews and becoming really great friends."

Early that Good Friday morning, Bayyari drove me to a Starbucks perhaps five minutes from his Johnson office. Between howdys and hiyas to friends picking up their morning lattes, he pondered why this Bible Belt community had created what he considered to be a deeply nurturing environment for its minorities. Good economic times, he believed, had had a lot to do with it: "Wal-Mart, Tyson's, and Hunt have all had incredible growth in the last five years. And, of course, this town has been growing ever since I got here in 1980, and we probably have another twenty years ahead of us." For him, the boom town had supported personal prosperity, which had, in turn, supported religious and ethnic tolerance.

Certainly, having more than enough jobs to go around has been one reason for widespread local acceptance of newcomers from disparate backgrounds in Northwest Arkansas. In addition, from the moment in 1994 that Wal-Mart sought to hire outsiders, it began to educate its insiders— that is, its home office associates—by initiating regular diversity seminars and workshops to help its new hires find their bearings in the community.

Most people in the area, however, credit the fact that they get along so well with people of other religions and ethnicities to their faith. No matter the cultural differences, they say, the bonding substance, the communal cement, is the intensity of that faith, even if the mode of worship differs from group to group.

Bayyari is someone who practices his religion in private; publicly and exuberantly, he embraces assimilation and things American, from his signature jeans and baseball cap to his consistent Rotary Club presence and, as a way of giving back to the community for his extraordinary success, a willingness to help finance local community efforts, be they schools, parks, churches, or synagogues.

· · · · · · · · · ·

By January 2008, however, the boom town, impacted by the subprime mortgage crisis, had already hit a glitch and would in the next year begin to implode. Even then, Bayyari conceded, building was slowing down, but as a result, the price of materials and labor was falling, which was some small consolation.

Ten months later, he soberly acknowledges the depth of the economic crisis. "Residential real estate is dead," he says, "but we do mostly commercial. We're able to keep going by building more and making sure that we're taking care of our existing tenants. We just have to work harder. It is also a good time to concentrate on acquisition."

With fewer construction jobs available, the Hispanic workforce has thinned out in recent months. I ask Bayyari his viewpoint on the area's exploding Hispanic population and the current crackdown on undocumented workers. "Hispanics are hard workers," he says carefully. "I have Hispanics working for me, great people. But the problem is that our immigration department is not screening who comes through our borders." Like so many immigrants who have waited their turn to become American citizens, Bayyari does not support illegal immigration. "I came in the front door—legally—and believe all people should," he says. "You know, we want the best of all people here. We don't want the rejects of the world."

Then he returns to the Temple Shalom project, which survived a precarious capital campaign and is still in the process of putting together a total of $1.3 million to finish construction. Bayyari's gift of free labor and materials provided at cost will save the synagogue at least $250,000.

Although all the money is not yet in place, the temple and Bayyari broke ground on October 14, 2007, in a ceremony attended by dignitaries from all the religious communities in the area—except, ironically, the Jews of Congregation Etz Chaim in Bentonville, a few of whom claimed, privately and bitterly, that they had not been invited. Bayyari had wanted to get started by then so that the foundation and shell would be up by the rainy season. By October 2008, he had made spectacular progress, having completed the foundation, which, he says, "we've got under a roof. And we'll be installing doors and windows in the next couple of weeks. We're putting it on the fast track, and I have a feeling that six months from now we'll have it finished."

It was not.

Although the community has struggled to raise completion money, help came from an unexpected source—St. Paul's Episcopal Church, which provided a meeting room for an elaborate sit-down dinner and fundraiser in September 2008. "I was one of the sponsors, and more than two hundred people came," Bayyari says, adding that the chancellor of the University of Arkansas gave the keynote speech. "We had entertainment and both a silent auction and regular auction. And I stood up and said, 'This is for interfaith reconciliation, and I need to see you guys open your minds, your hearts, and your pocketbooks.' It was a really great coming together of Muslims, Christians, and Jews to help our Jewish brothers in their efforts to have their synagogue." In the end, the event raised $45,000. "It really touches my heart," he says.

For Bayyari, the true assimilationist, helping out the Jewish community by engaging the Christian community perfectly summarizes the man he has become. Indeed, he is the first to acknowledge that living in the United States has broadened his social and religious horizons. "This is the land of milk and honey," he says. "Pretty quickly I realized it's nice to be tolerant and loving rather than hostile. I've made friends here of all religions— Jews, Baptists, Catholics, Hindus, you name it. Long ago I decided this was the ride I wanted to take in my life."

As for his own brand of philanthropy, learned at the feet of the Wal-Mart veteran Willard Walker, Bayyari is philosophical. "You figure it out as you go," he muses. "At some point I started to feel that whatever I've got is not really mine. We come in with nothing and leave with nothing. The Lord has blessed me with a great deal, but I am no more than a custodian. And being a custodian means to honor that calling by doing what is right."

A Shul Is Born

··········

On a balmy Tuesday evening in December 2006, Sheldon Hirsch and his wife, Nicole, brought a menorah to the Christmas concert of their three-year-old son, Justin, at his preschool, the Helen R. Walton Children's Enrichment Center.[1] And a few days later, they conducted a preschool "outreach" by visiting his class. Nicole, a tall woman with reddish curls spilling about her strong face, arrived armed with latkes (potato pancakes), applesauce, picture books about Hanukkah, and a dark, bearded doll called Hanukkah Harry. The mission? To let Justin's twelve Christian classmates celebrate Hanukkah—and Judaism. Unfortunately, Harry, with his scowling face, frightened one boy to tears.

··········

It is perhaps no surprise, given the larger history of the Jews, that here in Northwest Arkansas the Jewish community is struggling to define itself, unclear when to cross that delicate line between blending in and asserting itself as a community with particular needs of its own. This is especially true at holiday time. The Hirsches, who are committed to this outreach, are among those who feel confident enough to share—and explain—their Jewishness, even to the seesaw set.

Sheldon Hirsch, burly and balding, with glasses, mustache, and a wisp of a goatee, has been living in Northwest Arkansas for more than fifteen years, and he continues to be happily surprised by the inclusive way that Bible Belt southerners welcome him. They are amused rather than put off by his decidedly honking New York accent. "Especially when I was first down here," he says, "they were just so intrigued by it. And they loved to listen to me talk."

Hirsch, who in 2007 joined Wal-Mart's operations group after a lengthy job search, originally migrated to Bentonville from New York fifteen years ago for two reasons. First, he was recovering from a cocaine habit that had hit him hard in his twenties, and he figured that Arkansas would offer up healthier living. Second, he was working with his father and brothers as vendors of business gifts and small items for the home, and shortly after his father's death he moved down to the Bentonville area to represent their company. But soon the brothers, without their father as anchor, began to fight among themselves, and in 2004 their business collapsed.

In the meantime, Hirsch was determined to establish his own Arkansas roots. But down in the Bible Belt, Jewish girls were as difficult to find as blintzes (a special kind of Jewish pancake) at the Rogers IHOP. "That was the toughest thing," he says, "being single *and* Jewish."

And when Hirsch drove the thirty minutes down Interstate 540 to Fayetteville for Shabbat services at the University of Arkansas Hillel on Friday nights, he inevitably felt awkward. (Shabbat is the Jewish Sabbath, which begins at sundown on Friday and ends at sundown on Saturday.) The Fayetteville Jews, mostly academic types connected to the university, seemed oddly aloof, and Hirsch, with a combination of hubris and naivete, couldn't help wondering why they didn't snap him up for a Shabbat dinner or try to make a *shidduck,* or match, for him with a nice Jewish girl. After all, he was that rarity—a single Jewish guy in Wal-Mart-land. "But the hand of friendship was not there," he says.

So he joined JDate. An exchange of e-mails, by turns funny and romantic, with Nicole Green, a vivacious woman from Buffalo, New York, deepened into a relationship and, eventually, marriage. Nicole moved down to Arkansas, and six years ago they plunked down $279,000 for a three-thousand-square-foot ranch set on a wooded acre in a small community of pristine brick-and-shingle houses, each one prettily different from the next. In her early forties by the time they wed, Nicole made no effort to hide her agenda. More than anything, she wanted to be a mom and was elated when Justin was born. Eight days later the couple flew in a mohel, or rabbi who performs circumcisions, from Houston and a pastrami from Kansas City, Missouri, for what was, they say, the area's first bris, or ritual circumcision.

With the birth of their child, the Hirsches became concerned about establishing a Jewish community. They wanted Justin to have Jewish friends and a Jewish education, but they knew few families with small children. So, as a way of networking, they tried Temple Shalom again. But Nicole, like her husband, could not quite connect with the Fayetteville Jews. "In Bentonville we're more, you know, Wal-Mart," she says. "We're about business. That is why most people have moved here."

. . . .

On the first night of Hanukkah 2006, Nicole Hirsch maneuvers the family van through the Arkansas dusk and pulls into a parking space on Bentonville's town square, which is already festooned with thousands of colored Christmas lights. In a few moments, a town official will throw the switch, and the giant menorah and Star of David will twinkle on the square as well. Nicole cheerleads the moment, trying to convey to her son its momentous nature. But Justin remains unimpressed, preferring to sit in his car seat and play with a small orange dreidel, a top marked with Hebrew letters used in a game played mostly at Hanukkah. "At the beginning, there were so few kids around," says Nicole, "that I kept thinking, 'What are we doing?' But we've had a baby boom here. At least fifteen babies have been born since I was pregnant. So Justin may even go to grade school with other Jewish kids, which I never expected to happen."

More and more, the Hirsches, like other transplanted Jewish families in the area, had felt the need to build a synagogue of their own. Carol and Paul Stuckey had also been attending the congregation at the Hillel in Fayetteville and chauffeuring their two daughters, one a grade-schooler, the other a tweener, to its religious school on Sundays simply because no other existed. They, too, felt the Hillel was not fulfilling their needs and became part of that thimble-tiny group of Bentonville Jews determined to build a synagogue to their own liking. Whatever that was.

The Little Congregation That Could

Getting the shul, or synagogue, off the ground was no simple task. The process actually began on July 13, 2004, when twelve Jewish families from the area came together at the Rogers home of David and Wynnie Hoodis with the sole purpose of trying to form a congregation. "We just talked: Did we have the commitment? The people? The fortitude? We knew it would be a huge undertaking," said Hoodis, a tall, dark-haired man of around forty who is vice president of operations at Wal-Mart. "And what would the synagogue and a Jewish community mean? What kind of affiliation would we have? How would we practice?"

The group was pretty diverse. There were Jews who had moved to the area from big cities such as Dallas, Chicago, and New York. There were reform Jews and religious Jews and a number, surprisingly, who had converted to Judaism, like the Stuckeys. There were also Wal-Mart employees, vendors, retirees, and a doctor. Some among these initial families had been in the community for as many as ten years, and many had small children who were not getting the Jewish education their parents would have liked. Temple Shalom in Fayetteville was not really a full-fledged synagogue anyway but a former frat house that had been converted into the University of Arkansas Hillel. And, like the Hirsches, other Bentonville business types were simply not comfortable there.

So, sitting on the deeply cushioned brown leather sofas of Hoodis's living room in the gated Pinnacle Hills community, the families decided to put up seed money of between $1,200 and $1,800 apiece. In the days that followed, they e-mailed one another and divided research responsibilities.

Then the Bentonville/Bella Vista Chamber of Commerce gave them the use of a meeting room in the advertising and promotions office on Sunday mornings for a religious school. Wynnie, small, dark-eyed, and with uncommon poise, says, "The school was the key. Once that fell into place, we knew we could make this thing happen."

Families with small kids and empty nesters alike knew how important a religious school was, and Betsy Rosen, whose husband, Marc, is a Wal-Mart executive, took that on. The Rosens had moved to town from Chicago, and, as Betsy told the *New York Times* in 2006, you don't need to belong to a synagogue in Chicago because everywhere you turn there are Jews. Here, however, she and Marc sent their son, Joshua, to a First Baptist preschool because it was among the best in the area, and she says,

"We were very happy with it." Until their child came home one day with a picture of Jesus.

Now that they had actually formed a group and were talking about this imaginary synagogue, the Wal-Mart Jews were determined to establish a Jewish identity in Bentonville. By August 4 they formally founded Congregation Etz Chaim and elected its board. By September 12 the religious school was operational. The modest little meeting room soon offered five classes every Sunday, functioning effectively for almost a year as a one-room schoolhouse. "By the time we started, we had more than twenty families—and about twenty-five kids showing up," Hoodis says. Today there are sixty-odd families and between thirty-five and forty-five children.

The group had also begun to hold informal Friday night services at the Boys and Girls Club in Bentonville. "We were fumbling through them, however, because none of us had ever led a service by ourselves," says Wynnie. "And no one could carry a tune."

But it didn't matter, really. It was all about the dream. And the community.

The Jews, says Hirsch, wanted to paint a cohesive picture of their growing presence. "We want to let people who are transferring here know that they don't have to worry about their children getting a Jewish education. My biggest fear was that my son would grow up and wouldn't know what being Jewish was all about," he says. "For a while, there was this restaurant, Eat This, which featured Jewish food, and I remember my wife saying, 'I never thought that my child would actually order matzoh ball soup in a restaurant in Arkansas.' But he did. And we did."

When the High Holy Days rolled around in late September 2004, if the new synagogue was not yet a fact of life, the new congregation certainly was. In concert with the Fayetteville Hillel, the Bentonville Jews kicked off the Jewish New Year by holding Rosh Hashanah services in Fayetteville, and then for Yom Kippur, the Day of Atonement and holiest of holy days, the two groups jointly rented the auditorium at the shiny new Northwest Arkansas Community College. It marked the first-ever High Holy Days service held in Benton County. "People came to services who had lived here for ten, twelve, or fifteen years and never did *anything* Jewish," says Hoodis. "And they were excited about it and about the potluck Shabbat dinners we were having on Friday nights."

Somewhat mystically, that October 4, during the week of Simchas Torah, the holiday on which Jews celebrate the Torah, the young congregation received a portentous gift. An older couple, Jules and Jo Feinberg, having heard about the effort to establish Etz Chaim, drove more than six hours north to Bentonville, bringing precious cargo: one of two sacred Torahs from their synagogue, Beth Israel, in El Dorado, Arkansas.

Like the ten other remaining synagogues in the state, El Dorado had for years been losing young members. With membership down to around fifteen, El Dorado was fighting the inevitable and hardly needed two Torahs. So the Feinbergs provisionally donated one to Etz Chaim.

A Torah is a sacred scroll containing the first five books of the Old Testament, handwritten in Hebrew. This Torah, the new congregation would discover, had a special history. In June 2006, after the *New York Times* ran an article about Etz Chaim, the synagogue received a letter from a man who identified himself as Jack Feibelman and explained his family's "very personal connection" with this particular Torah:

> When I escaped from Germany in 1936 I joined my elderly uncle Adolf Feibelman who lived in Camden, Arkansas, since 1886. My parents joined me a couple years later and brought to Camden the Torah snatched from the Temple in the Feibelman hometown of Ruelzheim [Rülzheim] (in southwestern Germany). That temple of course was destroyed. When the congregation in Camden closed, we decided on donating the Torah to the El Dorado congregation. So it came about that you now have this Torah in Bentonville as a symbol of survival from a congregation that was over 400 years old.

And it was an appropriate symbol. By the end of 2004, the number of families who had committed to joining Etz Chaim had already risen to thirty-two. Heady with success, the scrappy group started thinking about either buying or renting a suitable property.

It was serendipity when Steve Fineberg, a local commercial realtor and one of the synagogue's original members, informed the group that the Hispanic Assemblies of God Church on the corner of Moberly and Central was available for $225,000. Says Wynnie, "We knew we had to jump on it because that's a great corner in Bentonville."

The group closed on the new building on March 24 and spent the next six months cleaning, hammering, and painting with their own hands. By early May they were affixing the traditional mezuzah, or encased parchment, a symbol of God's watchfulness, on the doorpost; on May 20 they celebrated their first-ever Shabbat in the new building.

But still, there was work to do. The goal was to ready everything for the fall dedication. The Jews of Bentonville wanted to celebrate their first High Holy Days in a shul of their own.

The Dedication

At 6:00 P.M. on September 16, 2005—a balmy Friday evening, as it turned out, just two weeks after Hurricane Katrina had devastated New Orleans—an enormous white tent floated across the stubbly grass of the parking lot that stood next to the tiny white building at the corner of Moberly Lane and Central Avenue in Bentonville. Cars lined the streets and jammed the strip mall across the way. People dressed in their Shabbat best spilled out of the tent and milled about the modest building as the mournful strains of centuries-old Hebrew melodies filled the air.

It was a symbolic moment for the area's small Jewish population and also for the community at large. The dedication of the county's first synagogue, Etz Chaim, which means "Tree of Life" in Hebrew, signified that the Wal-Mart Jews were emphatically putting down roots in a state where not even a dozen synagogues remained. In fact, this was the first small-town shul to open in the South in fifty years.

And the congregation respected the gravity of the evening. It was celebrating its small victory—sheer existence—and so, along with families and friends, the members had invited all the prominent local political figures in the area—among them, then-mayor of Bentonville Terry Coberly; the mayor of neighboring Rogers, Steve Womack; and Bentonville's superintendent of schools, Gary Compton.

More important, even, the Jews, as a token of goodwill, had reached out to representatives from the Catholic and Baptist churches, the Bentonville Islamic Center, and the Northwest Arkansas Hindu Association, asking them to participate in the dedication, which was intertwined with the evening's Shabbat service. Each read excerpts from "A Prayer for Flood-Filled Days," a poem written by two rabbis to honor the victims of Hurricane Katrina, with a text comparing its devastating flood to Noah's Flood.

Rabbi Debra Kassoff, the director of rabbinical services at the Institute of Southern Jewish Life, had flown in from Jackson, Mississippi, to lead the evening's service. She created a blend of prayers, speeches, and traditional Hebrew songs that concluded with a procession of the Torah scroll in which the entire group, 250 strong—members, children, guests, and public officials—walked, singing, behind one of the board members carrying the Torah. The group circled the shul, then entered it. After the rabbi opened the ark, the cupboard designed to house the sacred scroll, the Torah that had been inherited from the struggling congregation 320 miles away was placed inside its new resting place for the first time.

"It was very moving," says Hirsch. "I cried. We all cried."

Rabbi Kassoff felt the enormity of the occasion as well. "The congregation was so proud of their accomplishment and what they had built for themselves, for their children, and the community," she says. "I was just blown away that I got to be a part of it."

Together everyone recited the blessing usually said over bread on the Sabbath, and guests from as far away as Chicago and Minneapolis drank wine, feasted on cakes and fruit, and browsed the interior of the synagogue, with its fresh coat of golden-yellow paint, purple carpet, and tangerine-cushioned wooden pews inherited from the building's last inhabitants. What visitors also found was the Judaica Walk—small tables set against the walls to display Jewish art and ritual objects. The home-style museum was the congregation's attempt to demystify Jewish traditions for visitors of other faiths. Members brought personal objects and wrote explanations for the menorahs, kiddush cups, and prayer shawls on display. One couple brought a rare family Torah; another, their ketubah, or Jewish wedding contract. Yet another exhibited a Judaic woodcut that his father had made.

The non-Jews proved genuinely curious. "When people find out we're Jewish, they have constant questions," Wynnie says. "We found we have to be very learned."

The Jews were also wary. Concerned about how the larger community might respond to the presence of a shul, they contacted the Bentonville Police Department, which agreed to put extra patrols on duty that night. They were not necessary.

"We didn't get even one nasty letter slipped under our door," says Hoodis. "Not ever." To the contrary, he says. The Christian community in the area, like most conservative evangelicals, is so pro-Israel that during a recent Israeli-Palestinian altercation, a local man came by and donated $500 as a gesture of support.

This suggests an irony of sorts: evangelical Christians support Israel not because both religions share a belief in a Judeo-Christian God, not because Israel exists as a rare democracy in the Middle East, and not even because its existence can be seen as reparation for the genocide of the Holocaust. Rather, evangelicals embrace the Jewish homeland because of simple biblical prophecy admonishing Christians that Israel's establishment, and the return of the Jews to their desert homeland, are necessary before the Rapture and Second Coming of Jesus can occur. The Left Behind series of books by Tim LaHaye and Jerry B. Jenkins, which have sold many millions of copies since the first volume was published in 1995, has gone a long way to popularize this view. So the evangelical embrace of Israel has nothing whatsoever to do with religious tolerance or political acceptance and everything to do with a literal reading of the Scriptures.

Whatever the reasons, much of Bentonville gathered to celebrate the birth of Etz Chaim, the Jewish community's formal declaration of existence. "The dedication was a great event for the whole community," said Rich Davis, vice president of economic development for the Bentonville/ Bella Vista Chamber of Commerce, who called the dedication "this consummate Chamber of Commerce evening."

"I still recall the invitation," he remembers. "On the front was a menorah and something written in Hebrew, and inside it said SHALOM, Y'ALL, which made me laugh. In the grand scheme of things, this event was exactly a reflection of the diversity that's occurring here."

Postpartum Papa

It is something of an irony that Sheldon Hirsch missed the first High Holy Days at Etz Chaim. In fact, his life took a dramatic downward shift in the days after his son's birth. "Nicole got her dream come true—to be a mother," he says. Yet he was unprepared for what that entailed and how her attention now fixed on their infant son, what he ate, how warm he was, why his nose was running or his cheeks were flushed. Hirsch bluntly says, "I felt abandoned."

Making room for his rosy, golden-haired son was a tough recalibration. Emotionally vulnerable, unemployed, still mourning the loss of his family business and the breakdown of relations with his brothers, Hirsch buckled under the weight of fatherhood and slipped back into the coke-eyed world he had conquered almost twenty years earlier. "I had troubles with becoming a father and being second to Justin," he recalls. "But my wife says that normal people don't go out and smoke cocaine [when they feel abandoned]. That's where I have to take ownership of my problems and of what happened to us."

But it was difficult to own up to dabbling in cocaine, staying out late, and disappearing for days at a time. Nicole became concerned by her husband's erratic behavior, and angry, too. "My addiction went into rapid form," he says. "I needed to do cocaine all the time. I wasn't a good father. I wasn't a good husband. I quit for a few months, but nothing long-term, because I just didn't turn it over to a higher power. And it became an issue."

The couple went for counseling together, and Hirsch went to individual therapy. Eventually, he entered a treatment facility in Springdale. This is where he spent the bleaker-than-usual Yom Kippur of 2005, because the rehab center refused to allow him to leave. "So I got a prayer book and did what I had to do," he says.

It was not just a difficult time but an embarrassing one. The Hirsches were reluctant to discuss the situation with members of their congregation for fear that it might affect his business prospects. On the other hand, Nicole, with an infant to care for, felt alone and overwhelmed. "And she said to me, 'How am I going to deal with this unless we tell our friends what's going on?'" says Hirsch. "And you know what, they were there. They helped Nicole, and they helped me. It's been an interesting journey."

Yet from the ashes of his self-esteem, from the mess he had made of marriage and fatherhood, came self-discovery, faith, and a surprising new friendship. While Hirsch was struggling with his demons in the Springdale rehab, an Orthodox Chabad rabbi, Mendel Greisman, known as Mendy, who had moved to town with his wife and young family in the summer of 2005, visited him regularly. The two would put on *tefillin*—two little black boxes filled with biblical verses, which Orthodox men strap onto their arm and forehead when they recite morning prayers—and pray. And they would talk about faith and God. "I had become spiritually bankrupt," says Hirsch. "I couldn't pray. I couldn't dial God anymore. And the more I worked with Rabbi Mendy, the closer I felt toward Him. I don't misdial now."

There is something surreal about the notion of a Jewish drug addict in small-town, Christian Wal-Mart-land who, in order to fight his "demons," turns, for comfort and advice, to a Chabad rabbi. After all, this is *Arkansas*, of all places. Yet bizarre though it may seem, it also happens to be a fact of Hirsch's life.

Like many who have been through rehab and twelve-step programs, he embraces and often uses such program buzz phrases as *spirituality* and *bonding with my higher power.* With Greisman as his guide, he has also committed to putting on *tefillin* every morning. Hirsch considers Greisman to be one of the blessings of Bentonville.

"Had we been in New York, would we ever be exposed to Chabad?" Hirsch asks, tipping his virtual yarmulke to the unique nature of their Bentonville friendship. "The only exposure would be seeing them giving out Shabbat candles in the truck or walking down Forty-seventh Street, the heart of the Diamond Center."

. . . .

These days Hirsch also considers Wal-Mart to be a major blessing. After his long struggle to cleanse himself of drugs, two years in the job market, and a lengthy interview process at the home office, he finally, in August of 2007, was hired by the company as a home office associate. "I go out into the field and get testimonials from the stores that have piloted new innovations to streamline the shopping process," he explains. "One of my responsibilities is to communicate to managers why we are making certain changes and why we would need to adjust schedules at the registers and among the managers themselves, according to when our customers will be there. What we strive for is to make their jobs easier and to make the shopping experience better for our customers."

Hirsch seems exuberant and genuinely grateful to Wal-Mart for this opportunity. As a youngster he suffered from attention deficit/hyperactivity disorder (ADHD) before medications existed to control it, and consequently he never finished college. "I couldn't sit still for an hour at a time," he explains. Now he is taking the appropriate medication, which, he says, "keeps me engaged in projects and allows me to do the things I have always dreamed of doing."

As with most Wal-Marters, Hirsch keeps a strenuous schedule, arriving at the home office at about 6:15 A.M. on most days because, he says, "At that hour you can get a good parking spot. By 8:30 you have to park all the way out." He takes one hour for lunch and leaves at 4:00 P.M. unless unforeseen work crops up. "And then I'm there until 5:00 or 6:00 P.M." If everything is under control in his area, Hirsch says, "then I am empowered to find new concepts to make the procedures or the stores better."

Hirsch sees Wal-Mart as a fount of possibilities. "That's the amazing part of being here," he says. "I could work in operations for a year and a half, then go into their marketing or merchandising divisions. When you look through the job listings, there's just so much opportunity. This week I took a leadership class. They are giving me the opportunity to be a great leader. I feel that what I am doing now is a start, not an end point. Can I be a vice president someday? Maybe. I think I am creative enough. Will it take work? Yes."

When I ask Hirsch whether he, as a committed Jew, feels that Wal-Mart culture is, at its core, too Christian, he insists that, having just experienced his second High Holy Days as a Wal-Mart employee, he has received only respect and curiosity from colleagues interested in learning about Jewish customs. Still, he says diplomatically, "There's a lot of work ahead of us on diversity. For instance, one of my colleagues set a meeting during the High Holy Days, and I e-mailed him to suggest that it was probably not the best of days for this. And he *did* change the date." Another associate told Hirsch that the company would make sure that the High Holy Days would be noted on future calendars. "He was trying to be inclusive," he says. "We're making progress, so I look at things as getting better rather than worse."

Meanwhile, he professes contentment with his job, all the while refusing to discuss salary or stock options. "I have a very nice package," he says tactfully. "Could I be doing better? Sure. But I don't let myself go off on the negativity. Money doesn't drive me right now. I have a beautiful family and a beautiful home and a job I love doing. I'm very fortunate."

Still, moments of guilt and sorrow haunt Hirsch. He tries to help other people by working at a local rehab center part-time and by telling his story because "I don't want them to go through what I did." His darkest fear, however, is that his son will, one day, relive his mistakes. "Unfortunately they say alcohol and drug addiction are hereditary," Hirsch says. "If I keep him informed about what happened to me, hopefully he will learn from it."

Recently, Hirsch introduced Justin to the tradition of *tefillin*, letting him share in his morning worship and his faith. That's part of the prayer, Hirsch explains, "'Teach it to your children and put a sign upon your houses.' I mean, it's holy to put on *tefillin*. And if I had never figured out my addiction, I would not be as close to God as I am today."

Stranger in a Strange Land

Monday night, December 18, 2006, brought a cold wind and a flurry of multiculturalism to Bentonville. Early on the same blowy evening, as thirty or so members of the Hindu community were preparing to descend on Etz Chaim, which they had rented in order to hear a traveling swami from Dallas deliver his quarterly lecture on spirituality, the Orthodox Chabad of Northwest Arkansas was throwing a Hanukkah skating party at Great Day Skate Place, the local ice rink, just a hop, skip, and a glide from the shul.

Outside, a bright neon sign announced the event: THE CHABAD OF NORTHWEST ARKANSAS—SKATING PARTY. Inside, the room and the rink were both reserved for the Jews. Forty or fifty men, women, and children wandered around the vast arena, mostly hovering near the buffet line set up for a holiday meal of kosher kugel and pasta, courtesy of the Chabad rabbi's wife, who also sells fresh challah bread for Shabbat each week. As for the skating itself, not more than five people actually ventured onto the rink at any one time, and most of those were children absorbed in kicking a plastic dreidel across the ice. The one figure who skated with surprising grace and sureness was Sheldon Hirsch, defying gravity and his own bulk as he raced around the rink. Later, he confessed to having played ice hockey back in his anti-Semitic hometown of Huntington, Long Island.

One person, however, who resisted the ice was the host himself, who stood at the rink's periphery, greeting guests. In truth, nothing could have been less congruous down here at Great Day Skate Place than this man throwing the party: Rabbi Menachem Mendel Greisman. Of medium size and wearing a long black jacket, he could have stepped out of a photograph of a nineteenth-century Minsk shtetl, or small Jewish town, dressed as he was in the Lubavitch Hasidim fashion, his appearance marked by a patchy brown beard; long dark sideburns, or *payots*; and a huge black hat with a wide brim. On closer scrutiny, Greisman was a very young man, not more than twenty-five, with a soft, pleasant voice, a pink baby face, and a relaxed, welcoming manner. Still, his Orthodoxy and odd attire has, more often than not, prompted the more secular Jews of Bentonville to dismiss him with a shrug of the shoulders and a roll of the eyes. It is as if, in this small Christian suburb, they worry that he is calling embarrassing attention to his— and their—otherness. Yet even in urban areas like New York, secular Jews behave just as intolerantly toward their Orthodox brethren. And Hasidim, in turn, often tend to be equally dismissive of reform and conservative Jews.

Not too far from her husband stood the Rabbi's plump and pretty wife, Dobi, wearing a dark ankle-length skirt and long-sleeved blouse, as well as a red wig (*sheitel*) in observance of the Hasidic principle of *tzeniut*, or modesty. On her hip she carried the youngest of her then-three redheaded children (ages one, two, and three; a fourth was born in September 2008). Together, the Greismans make up the entire Chabad community of Northwest Arkansas. They arrived shortly after the Jewish community formed Etz Chaim, and while they say that they are not here to proselytize, they are part of an Orthodox and sometimes mystical tradition that, subtly, does just that by offering hard-to-find services to local Jews. The Chabad Lubavitch Movement has sent more than twenty-five hundred representatives, among them the Greismans, into Jewish communities throughout the world, providing prayer, religious instruction, and kosher food to all who seek it. At the Bentonville ice rink, the couple sent their Jewish guests home with small tin menorahs and Hanukkah candles—considered by some a real service, since, as diverse as Northwest Arkansas has become, these items are unavailable at the local Wal-Mart.

Every Shabbat, on Friday night and at noon on Saturday, visiting Jews break bread at Greisman's kosher table in a small subdivision not far from the main highway in Rogers. It is a modest home whose bookcases, filled with scholarly Hebrew texts, line the yellow walls of the central space; once a living room, it now holds a large dining table at which the Greismans regularly host meals. One week, Greisman said, seventy-eight people dined at their table.

On Saturday mornings, Jews can join him in his own tiny Orthodox shul that he converted from a small adjoining garage, where, as prescribed by Orthodox tradition, men sit on one side of the white lace curtain that divides the room and women sit on the other.

Does the rabbi, imposing and odd-looking in his silks and hat and wispy facial hair, try to convert Christians, or even Jews, to his more Orthodox path? Absolutely not, he says. "I just try to bring the beauty of Judaism to Jewish people." Moreover, he welcomes the curious Gentiles who stop him in the aisles of Wal-Mart with questions about Judaism. "I provide answers, but I don't try to convert them," he says. "Ever."

Granted, living on a small suburban street in a Bible Belt town such as Rogers, surrounded by Christian families, cannot be easy for the Greismans. But Mendy, who moved into his modest home in the fall of 2006, says that his neighbors are welcoming. Perhaps. Still, back in 2007 his local property owner's association filed a complaint with the town of Rogers that on Shabbas there was "excessive vehicle traffic with parking congestion and excessive pedestrian traffic . . . as a result of the opening of the 'Chabad House,'" which had not been zoned for religious services.[2] Today the rabbi insists that the issue, fanned by one irate family, has been resolved. "My neighbors are very, very nice," he says. "They invite me to their homes. They know they can't give us food because we keep kosher, but we spend time visiting."

Born into a Chabad family in Israel, Greisman grew up in the city of Zefat. He says that it was the rabbi of the Little Rock Chabad who, back in 2004, suggested that he look into setting up a shul in Northwest Arkansas. "He said, 'I'm reading in the paper that there's tremendous growth there. People are calling all the time because there's no rabbi. Why don't you go look at the area?'" So he did.

Greisman sees one of his major responsibilities as that of servicing the Wal-Mart vendors. "At least a hundred Jews pass through here during the week," he says. He offers them daily prayers and kosher catering. In exchange, they bring goods he cannot get in Arkansas—a case of frozen kosher chickens here, a case of frozen kosher milk there.

The situation, he recognizes, is much easier for him than for Dobi, who spends her time chauffering her kids to carefully chosen play dates with local Jewish moms, cooking for the family and its army of Jewish visitors, and preparing for Shabbat. Recognizing how isolating life in Rogers is for his wife, Greisman simply says, "I appreciate her every day. I couldn't do anything without her around." Dobi, indeed, maintains an aura of cool competence in the midst of chaos. At a Shabbat lunch, not even the arrival of guests, the presence of her visiting mother, or the raucous play of her three tots, climbing up and down steps, laughing, and fighting, ruffles her nonchalance.

To fulfill the tenets of their Orthodoxy, the Greismans separate themselves from Reform Jews, Gentiles, and Muslims alike in some striking ways. They plan to homeschool their children and then, possibly, to send them to a religious Jewish school in Little Rock when they are older. "We want to make sure that from a very young age our kids get the education and values we believe in," Griesman explains.

He and Dobi live a world apart in other significant cultural ways. They are unable to eat at any restaurant in town because none serves kosher food. Also, they do not own a television or go to Hollywood movies, unwilling to expose themselves or their children to entertainment that they consider immodest. Says Griesman, "It's a personal choice because we feel that today's movies are not pure and holy."

Their focus on modesty is reminiscent of the Muslim women who wear the *hijab.* "Even on the hottest summer day, you won't find my wife in shorts and a tank top," he says. "It's a challenge because her long skirts raise eyebrows sometimes."

The Greismans, used to being stared at here in Northwest Arkansas, say they don't mind. While their unusual dress code and strict rules of observance may prove embarrassing to some secular Jews in Bentonville who may be eager, even desperate, to blend into the community, the truth is that this Lubavitch rabbi also projects an empathic nature that is remarkable in a man so young. It is this empathy that was such a lifeline for Sheldon Hirsch.

And it just may be that in the souped-up religious atmosphere of the Bible Belt, a man of the cloth—even though the cloth be cut by an Orthodox Jewish tailor—curries respect. And acceptance.

Jews? In Arkansas?

"Down here the first thing people say is, 'So what church do you go to?'" observes Betty Goldstein, a Brooklyn native with a booming New York voice who moved to the area nine years ago with her husband, Martin. "It's *very* Bible Belt here. They're *so* gung ho. It's really something."

One of the unexpected and pleasant truths about Arkansas is that even though it is so emphatically Christian, it has always been Jew-friendly— and this while few Arkansans have ever actually seen a Jew. Jewish immigrants from Europe began to arrive in the state in the early part of the nineteenth century but never in great numbers. In 1825, Abraham Block, a merchant, moved to the town of Washington in the Arkansas Territory, not far from the Texarkana border, and opened a store. Catering to farmers and field hands, who composed the largest part of the population, he soon emerged as one of the region's wealthiest men.

By 1859 enough Jews lived in and around Pine Bluff, Arkansas, to begin meeting regularly. That same year a mohel traveled the countryside on horseback, plying his trade as a ritual circumciser. And the Reverend L. B. Sternheimer of Columbus, Georgia, took an ad in the *Occidental Advertiser*, noting that he had already performed similar functions in Arkansas and could provide recommendations from satisfied Jewish clients on request.[3]

In the post–Civil War years, as Arkansas became increasingly more mercantile in nature, it also became increasingly more hospitable to Jewish peddlers and wholesalers who brought goods into once-isolated areas, and, by doing so, actually helped to develop them. In fact, fourteen Arkansas towns were founded by Jews or named after early Jewish residents, including Altheimer and Goldman in Jefferson County, Berger in Pulaski County, and Felsenthal in Union County.

By 1866, B'nai Israel, the first Jewish congregation in Little Rock, was formed, and by 1878 almost fifteen hundred Jews lived in the state, most of German origin. They proved themselves so hardworking and lived so harmoniously with the rest of the population that an article in the *Pine Bluff Graphic* on October 18, 1889, described them as "the most wonderful people the world ever produced, their history and achievements largely entitle them to the claim of superiority."[4]

As a result of the great early-twentieth-century immigration, the Jewish population of Arkansas, aided by Jewish resettlement groups, grew until, by 1927, there were 8,850 Jews in the state. Sylvia Greif remembers her childhood in Marianna, a small town in eastern Arkansas, about forty miles southwest of Memphis, Tennessee. "In my area it was rare to be a Jewish girl," says Greif, who was born in 1920. "Of course, when I was young, the smart alecks would call me 'Jew baby,' but I'd answer, 'I'm proud of it. I am God's chosen people.' It was better than running home and crying to Mama. Finally they saw they couldn't get the best of me and shut up. Some Jewish families actually left town because of the bad time their children were having, but I did *not* have a bad time in Marianna."

Although Jews were alien to the Baptists and Methodists, who were part of the dominant culture, they integrated comfortably into the Arkansas landscape. One reason was that Judaism was the basis of the Judeo-Christian tradition. Also, Stuart Rockoff, a historian with the Goldring/Woldenberg Institute of Southern Jewish Life in Jackson, Mississippi, says, "Part of it has to do with race and racism. Jews were treated as white people, and in the South white and black is really what mattered. In the big northern cities, where all sorts of immigrant groups existed, a whole different racial dynamic existed. But Jews have a history of fitting in, and in the South they benefited in some ways from racism."

Not even the rise of the Ku Klux Klan in the years after the lynching of the Jew Leo Frank, in Georgia in 1915, significantly impacted the Jewish community, Rockoff insists. "When the Klan developed in the late teens and early 1920s," he observes, "Jews were part of their ideology, but the Klan was much more focused on Catholics in the North and blacks in the South."

As the Klan swelled—in 1922 it boasted more than four million members—Jews kept an ever-lower profile. By the late 1930s, Little Rock, with twenty-five hundred Jews, emerged as the largest Jewish community in the state. Yet, they remained a minuscule presence—they were never even half of 1 percent of the state's population. Today, it is estimated that a mere sixteen hundred Jews live in Arkansas.[5]

Despite their modest numbers, Jews distinguished themselves in Arkansas life. "In looking at these small towns, I'm struck by how many served on school boards or city councils," says Rockoff.

Prominent Jewish politicians in Arkansas cities include Jonas Levy, who was Little Rock's mayor throughout the Civil War, and Charles Jacobson, a state senator. Jewish merchants owned leading department stores in the state. Julian Waterman became the first dean of the University of Arkansas Law School. And Cyrus Adler, a prominent educator and scholar from Van Buren, served as president of the Jewish Theological Seminary in New York, the American Jewish Committee, and the American Jewish Historical Society.

Why, then, did the Jewish population of the South, and of Arkansas in particular, dwindle? For one, it was part of a huge general migration during the second half of the twentieth century as young people from small towns headed to big cities, seeking new and brighter opportunities. What's more, over the last several decades, Jewish retailers—whose working lives in the South had always revolved around the ownership of small stores, predominantly, dry goods, groceries, and jewelry shops—were forced to reinvent themselves as the retail industry metamorphosed, largely because Wal-Mart and other big chains were devouring mom-and-pop shops, one after another.

And so, for the most part, the story of small-town Jewish life also became the story of its decline, as instanced by the fact that during the last few years the synagogues in both Helena and Blytheville have closed down.

Yet Bentonville has emerged as a surprise. It's a small but healthy Jewish community, with the second-largest Sunday school in the state. "To me," says Rockoff, "the number of kids in religious school is the best barometer of a community's health."

Rockoff, however, sees Bentonville as the exception that proves the rule. "It's growing, but why is it growing?" he asks. "Because of a corporation. And who are the Jews of Bentonville? Are they merchants? No. They are corporate executives. It's pretty clear that if Wal-Mart were in St. Louis, there would be no Jews in Bentonville."

The irony, of course, is that these Jews, once independent retailers themselves, are now corporate executives working in the service and the shadow of Sam Walton's Christian merchandising behemoth.

Making Noise—but How Much?

It is something of a phenomenon that so many of the Bentonville Jews have felt comfortable asserting their rights as Jews in order to ensure that they were part of the overall community. It was almost as if the transplants, many from cities such as New York or Chicago, have had to do the work that local Jews were not comfortable doing. "In these small towns, southern Jews have always been more willing to let things go, to not make waves," says Rockoff. "That's how they fit in. Someone from Chicago is less likely to say, 'Oh, it's okay if they mention Jesus during the city prayer.' Things like that."

Even before the establishment of Etz Chaim, the Jews of Bentonville began to flex their muscle. Soon after 9/11, Lee Paull, a former Wal-Marter, spoke to the mayor, Terry Coberly, about adding Hanukkah symbols during the Bentonville Square tree lighting that year. From the beginning she was amenable. And so that December, Jews gathered on the square for the first time in order to say a blessing, to switch on the lights of the menorah and Star of David—and to make their presence known.

There is little doubt that since then they have become increasingly emboldened. For one, as a group they have lobbied the school system to be more inclusive. Now, instead of "Christmas vacation" and "Easter recess," local schools break for "winter vacation" and "spring recess."

Some, like Paull, prefer to fight these battles alone. "When my kid was in the fifth grade in the Rogers school system, they were passing out Bibles to students. I put a stop to that," he says, sounding like a one-man vigilante committee. "And they used to mark a kid absent during the High Holidays. I put a stop to that, too."

Superintendent of schools Gary Compton also takes credit for the school system's recent gestures of inclusiveness. "We try to be sensitive to multiculturalism," he says. "Hanukkah, Kwanza, and Christmas are all joyous holidays. We don't need to fraction ourselves. What's wrong with saying, 'Hey, it's holiday time'? Teaching how all these holidays evolved seems like a much better option."

Supportive words like these are nice. Always, however, the Jews must balance their needs with the fact that they are living in an overwhelmingly Christian culture. How do they fit in? When should they be difficult and scrappy? How often should they underscore their differences, their otherness? What is that fragile hairline between assertiveness and trouble?

The truth is that many Wal-Mart Jews, especially those highest up in the executive suite, seem uncomfortable speaking publicly about their religion or their experience of being Jewish in Bentonville. Perhaps their caution has been fanned by Wal-Mart's internal culture of privacy; just as likely, it is the natural reticence that has become part of the post–Holocaust Jews' survival instinct—a reticence that by now seems ingrained in their DNA. "Some Jews here are very careful," Sheldon Hirsch observes about his colleagues. "Just as some people are careful outing themselves as gay, others are careful outing themselves as Jewish. They're very private with their personal life when it comes to Wal-Mart. Down here, people don't necessarily recognize Jewish [names]. And Jews are often very timid with the press because they are afraid that their comments may be misconstrued. I'd rather let people out themselves."

In some impressive ways, Northwest Arkansas is beginning to take its commitment to diversity seriously. As part of the area's 2006 holiday commemoration, the Rogers Public Library integrated a Hanukkah celebration with its Saturday Family Story Time series. "We don't actively go into the schools, but because we're the only synagogue in town, we get calls," explains Wynnie Hoodis, whose basic philosophy of outreach is more conservative than that of the Hirsches.

Religiosity defines differences, but it can also work as a major perk, or calling card, for Jews in Arkansas. Because godliness and worship are critical to the Bible Belt, many in the community feel that Jews can best find their space by, well, being Jewish. There is no better way for them to fit into the faith-based culture that surrounds them than to create, or join, a synagogue. "There is great respect for Jews among many Christian denominations, and this is especially so with the rise of the Christian right and its embrace of Israel," says Rockoff.

And because religion is so culturally important in the region, the Jewish religion becomes that much more meaningful to Jewish people, suggests

Rabbi Kassoff. "The cultural current is that you go to church and identify with your religious community," she says. "For Jews, a double force is pulling them toward the Jewish community. First, that's what you do in this part of the world. And second, almost as a reaction against the overwhelmingly Christian culture around you, you need to work harder to cultivate your Jewishness here than in a more secular environment."

While most Jews in the area dismiss the notion of local anti-Semitism, online responses to newspaper articles about the Jewish presence here often suggest something else altogether. On June 20, 2006, a reader of the *Arkansas Democrat-Gazette* sent in this reaction to a story about the Etz Chaim Jews:

> I sure hate hearing about the kikes having made a kike-haven out of such pretty country. Hopefully some of the locals can see them for what they are, hopefully one of those few will violently protest them being there. Hopefully that will start a chain reaction. Hopefully, hopefully, hopefully . . .

Was he voicing the feelings of the majority? Or was he simply a crackpot looking for a public forum?

Often, too, Jewish children find the climate more uncomfortable than their parents do—or are more apt to give voice to the prejudice they experience. Two Jewish brothers, ages eight and ten, complained that at school Christian children approach them regularly. "They say, 'You don't believe in Jesus. You're an Israel man,'" one boy complains. Just as Sylvia Greif did nearly a century earlier when kids called her a "Jew baby," these boys have learned to handle hostile comments with low-key wisdom. Their strategy: they each said, "I ignore them."

Not too long ago the teenager Rachel Stuckey was perturbed for another reason: friends were trying to convert her, a gesture that might have been ironically amusing to an outsider, since both her parents had themselves converted *to* Judaism. The most overt attempt, says her stepfather, Paul Stuckey, was by a girl whose father was a Christian Fundamentalist preacher. Did it at all appeal to Rachel, who was then sixteen? "No, it made her mad," says Stuckey. "So I had to point out to her that *because* they believe she is going to spend eternity in Hell unless she accepts Jesus Christ as her personal savior, they are going to try to convert her—and, in *their* minds, to save her."

Stuckey worries that these teenagers are still too young to understand the line between what is acceptable behavior in this regard. In addition, he believes, children of his daughters' ages have less self-confidence than adults when it comes to speaking out. "So it's harder for them to say, 'Well, this is inappropriate. I have my own religion. Thank you, but no thank you.'"

A Patchwork Congregation

Paul and Carol Stuckey, among the founding members of Etz Chaim, are unique for a number of reasons. They are, first of all, the synagogue's only couple who were born and bred in the South—she hails from Jackson, Mississippi, and he, from Central Arkansas. Second, she grew up Catholic; his background was Methodist. And they came to Judaism in different ways and at different times.

Carol, who converted more than twenty-seven years ago, says, "I was extremely unhappy in the Catholic religion." She was also a recovering alcoholic who had been sober for a few years. "And I was looking to find a relationship with some sort of higher power." She had started visiting different church denominations for spiritual nourishment. "But every time I went to a church, I'd get frustrated," she remembers. "I didn't like any of it. But I really wanted to stay sober and come up with some sort of spiritual path."

Then a friend who had married a Jew invited Carol to come to synagogue with them one day. "And it was a revelation," she recalls. "It was like I was home. And I was so surprised because I didn't even think you could convert to Judaism. I thought either you were a Jew or you weren't."

After reading about Judaism, Carol started attending synagogue and eventually decided to convert. Telling her parents, she says, "was horrible. My mother felt like I'd slapped her. She showed up at the conversion ceremony, which occurred the day after terrorists in Israel had entered a synagogue and massacred a group inside. And she kept asking, 'Are you sure you want to do this?' I was very young, maybe twenty-three, and I asked her if she wouldn't rather I had some spiritual life than none. But she didn't see it that way."

Carol began studying Hebrew and taught Sunday school in Jackson. When Rachel was born, she raised her Jewish, even though the girl's birth father was Episcopalian. Then the couple broke up, and Carol met Paul Stuckey. They married eleven years ago and moved to Northwest Arkansas, where Paul, a physicist, works as a consultant for Benchmark, the largest engineering and architecture firm in Arkansas; its biggest client is Wal-Mart. Carol is an accountant in the real estate department at Wal-Mart. Soon the couple had a daughter together—Rebecca, whom they were also raising Jewish, even though Paul had not yet decided to convert. The family lives in a rustic farmhouse in Bentonville and attended the congregation at the Hillel in Fayetteville simply because no other existed.

When the Stuckeys heard that the Jews of Bentonville were forming a new synagogue, they became founding members. And Carol began teaching in their makeshift religious school. "I had learned Hebrew many years ago but forgot it," she says. Since her Hebrew was so rusty, she literally learned the lesson plan the night before she taught it.

Finally, after more than a decade with her, Paul decided to become Jewish as well. He had been a practicing Buddhist during college but says that the religion was ultimately "too foreign" for him. After rejecting it, he became an agnostic for fifteen years. "I had no strong religious belief of my own, so we continued on without my ever thinking that I would convert," he explains. But he attended synagogue with his family every week and participated in the community's functions. So in 2006, he says, "I concluded that it was the right time."

Stuckey began the conversion process, long-distance, with Rabbi Kassoff, who was living in Jackson, Mississippi, at the time. He completed it in April 2006 with the traditional *mikveh* (cleansing bath) and Beit Din, or rabbinical court, and a commitment to keeping kosher. Although he was not required to learn Hebrew, he says, "I did have to learn some of the prayers in Hebrew, especially the Sh'ma."

One reality of living in the South, and in particular the Bible Belt, observes Rabbi Kassoff, is that most people are forced to confront what it is they believe and who they are, spiritually. A person raised in a nominally Christian faith in the North can coast along if his religious tradition of origin doesn't speak to him. "But in the southern communities," she explains, "it's more important to take a stand and say, 'This is my faith; this is what I believe.' If someone is born into a faith that doesn't make sense to him, it's more important to find that resolution somewhere else."

For some, such as Carol and Paul Stuckey, that resolution was Judaism.

A Steve and Eydie for an Offbeat Shul

Although by the fall of 2005 the Jews of Wal-Mart had a working synagogue of their own, it took another nine months before they found a rabbi.

One issue for Etz Chaim was that, as Tevye the Milkman from the musical *Fiddler on the Roof* said about his daughter's impending mixed marriage, it was neither fish nor fowl. In other words, the brand-new congregation had not yet chosen a formal identity. It was neither reform nor orthodox, conservative nor reconstructionist—identities that often create divisiveness within Jewish communities—nor is it any one of these today. That led some Jews in the community to turn their backs on it.

What's more, the tiny membership could not afford a full-time rabbi. So after six months of auditions, Etz Chaim finally hired the Tulsa-based rabbi and personal injuries lawyer Jack Zanerhaft, and his wife, Debbye, to spend one weekend a month in Bentonville to lead services and give direction to the children's religious studies program.

The amiable couple feels that for the price of one, the congregation got two—the rabbi *and* the cantor, a musician trained in singing the liturgical Hebrew texts and chants, a crucial component of most prayer services in a synagogue. Actually, Debbye, who bills herself, more aptly, as a "cantorial soloist," with a voice that is neither heavy nor operatic, functions, in the best sense, as a cantor-lite, strumming her guitar and infusing the Hebrew repertoire with a cheery, cabaret-like style that is particularly appealing to the congregation's young children.

The rabbi remembers talking that first weekend with one of the temple's board members. "And I said to him, 'Debbye and I are like Steve and Eydie,' meaning Steve Lawrence and Eydie Gormé, the popular singing couple of the 1950s. And he was too young to have heard of them, so he said, 'Who?' Then I said, 'You know, Captain and Tennille.' I got another blank stare. Finally, I mentioned Donny and Marie, and he got it. Debbye and I feel very lucky. After all, how many people get to do something they love *with* someone they love?"

Zanerhaft has invested considerable pride in what he considers the trailblazing nature of the synagogue—the fact that to this day it remains unaffiliated and has so many converts and blended families. "I like to think of them as Jews by choice," he says. "We are an important symbol of what Judaism could become. Instead of having boundaries, at Etz

Chaim we are inclusive. Remember, Abraham's tent was big enough for everyone—for Jews, for those married to Jews, and for anyone who *cares* about Jews."

Life and Death Issues for a Tiny Community

Today, more than four years after Etz Chaim officially dedicated its building and opened its doors for worship, sixty-three families—almost double the initial number—are members. But the synagogue faces problems, some typical and some not. The first, putting worshippers in the pews for services every Friday night and Saturday morning, is a challenge that every congregation must deal with. Here in Bentonville, it is sometimes impossible to pull together even a minyan, or number of worshippers, usually men, required for certain prayers or ritual obligations.

So the social whirl meant to bond the Jewish community—Purim and Hanukkah parties, wedding renewals and bar mitzvahs, movie nights and kids' programs—also becomes a way to increase the turnout. The only surefire attendance bonanzas, however, have been the High Holy Days, where, every year, families are spilling into the aisles. More than one hundred adults, a full house, showed up for Rosh Hashanah services in 2008; and at Yom Kippur's closing service, Rabbi Zanerhaft enchanted a flock of perhaps forty children under age ten who listened, rapt, as he dramatically recounted the story of Jonah and the whale, allowing his mini-congregation to punctuate the drama every few minutes by blowing into fish whistles he had distributed before embarking on his fish tale.

"Our slogan is: 'Building a Jewish community together.' And we're going to be building this thing for a long time," says Hoodis. "So if someone is not spiritual and just wants a movie night, good. We've got to make sure we can serve our entire population."

Another equally pressing issue among congregation members is the natural attrition of the community. Although Etz Chaim can now boast that its enrollment of families is five times the meager number that signed on when the synagogue started up (twelve), newcomers arriving to work for Wal-Mart's vendors usually do a tour of between two and five years, after which their companies relocate them elsewhere. This makes the synagogue's membership fluid and unstable.

Interestingly, as Bentonville has become wealthier, these suppliers, who once eagerly uprooted their families and scurried back to the big city on completing their Bentonville assignment, have begun to protest these transfers. Now they are interested in putting down roots in the area. The schools are too good; the cost of living, shockingly low. As one Jew, a consultant to a Wal-Mart vendor and a New Jersey transplant, put it, the housing dollar buys a tremendous amount down here—and always did, even before the mortgage crisis. "Now," he says, "I have a bigger home and more rooms than I know what to do with."

Rich Davis, of the chamber of commerce, says he has heard the horror stories. "Vendors come down here kicking and screaming and saying, 'Oh, my God, we're being sent to perdition because, I mean, it's *Arkansas*.' They come in for a few years in anticipation of getting transferred somewhere else afterward. And lo and behold, they now would rather change jobs, working for a different supplier in town, so that they can stay. We call it 'vendor-hopping,' and executive search firms have sprung up here to facilitate this."

Some Wal-Marters as well—merchandise buyers and IT workers, among them—even choose to vendor-hop, crossing over from buyer to seller, from Wal-Mart employee to IBM, Schlitz, or Procter & Gamble employee. They do this because vendors' offices tend to be plusher and more attractive; their hours, shorter; and their salaries and benefits, better. So crossing over often provides an irresistible opportunity to make the perks of life in Northwest Arkansas more or less permanent.

Of greater concern to the Bentonville Jewish community than job-hopping are issues surrounding life and death. Life issues embrace baby namings for girls and the bris for boy babies. Death issues involve acquiring funeral homes and cemeteries that will prepare bodies and bury them according to Jewish tradition.

Having guided his congregation into existence, David Hoodis admits that for now the synagogue is still trying to define itself. "We're young," he says. "We don't have anyone yet who has amassed a fortune here and wants to sustain Jewish life with a donation."

Jack Zanerhaft applauds the congregation's pioneer spirit and points out that one of the fastest-growing segments of Jewish life is the nondenominational synagogue. "Perhaps Jewish America can learn from tiny Bentonville," he says. After all, its patchwork membership—a handful of Jews from orthodox, conservative, reform, and reconstructionist shuls across the nation, as well as Jews who have converted or have interfaith marriages or blended families—has converged to work in harmony at Etz Chaim. "And they've managed to build a unified, bracing, traditional, and authentic synagogue and Hebrew school in an area that had never seen a shul before. Who'd believe that? And who'd believe that we could create a holiday celebration and a way of studying our sacred text that would be meaningful to everybody? It's mind-boggling."

Men Cooking Latkes

Ignoring the nip in the December air, the crowd milling about Bentonville Square gasps as the five-foot-high electric Star of David and Hanukkah menorah, side by side on the lawn in front of the courthouse, light up a corner of the Arkansas night.

It's a measure of awe usually reserved for July Fourth fireworks, but early on this first night of Hanukkah, the ceremony is awesome for another reason—the Jews of Bentonville have miraculously integrated their tradition into this Christian community's celebration. Yes, wreaths and lights blanket the fountain in the square and entwine themselves in trees and along the rooftops of the Wal-Mart Museum and Station House Cafe. But what's so stunning is that now the Jews can also count on the fact that every December the Confederate soldier on the square will be silhouetted in the glow of candelabra, honoring a battle of another kind—Judah Maccabee's victory over the Syrians more than twenty-three hundred years ago.

But what catches the eye of little Justin Hirsch is the illuminated diorama of the Nativity across the street. He stares at the mini-manger until his mother drags him away.

Twenty minutes later, half a dozen men are mingling in the synagogue kitchen. As wives and kids arrive, the fragrance of latkes sizzling in hot pans envelops them. It is a Norman Rockwell scene gone screwy and Jewy, marked by biblical storytelling, exuberant singing, and eating.

Justin Hirsch's eyelids flutter and close, and his father lifts him onto his broad shoulders. "People fall back on religion when things get tough," Hirsch says. "But when things are good, religion is important, too. I'm a spiritual guy. My spirituality is for today. It makes me who I am. My religion is for tomorrow; it's going to save my soul."

Hirsch's journey toward faith is as American as his stumble and rehabilitation, as his finding a way to a second chance—which is why Etz Chaim is so important to him. "For me, to realize this synagogue after being here for nine years without a place to worship was a dream," he says as he carries his sleepy son to their van. "Now, with Etz Chaim, we've planted ourselves. Bentonville is no longer just a resting point. It's home."

4

A Hindu Family's
Delicate Balance

· · · · · · · · · ·

There is something wonderfully incongruous about the swarm of Hindu children sitting in the sanctuary of the synagogue on Moberly, chanting, *"Ommm,"* and repeating their lessons against a backdrop that includes a wooden replica of the Ten Commandments leaning against a wall, a portrait of a bearded rabbi propped on a chair, and, of course, the simple wooden ark that holds Etz Chaim's precious Torah. Moses would have been encouraged—and possibly a tad bewildered.

The children, all dark haired and dark eyed, most between six and twelve and wearing jeans and brightly colored shirts, look like a million other kids across the country, but they sound emphatically different: *"Ommm,"* they obediently repeat. It is part of their Sunday meditation. From time to time they glance at notebooks in which they have phonetically written out a variety of Hindu prayers.

The Hindus hold dear a tradition called Balavihar, in which they get together and teach their children the principles of their religion and ancient culture. "The literal meaning of *bala* is 'kids,'" Sudhir Katke, the former vice president of the Hindu Association of Northwest Arkansas, explained a few days earlier. "And *vihar* is like a house or environment. So this is an environment for kids."

For years the Wal-Mart Hindus re-created this environment in their homes every other Sunday until the number of children—sometimes more than sixty—became too unwieldy; and so in 2008 they rented out the synagogue on Sunday afternoons. Here the children receive instruction from local parents, using religious material from the Chinmaya Mission in Dallas to support their spiritual lessons.

"Our belief is that if we teach our children our culture and what we stand for, they will eventually make the right choice in life," adds Katke.

One damp and cloudy morning a week before Christmas, two dads, Ajaydev Nallur and Nuresh Sunkireddy, are discussing with the youngsters ways to improve their goodness and empathy. Today's lesson will address possessiveness and the notion that "It's only mine."

Nallur, known as A.J. to friends, works at Wal-Mart by day and is the father of two girls who usually participate in these classes. Today three sections fan out through the synagogue—one occupying the classroom; another, the spacious kitchen; and the third, the sanctuary.

"When you don't want to share something," he asks his group, "what is the cleaning agent?"

After a moment, a small voice pipes up: "To share."

"And why should I share?" asks Nallur.

The children are silent.

"Because *everything* belongs to God," he tells them. "It's not *your* toy; it's God's toy that he gave you to play with. So you should pass it on."

Later, Nallur asks each child to write down her name and "two good things that God has given you as a gift." The kids then open one another's notes and read them, occasionally laughing or scrunching up their faces, amused or embarrassed at the way their friends have characterized themselves.

Nallur then instructs them to each write down two good things about the person who has just read their notes. One girl protests, "I don't know him that well."

"You need to learn to develop how to see good things in others," Nallur explains, suggesting that each child write down what comes to his or her mind about the other. "It's very sad if you can't find two nice things to say about someone else," he chastises them gently. "If we can find good things in everybody, there's no need to feel jealousy."

Nallur tells his Sunday school class a story that he hopes will illustrate an antidote to possessiveness: "Everyone went to the hall where God was giving a party. There was lots of ice cream and pizza, and God told them, 'You can eat as much as you want, and you won't grow fat or get a stomach ache. But there's one condition: you *must* eat without bending your elbows.

"Everyone was angry and indignant. How could they eat without bending their elbows?"

The children think for a moment. Not one wiseacre suggests putting his head into the food. They simply wait—expectant, compliant, respectful.

"They feed each other," says Nallur with just a flicker of triumph in his voice. "Think about it, they did not need to bend their elbows to feed each other. The story shows that if you share and work as a team, you can be happier than if you don't share."

This is the season of giving, the dads remind their students, then ask how many of them ever give gifts to friends. Four raise their hands. Do you feel happy when you give friends a present? he asks.

"Yes," the children chirp.

"Do you feel happy when you keep the gift for yourself?"

"No," they shout.

As the class winds down, the dads remind their charges that for their next meeting they will need to make up a story for each negative value or feeling they have discussed—jealousy, vanity, and guilt. There is something touching and important about these lessons. The class, apart from its religious value, emerges as a primer for empathy, generosity of spirit, and thoughtfulness.

Balaraman Kirthigai Vasan, known as B.K. and the former president of the Hindu Association of Northwest Arkansas, explains it this way: "You need to love every human being. You need to have compassion. That is God's quality."

Who can argue against such ideals?

Many Acquaintances—but Few Friends

Early on a weekday evening Nallur shows me into his two-thousand-square-foot home in a respectable Bentonville subdivision. The living room, painted a warm yellow-gold, also boasts a large, open kitchen, a massive brown leather couch, and a huge LCD television screen. In a preferred spot over the fireplace sits a portrait of Matha Amrithananda Mayi, a humanitarian known as the Hugging Saint or the Great Hugging Mother to her millions of devotees, including Nallur, because she hugs everyone who approaches her; she has been known to hug more than fifty thousand people in one day, and the story goes that she has hugged more than thirty million to her ample bosom over the course of the past three decades. (A film about her called *Darshan—the Embrace,* was shown at the 2005 Cannes Film Festival.)

Nallur arrived here from Kerala, India, in January 1995, by way of a two-year stint in France, to work for a small technology company. He brought along a beautiful young wife, a baby daughter, and a commitment to his Hindu tradition.

That December he joined Wal-Mart as an IT technician, working in a group alongside ten Americans and writing programs for various store applications. "It helped the managers look at how many items were sold," he explains. "It helped them see what worked best for us."

But in 2008 he moved into a new position at the company. Now, with the official title Project Leader for ISD, Computer Division for Pharmacies, he oversees the writing of programs that pharmacies in the Wal-Mart stores will use to fill prescriptions. "This helps the pharmacist and the technician inside the pharmacy," says Nallur, "to make sure that each prescription is correct and that each bottle has the right number of tablets."

As with all other home office employees, Nallur participates in monthly team-building lunches with colleagues and mandatory Saturday morning meetings, which management in 2008 cut down to once a month. Was that because the rank and file, desperate for more sleep and family time, rebelled?

Nallur smiles. "Mainly it's a move to cut expenses," he says. "Also they reorganized things recently so that regional managers now live in the areas that they manage and no longer work at the home office."

Nallur works the protracted Wal-Mart hours from 8:00 A.M. to 6:00 P.M., with an hour off for lunch, and acknowledges the demanding workload. "There are times that we feel, 'Hey, there's so much stuff coming down the pike, and we don't have enough people,'" he says. "What I've seen Wal-Mart do—not overnight, but eventually—is to go in the right direction [and hire more people]. The company was always humane, but there's pressure from the outside as well. You can't tell Target or other competitors, 'Hey, hold back.' There are times when pressure is applied and we've got to perform. That's part of the business. And you know that phrase, 'If you can't stand the heat. . . .'"

. . . .

As the head of a Hindu family, Nallur, like so many who have relocated here from other cultures, be they Hindu, Muslim, Marshallese, or Hispanic, struggles to retain his old values and yet to make a modern American life in a sometimes alien new world. His eldest daughter, Saranya, just seventeen, attends Bentonville High School, and her sister, Varenya, eleven, is a junior high student. Subha, his wife, whose English is still shaky after more than fourteen years in the United States, took a job two years ago at a local nursery school and seems pleased though slightly intimidated by it.

The family attends numerous dinners and festivals within the tight-knit Hindu community. Later this evening, in fact, they will host a rehearsal for a devotional choir that will perform at their temple in Gentry. Yet Nallur expresses profound feelings of social isolation and a longing to develop deeper friendships with Americans.

Nallur, who at first seems like an informal kind of guy, is actually shy and almost obsessively concerned with protocol. But he has not been able, or willing, to integrate more successfully into the larger white community. When asked the most difficult part, he says bluntly, "It is not being able to socialize with them like we do with Indian families. The people at work never say, 'A.J., come to my house for dinner, come to my home.'"

At the same time, he admits, he has not invited them to his home either. "This barrier is a little strange," he says. "We have a professional relationship with the Americans. Nothing more."

Even on "food days" at work, which are designed to encourage multiculturalism, and where people of different ethnic backgrounds bring their native dishes to the office for others to experience, Nallur finds it difficult to share his culture. He worries about how colleagues might respond to the spicy and savory Indian cuisine, and when it is his turn to bring a dish, he buys potato chips and bottled drinks instead. "I hesitate to take Indian food," he says. "I do not want them to say, 'Eeeew! Too spicy.'" He pauses, then blurts out, almost remorsefully, "It *is* me, I think. Others may be shy to open up, but I am not opening up, either."

Later he concedes that remaining aloof from his American coworkers may offer another more profound kind of barrier. "It may be that we also want to make sure our kids are not too much influenced by American culture—the bad part, where they think dating, or staying with another person before marriage, is okay," he explains. "We don't want that kind of influence, so that may be in the back of my mind." It's easier to reject American culture than to have to explain it to a child who is smitten by it. "We don't want too many social gatherings where the kids think, 'This is normal,'" he explains.

His social reticence notwithstanding, Nallur is still drawn to life here in the United States. "The United States is really a bighearted country," he says. "I know. I have been to France, and they do not welcome immigrants the way the U.S. does."

The Indian Influx

The explosive growth of the Northwest Arkansas Hindu population began about fifteen years ago, says B.K. Vasan, who emigrated from Chennai in southern India in 1994. He and Sudhir Katke are sitting in the empty breakfast room of Bentonville's Courtyard Marriott Hotel on a December evening. "When we came to live here, there were maybe twenty Indians," says Vasan. "Now there are between four hundred and five hundred families." Around two hundred additional single men have also arrived in recent months to fulfill short-term contracts, he says, and will probably return home within the year.

Back in the early 1990s, only a few hand-picked graduates of the Indian Institute of Technology, one of that nation's premiere universities, came to the United Sates to work, Vasan says, explaining, "They were extraordinarily brilliant." But then, right around the year 2000, opportunities here in the United States opened up, compounded by the dot-com boom. "At that time, if you asked an Indian student why he was studying computer science, he would say, 'I want to go to the U.S.,'" he says. "We knew if we joined these multinationals, we'd get an opportunity to come here. It was a dream for a lot of us in India."

Vasan, arriving in Bentonville with a master's in computer science to work for Wal-Mart, had first been a consultant for Tech Data Corporation in Clearwater, Florida. He recalls that originally all the young Indian immigrants, whether single or married with young families, found inexpensive accommodations at the Lost Springs Doubletree Apartments in Rogers. "We pretty much knew everyone," he says. "Then it grew from twenty people to forty to one hundred. Even today, one of the best things about this area is that all the Indians bond together. We are still close."

But ten years ago the community was very different. "We were quite isolated," he explains. Even then, he says, he never experienced any prejudice.

"Nor have I," adds Katke—with one exception. Shortly after 9/11, local behavior toward the Indians changed because people in the area were confusing Hindus with Muslims. Katke, who at the time wore a goatee, took his son to a soccer game, where one father asked him bluntly if he was from "that" part of the world. "Some others asked me, 'Do you have a mosque?'" he says.

Interestingly, none of the Muslim families I spoke with in the area ever mentioned that they had been mistaken for Hindus. Most likely, the higher visibility of Muslims in our culture and the negative publicity that has been heaped on them since 9/11 accounts for this reactiveness.

But Katke's Wal-Mart managers were sensitive to the problem. "One came to my house," he says, "and assured me, 'If you have any problems from anybody, let me know. I will handle it.'"

. . . .

Sudhir Katke hails from Mumbai, India, and arrived in Bentonville in 1997 to work as a systems analyst for Informix, a company that IBM eventually bought. He remains an IBM employee and works on database systems for Wal-Mart. "Everybody treats me as a Wal-Mart employee," he says.

Both Vasan and Katke unabashedly support Wal-Mart. "Its strength is that it has three basic beliefs," Vasan explains. "The company has respect for the individual, it believes the customer is always right, and it strives for excellence. Also there is an open-door policy so that we definitely feel we are part of the company." What he says may be true, but it echoes, almost word for word, the way others have described Wal-Mart; it also happens to be precisely how the company describes itself in an internal corporate video.

The men attend Wal-Mart's 7:00 A.M. meetings on Saturdays, which provide a combination of company cheerleading and business updates. "We go once every month," says Vasan. "It used to be required to attend every other week, but I went every time because that way I learned about the business." He insists that the company offers excellent salaries and benefits, adding, unsolicited, "We are all very well paid. I don't have any regrets, and I don't think I'll work anywhere else."

(Of course, the Bentonville area does not offer the plethora of jobs for computer programmers that a big city might. As for salaries, few middle managers whom I spoke with were comfortable sharing what they made. However, a former Wal-Mart attorney told me that he could have made two to three times as much as general counsel for a big-city corporation as he did working overtime *and* seven days a week in Bentonville.)

Both Vasan and Katke come from privileged Indian families. They grew up with maids and cooks at home; even at Indian hotels, a surfeit of porters and bellboys helped with baggage and driving. Both say that one of the most daunting adjustments they have had to make on moving to America was that of doing things for themselves. "Here, you take your car, you fill it up yourself, you drive to work yourself," Vasan says.

"Back in India, you can call somebody like a maidservant to clean your utensils, wash your clothes, and mow your lawn," Katke adds. "Here you don't have the luxury, and you do your own chores because these services are very expensive here."

The families also had to deal with language problems and food problems. Vasan, like many Hindus, is a vegetarian. "When I first got here," he says, "people didn't know what that meant."

There were also problems getting around in a community with no public transportation. "For about a year, my wife didn't know how to drive," says Katke. "That's one of the challenges of living here."

Finally, there were people problems. In India, Vasan's wife had been surrounded by a large extended family that helped her care for the children. "All day she was sharing and caring," he says. "Here she's alone most of the day." (Subsequently, she solved that issue by getting a job in Wal-Mart's financial support area.)

....

As cohesive as the Hindu community is, being such a unique minority in Arkansas offers cultural and religious challenges. Christmas, Vasan says, is a much more religious holiday in India. "There it's about Christ; here, it's about Santa," he says. "We celebrate the Santa portion because our kids are fascinated with him. So we have a Christmas tree here, and we put gifts under it for them. But we don't worship Christ. We worship Krishna. And we believe in reincarnation."

Hindus believe, too, that the god Krishna, an avatar of Lord Vishnu, sent down his message of harmony and knowledge in such Hindu holy texts as the Bhagavad Gita, the Vedas, and the Upanishads. These texts, which set down a system for living based on the teachings of ancient Indian sages, concentrate on ethics, spirituality, and devotion to goodness.

Sometimes, says Vasan, various churches send representatives to their homes with flyers explaining Christ. "The beauty of our Hinduism is that we are very tolerant because we are clear what our goal is," he adds. "We believe every path leads to God. And we have gone to two or three churches this past year to talk about Hinduism."

Keenly aware of the Christian community, the Hindu Association feels an obligation to educate non-Hindus. Toward that end, both Vasan and Katke have given interviews to local newspapers and held public festivities at their brand-new temple in Gentry, about three miles from the airport. "We were thinking of perhaps having a Hinduism Awareness Day where we can bring the swamis or other learned people here. Our goal is not to preach or convert anybody," he explains, "just to educate them so that next time, when I say 'Hinduism,' you can go, 'Oh, yeah, I know what they mean.' After all, we are the third-biggest religion in the world." Indeed, more than a billion people consider themselves practicing Hindus.

Even with the acquisition of the temple in Gentry, the Hindus rent out the more conveniently located Jewish synagogue, Etz Chaim, on Moberly in Bentonville for both their Sunday school and their quarterly lectures from Swami Udhava Chaithanya of the Chinmaya Mission in Dallas. On a brisk winter evening in 2007, while the Jews enjoyed a Hanukkah ice-skating party thrown at a local rink by the Chabad rabbi, about thirty Hindu men and women and a few children showed up to hear the swami discuss the Hindu holy book, the Bhagavad Gita. "He gave us all clarity," says Vasan.

With religion so central to Hindu life, almost every Hindu family in Bentonville has set aside a special prayer room for worship. "Unlike the Muslims, we don't have a prescribed number of times to pray. Our Scriptures say that we need to think about God all the time," says Vasan. "And so sometimes we pray and meditate in the Lord's name for five minutes before work. On the weekend, we spend more time. But it's not forced. It's up to us."

Hindus, he says, do not proselytize; they accept. The religion, the basis of Buddhism, Sikhism, and Jainism, is about learning in order to achieve peace, happiness, and compassion.

"Trying to convert others would mean that we all have different gods. But Hindus believe that Christians, Jews, Muslims, and Hindus alike share one God. Those are all paths you choose to reach God," he explains. "They are all perfectly acceptable. What counts is that you are a good, strong religious and spiritual person."

The Children Speak Out

In almost all these diverse communities—Muslim, Hindu, Jewish, and Hispanic—the adults largely refuse to acknowledge, or notice, prejudice. But encourage the kids to speak, and the results are different.

Varenya, Nallur's younger daughter, says, "Someone told my Hindu friend that Christianity was like a flower, but that she was a weed."

After all the love lessons preached in the morning's Sunday school class, one boy confesses, "Some people say to me, 'Do you know Jesus Christ?' 'Not really,' I tell them. Last year they said Jesus is the only God. I can't believe I'm saying this, but I just felt like pushing them off a cliff."

Another boy shakes his head in agreement. "They don't even know that Hindus pray even more than Christians," he says. "And we give to charity just like they do."

"I don't understand what a Bible is or what they do at churches, or if they get toys or what," a ten-year-old girl offers. "I've felt like talking about it, but I'm scared they'll tease me or hate me. I don't know what to do."

But taunts often have nothing to do with racism or religious intolerance. They are simply about kids harassing one another and latching on to anything different. "People tease me and say, 'He's from India-India. He likes peanuts-peanuts,'" one boy complains. "I don't know why they think peanuts are from India. *Everybody* teases me. Sometimes they call me 'monkey ears' or 'elephant ears,' but I don't care. I just think it's dumb."

When Saranya Nallur suggests that the white boys who had been pushing over the Indian girls' lunch trays in the school cafeteria a few days earlier might have been trying to make fun of them, her father immediately stops her. "The danger is in our perceiving a normal act in a different way," he says, being very practical and conciliatory. "You have to be cautious before running to that judgment."

Nallur, the wise father, advises his girls never to talk in general terms or put nationality into their conversation. "If you do that, you encourage a stereotype," he tells them. "For your own sanity, it is better *not* to dwell on those things."

An American Teen, Hindu Style

Yet the difference in cultures is something that consumes Nallur. In early 2007 when I first visited the family, Saranya, then fourteen, curled up beside her younger sister on the sofa in the family's living room and declared, "Our family is very into religion."

Back two years ago, she talked about her after-school ballet classes and bowling outings with her Indian girlfriends and said, "We do not really go out to the movies."

At Bentonville High School, where there are few Hindus, she also hung out with American girls—but cautiously and under her father's ever-watchful eyes. "May I explain something?" he asked, noting that he and his wife had reservations about their daughter mingling with Americans. "We are trying to make sure she understands our culture, and we are afraid of her hanging out with these people"—non-Indians—"because they have different standards about dating and boyfriends. She understands that these are limitations, and hopefully, when the time comes, they will make sense to her."

"It's just really the boy thing," Saranya insisted calmly, perhaps not fully ready to acknowledge the restrictions her father was placing on her future. "I mean, I should be concentrating on school now, and that is what he is worried about." Besides, she said matter-of-factly, "We do not date at all."

Yet, was that an ever-so-subtle roll of the eyes in her response? A suggestion of impatience? Had she heard his point of view too often and not been completely convinced? Still, the deferential daughter offered up the preferred point of view. "I mean, I could choose if I like the person or not," she explained. "If they choose him first and I do not like him, I do not have to date him."

Of course, the big unanswered question is whether or not leaving the Hindu fold for college will present the temptation to meet and fall in love with a non-Hindu boy. "I hope that will never happen," said her father quietly. "Once she has the maturity to do the right thing, I will not hesitate for her to be with her friends. But right now I have to protect her."

Nallur holds the Hindu belief that marriage, arranged or otherwise, means learning to accept one's mate. "If you do, that will decide whether your marriage is successful," he said. "I believe that the human goal is to realize God, and if you want to do that and know of a certain path, it would be nice to have a partner who also believes in that path."

The patience and acceptance required of an arranged marriage can even improve a person's work life, Nallur suggested. "In the workplace you come into contact with all different people. And if you know how to accept them for who they are, you become a better team player than a person who, if he does not like something, only knows how to throw everything out." Teamwork, by the way, is critical to success in the Wal-Mart workplace.

· · · · · · · · · ·

Nallur and Subha, like all the Hindus with whom I spoke in Bentonville, were married in India by arrangement. There was a matchmaker, she explains, and a bit of astrology to see whether they were compatible. Then, Subha's parents brought his picture to her. When she approved it, Nallur and his parents came to visit.

Whatever misgivings Subha may have had about this institution, she certainly was not going to explore them publicly. Asked whether her daughters should follow in her footsteps, she says without irony, "I go with my husband. I think what he thinks."

"An easy way out," Nallur acknowledged lightly, but he was pleased. "She leaves the tough decisions to me. This is the way it is in the household."

While most demographers calculate that divorce rates for American nonarranged marriages have "never exceeded about 41 percent,"[1] it is, though anecdotal, not an impressive argument for choice; at any rate, it is difficult to imagine that arranged marriages can fare any worse. "We believe love and respect will come later," Nallur says. "It has to be slow and gradual. That is a stronger bond than infatuation."

Or, as Vasan explains, "We still believe in one man and one woman for a lifetime. And we learn to live with compromise. It's not like we love each other all the time."

· · · · · · · · · ·

For Subha Nallur, coming to the United States with a husband and a two-year-old daughter was especially difficult, since, unlike him, she had only a halting knowledge of English. Malayala had been her native tongue and the language she spoke in Kerala. For more than ten years she picked up whatever English she knew by talking to other Indian wives, since most do not speak Malayala. But it had been a torturous and slow process.

On first arriving here, Subha wore a sari, an Indian garment usually made from colorful printed cotton or silk, which she carefully draped around her body. Although nobody stared or asked questions, within six months the demure young woman chose to leave traditional dress behind, except for special occasions. Even so, so many Indians now live and work in Northwest Arkansas that it is not unusual for them to wear saris to the office.

In September 2007, Subha took a big step toward assimilation by accepting a job at the Stepping Stone Children's Academy, where she works with American women, taking care of three- and four-year-old children. Much to her surprise, it brought her the seeds of a social life, the very kind that had been eluding her husband. Once a month, she said, she was bringing a dish to a potluck lunch and was, in the process, making friends.

But Nallur immediately qualified the situation. "When you say 'friends,' yes, there are people at work, but if you talk about meeting socially, it is rare," he explained. While trying to help his wife with her nascent English, he was also speaking from his own experience of thwarted friendship—and from his complicated motives for remaining separate.

Sunny Days

A fine, crisp October morning in 2008 also happens to be Saranya Nallur's birthday. She is sixteen and plans to celebrate with girlfriends by going to lunch at a local Mexican restaurant and then to a movie. She is over the moon at the prospect.

Actually, the entire Nallur clan seems happy—happier than during my visit a year earlier. Subha, whose English is much improved, seems more relaxed, and Nallur no longer feels the need to answer—quite literally—for his wife. In fact, the entire family dynamic seems much sunnier. When asked why, the Nallur teens, both of whom are now sporting braces, laugh and gesture toward the backyard, where a frisky three-month-old golden retriever is happily attacking a patch of grass. "Sammy," they say. "Sammy has helped a lot!"

As proof, they bring Sammy into the living room, where he leaps about and gnaws on my shoe and hand until the girls, giggling delightedly, drag him back outside. Sammy, Subha adds, was an early birthday present for Saranya, who had been longing for a puppy since she was five.

Before Saranya heads off for her birthday celebration, I ask her if she ever wants more freedom. "Freedom from what?" she asks, baffled.

Freedom to hang out with boys, I suggest.

"That's not very important right now," she replies, sounding mature and much like her dad. "My studies are pretty important. I see a lot of people get distracted by boys. I want to wait until I'm safe." By "safe," she means post–medical school—light-years away. "I'll be kind of old by then," she observes.

Meanwhile, Saranya focuses on achievement. Currently she ranks fourth in her class of seven hundred students. She takes three advanced placement classes, studies tennis and classical piano, and almost every Sunday plays piano for the seniors at the local Apple Blossom Retirement Center.

Saranya usually practices on the family's upright piano, located in its prayer room, while Varenya plays duets with her on a keyboard, which now sits in the living room under the photo of the Great Hugging Mother. For India's Independence Day the sisters played an Indian song, "Veer-Zaara," at a concert at the University of Arkansas. "It's a film song that a lot of people know," Varenya says. "My sister is the melody. I was the background."

Mother and daughters all agree that life has brightened now that Subha's English has improved. "We always used to invite Indian friends over," Varenya explains, "but now my parents are comfortable for us to invite American friends, too."

True, says Subha. "Nowadays I can talk with my neighbors without any hesitation. Before, I was so uncomfortable, I used to go and hide."

She has also discovered the benefits of friendship. One woman from work invited her to her wedding in Cedar Valley, Missouri, a few weeks earlier. "It was my first American wedding," says Subha who attended without A.J. "I was a little scared. But it was good. The bride wore a fancy gown, and we all sat together and talked."

"And I didn't feel separate or anything. I was comfortable."

Valentines for Wal-Mart

Nirmala Kulkarni, a slender, angular woman in her mid-thirties, and her husband, Balu, sit primly at the head of their rectangular wooden dining room table early on an Easter Sunday evening. They are joined by their good friends, Padmaja Voosa and her husband, Murthy Kolluru, as well as by Nirmala's mother, Parvathi Dugganapalli, who is visiting from India. All three women have adorned themselves in lovely brocade saris in luscious shades of lavender, cinnamon, and tangerine; the men, both mustachioed, wear American button-down shirts and sweaters.

The Kulkarnis, parents of twin toddlers—a boy and a girl—live in a modest but cozy home in the same subdivision as their friend, Vasan. An electrical engineer, Nirmala came here from Bangalore in August 1998 as a consultant for Wal-Mart, and six months later the company hired her as a programmer. Today, as a solutions architect, she specializes in technological strategies.

Balu followed two years later, joining Wal-Mart's information systems department. He now works on the business side in the home office's diversity group. Although theirs, too, is an arranged marriage, it was Nirmala's brother, while attending college with Balu, who introduced them.

Murthy Kolluru, who earned a master's degree in computer applications, arrived here from southern India even earlier, in February 1997, to work in Wal-Mart's IT department as a pricing manager. "We created pricing system for the stores—merchants use them to create rollbacks, markdowns, and to decide the price of merchandise," he explains. After returning home that December to marry Padmaja, he brought his new bride back to Bentonville, where they are now raising their two elementary-school-aged daughters.

Even so, Padmaja, with a master of arts degree in political science, has managed simultaneously to work full-time at Wal-Mart since 2002 and to mother their girls. Although she began as an auditor in the financial area and spent almost seven years there, working on an hourly basis on vendor and overcharge claims, six years later she moved over to the IT department and is now a computer programmer on the management side.

How does a social sciences graduate without the engineering background of most IT workers become so adept at computers? Padmaja laughs, then explains that after earning her master's she took courses in computer programming and aced a number of refresher classes that Wal-Mart offered.

"I am very happy about this change," she says. "I'm in the replenishment area, and my platform is mainframes. This job is much more challenging and satisfying."

Upward mobility seems to be a positive characteristic of Wal-Mart life. Consider that Murthy, too, has moved into a different slot at the company. "Now I'm on the business side," he says. "It is a little better than IT, timewise. There, you had to work forty-five hours a week. Plus, with four people on an IT team, you were on call once every four weeks [in case of a systems breakdown]."

Murthy also wanted to be part of management. There he could learn the business and—although he did not say this—participate in bigger bonuses and stock options. Now, as a middle manager, one of only twenty-four in the company, he uses the pricing systems that he developed to decide the price of electronics such as TVs, computers, flash drives, and printers.

"For instance," he says, "if Best Buy's weekly bulletin offers a flash drive for $29.99, I have to figure out how we can beat this in Wal-Mart. First we decide the strategy for the department, and next for each category of item. Then we ask, 'Who are the major competitors, how are they pricing the item, and how can we beat them?'"

Murthy holds team meetings, attends department meetings, and then, after coming up with a strategy, talks to Wal-Mart merchants. "When I implement my pricing, I talk to the replenishment managers, category managers, and several other people so that they do what they are supposed to do," he says. "Suppose I take down the price on a TV by $200. A huge demand in the market will follow. So the replenishment team should know in order to fill the store with inventory for that demand." Murthy also travels a few days each month.

For all his effort, does Murthy consider himself to be sufficiently compensated? "They pay well enough," he says cautiously. Well enough on a national level or an Arkansas level? "The last time I heard, we were competing nationally," he answers me politely.

And how do the stock options, which made fortunes for many early Wal-Mart managers, pan out these days? Are they more important than salary?

"No," says Murthy, who explains that managers receive options equal to a percentage of their salaries—in his case, about 30 percent. These options mature within three to five years, but the stock price needs to rise and the manager needs to have available money to actually purchase the stock in order to make a profit. (Still, as Coleman Peterson has pointed out, compensation should be evaluated on not only salaries and stock options but also 401(k)s, pensions, and health insurance.)

Murthy's community commitments extend beyond Wal-Mart and family. He finds time to play on one of the home office's three cricket teams and is also president of the Hindu Association of Northwest Arkansas; as such, it is his charge to raise funds to build a permanent Hindu temple in Gentry. "When we bought the land, a barn was there, which we converted into a prayer hall," he says. "That's where we celebrate all our festivals. At any festival we have between three hundred and four hundred people."

Because this temporary temple is usually bulging at the seams during celebrations, the Hindu Association plans to go forward and build the real thing when its fundraising tops $500,000; at the moment the group is $200,000 short but hopes to reach its goal by 2010. "If you go to any other community like Chicago or New York, the highest donors are either doctors or business owners," Murthy says, repeating the concerns of the Jews in the area who also worry about future financial contributions. "But it is difficult to convince computer professionals to pay money for the temple. That is our biggest trouble." A fancy black-tie dinner in 2008 raised $60,000, thanks to donations from J. B. Hunt, from Tyson's, from such vendor companies as Procter & Gamble and Kimberly-Clark, and, most especially, from Wal-Mart's Diversity Relations Team.

In return, the Indians profess loyalty and almost unnerving enthusiasm for their employer—so much so that sometimes they begin to sound like Stepford workers. Surely theirs is not the same corporation that journalists, former employees, and lawyers alike subject to daily barbs, not to mention class-action lawsuits? Yet Wal-Mart has been paternalistic in the best sense, its hometown employees insist. "You talk about opportunity, and you have it with them," says Nirmala. "You talk about growth, you have it. And you talk about taking care of families, and you have it."

She uses her own pregnancy as an example. Both she and Balu had to take time off for doctors' appointments; after all, carrying twins made her pregnancy that much trickier. "And our supervisor were very kind to make sure that we took care of our stuff," she says. "If I wasn't feeling well, they sent me home and even called to see how I was doing. They really emphasize that family comes first."

As another example of how stellar an employer they believe Wal-Mart to be, Balu tells how his home was hit by a tornado early on a Monday in March 2006. The windows were shattered, the bedroom was torn apart, and the entire house, he says, "was a mess." So he phoned his supervisor and explained that he would not be able to work that morning because he had to clean up.

"A little while later," Balu recalls, "he called back and asked, 'Is it okay if we come by and help you out?' And I said yes."

Within twenty minutes, a small army of helpers, about fifteen people in all, showed up to clean the house and yard. The troops vacuumed, picked up the glass and breakage throughout the house, and made it livable. They also brought flashlights and boarded up the windows until Balu could get them fixed.

"My next-door neighbor asked me, 'Where did you get these people from?'" he adds. "And I said, 'They are all my colleagues, and they just decided to help out.' That's how things are here."

The Kulkarnis and Kollurus all work either the 8:00–6:00 or 7:30–5:30 shift with one-hour lunch breaks, and they religiously attend Wal-Mart's Saturday morning meetings. "And at night we go home and watch our Indian TV channels on our satellite dishes," says Nirmala. "Almost every day we cook Indian food. And on weekends we do community things together—birthdays, housewarmings, baby showers."

In August 2008, the Kulkarnis threw a big party at home to honor the first birthday of their twins, Anaga and Anish. "It was really a wonderful celebration," observes Padmaja.

Feeling comfortable within the Hindu and corporate communities, both couples claim to have integrated more easily into the dominant white culture than the Nallurs had. "We have American friends who invite us over," Balu says. "This is not an issue."

The Kulkarnis socialize with whites, blacks, Hispanics, and Muslims. "We go out," says Nirmala. "And they come to our place, too—they like our food. One thing I like about this county is that people are so nice to you."

What *was* a problem, Padmaja says, was the language. Unlike Subha Nallur, Padmaja spoke English when she arrived here, but all the Indians agree that understanding American accents and making their own thickly Indian-accented English understood in Arkansas emerged as a bigger challenge than expected. Eventually, however, they resolved the issue, so much so that both couples have since become American citizens.

While life in Northwest Arkansas offers endless comforts, one sore point for the Hindus has been the way in which Americans confuse them with Muslims. "We all basically look the same," says Murthy, who, like Katke, had also had a post-9/11 experience going to the McDonald's drive-through and hearing locals making ugly comments. "People have a fear of the unknown," he says. "They know our religion is different from theirs, but they don't know how. I would like them to be aware that our religion teaches nonviolence. That may help people understand us better."

Nirmala praises the home office for respecting her Hindu customs and traditions. "We have so many festivals in our religion," she says, "and if I ask for a half day off, my managers understand. Also, they make sure not to put us on certain big schedules during festival days—and we have about fifteen a year. I've felt that it was very nice of them to accommodate us."

Like many Hindu families, the Kulkarnis and Kollurus have designated prayer rooms in their homes with shrines featuring paintings; sculptures of Hindu gods, goddesses, and mythological figures; and religious mementos. They usually pray here twice a day. "We are happy continuing our culture," says Nirmala.

Occasionally, too, they explain their religion to church groups. "And we are also learning the Christian culture," adds Balu, pointing out that they sometimes visit local Bible study groups and have gone to Easter and Christmas prayer services and to the synagogue's dedication. "It was awesome."

"We are all open-minded about each other's cultures," says Murthy.

And how do the Kulkarnis envision their twins' futures? The family may one day return to India to live, but Balu says, "I prefer to raise them here."

As her husband speaks, Nirmala smiles mysteriously. "We will take it as it comes," she says.

A Marshallese Security
Guard "Talks Story"

....

Saimon Milne was furious. The Marshall Islander and his wife had brought their pregnant daughter into the emergency room of Springdale's Northwest Medical Center on a humid August afternoon, and the young man in charge was ignoring them. How is this possible? Milne wondered. The nineteen-year-old mother-to-be, six months along, expecting twins, and with a history of serious heart problems since childhood, was screaming with pain.

Not the type to lose his cool or to chalk up somebody else's bad behavior to anything as gross as prejudice, Milne, after begging and cajoling to no avail, finally did both.

First, however, he needed to act fast. He gathered up his family, loaded them into his car, and sped down I-540 to Willow Creek Hospital in another part of Springdale. His daughter, as it turned out, was already in labor. She gave birth to her premature twins in the parking lot of Willow Creek, and the babies were airlifted back to Northwest Medical Center for prenatal care.

Then Milne unloaded his anger at the attendant. "I was really pissed," he said days later, still furious. "Is this guy a racist, or what? He does not like me? How can he not understand that my daughter was really sick? He cannot tell first priority from second priority, and so on."

And so after the emergency team took over, Milne made his way back to the ER. "My wife said, 'Do not go. You're crazy.' But I went back. I said, 'Hey, mister, you know what? My daughter just delivered her babies in the parking lot. She was really needing help.' In my life, this is one of the things I will never forget."

Coming to America

A charmer with a craggy, lived-in face and a gruffly confident demeanor, Milne came to the United States—and Springdale—for the first time, he says, "a few days before they hit the tower in New York. And at first we couldn't go back because the airport was closed. But my wife kind of liked it here. She told me, 'Go back and quit your job and come back here.' And I was thinking about my daughter because schools are better here than back home. So I said OK. And soon I came back."

Milne immigrated here with his wife, Helena, their daughter, Selena, then twelve, and two of his four older children, who have since returned home. They came in part to visit another older daughter who lived here with her family, and in part because of Springdale's status as having the largest community of Marshallese in the United States—between six and eight thousand.

There were economic factors, too. "Marshallese are easygoing. They don't work, work, work," says Milne. "In California a one-bedroom apartment costs $2,000. Here, three bedrooms are $800."

He had hoped that Selena, especially, would get an American education and not drop out, as so many young Marshallese do. But she left high school at age fifteen and moved in with her Marshallese boyfriend instead. Milne was disgusted but eventually accepted it. "What could I do?" he asks. "I don't know."

Another lure of Springdale has been the abundance of work available for unskilled laborers. Quickly, Helena, who had never before held a job, was hired to pack chickens on the line at Tyson Foods, even though she was on the far side of fifty. Although it is not the custom for women to work in the Marshall Islands, Milne informs me, "I told her to work so she can get Social Security benefits. And while it seems kind of tough, she says she likes it. But my wife is a tough lady."

Milne quickly found himself a job as well. But after a year working at Rogers Car Mart, he became ill and discovered that he did not have the health insurance he thought he had. So he left. Serendipitously, on a Sunday soon afterward, the pastor at the Marshallese church that Milne attended announced that the Jones Center, the sprawling nonprofit campus and recreation facility in Springdale, was looking for a security guard. "And I'd been bringing my grandchildren here," says Milne, "and I saw the other Marshallese kids' behavior, which is really different from back home. They came here and changed. They no longer had respect for their elders."

So when Milne applied for the job, he told his future employers that he wanted to work with Marshallese children and teach them manners. They liked that. He got the job instantly.

"You talk to these kids, and it seems like they don't care what you say," he says. "When I see them all running, I say, 'Walk, please.' And when they are yelling, I say, 'Stop, please.' I deal with a lot of kids now, not just the Marshallese."

For six years Milne has been working here as a security guard. He and his wife rent, for $400 a month, a small, single-story bungalow about four blocks away in a dreary, treeless neighborhood dotted with dried patches of grass that pass for lawns. But Milne, sitting on his couch one afternoon, looks happily around his modest digs—two tiny bedrooms, a kitchen, a bath, and a small living room festooned with silk flowers, shell necklaces, American flags, and family photographs. "It's more than what I need," he says of the cluttered cottage that he clearly sees as palatial.

An Island Paradise, an Island Hell

Most Americans know little about the Marshall Islands, a collection of twenty-nine Pacific atolls and one thousand small islands about twenty-five hundred miles southwest of Hawaii. With a population of about sixty-two thousand, most of whom are of Micronesian descent and speak Marshallese, these islands' major atolls are the capital, Majuro, and Kwajalein, the largest island, which was occupied by the Japanese during World War II until the United States invaded and captured the Marshalls in 1944. By

1946 the United States had begun testing the first nuclear weapons on the Bikini and Enewatak atolls, and in 1947 the entire group of islands was made a U.S. territory.

The United States utilized the Marshalls as an atomic-testing site through 1958, detonating sixty-seven nuclear bombs in all. Among them was the ironically titled Bravo shot, which exploded over the Bikini atoll on March 1, 1954. This fifteen-megaton hydrogen bomb, said to be one thousand times more powerful than the atomic bomb dropped on Hiroshima, has the distinction of being the largest bomb this country has ever tested. (Every year Springdale's Marshallese community commemorates these bombings by teaching about their devastating consequences.)

Kwajalein as well became the site of an intercontinental ballistic missile test range. As a result, in the 1980s the U.S. government paid a $150 million compensation package to the victims of atomic testing—as it turns out, a mere pittance, since over time the population of the Marshall Islands has borne the horrific burden of that testing. Consider the 1999 Pacific Islands Report, taken from a University of Hawaii study, written by Dr. Neal Palafox of the university's John A. Burns Medical School, which found that in the Marshall Islands between 1985 and 1994, because of nuclear exposure and, to some degree, malnutrition, cervical cancer rates were 5.8 times higher than in the United States; lung cancer rates were 3.8 times higher in men and 3.09 higher in women; and liver cancer rates were 15.3 times higher in men and 40 times higher in women. While the researchers issued a caveat that even these levels were probably underreported because of local "underdeveloped health record-keeping systems," the report also noted that "increases in leukemia, breast cancer, and thyroid cancer after radiation exposure have been well established, especially in childhood exposures."

By today's standards, whatever reparations the United States made hardly seem enough. Still, in 1979 the Marshall Islands officially became the Republic of the Marshall Islands; in exchange, the United States was given permission to patrol the waters and lease an atoll for a naval base. More important, in 1986 the Compact of Free Association between the Marshallese and the United States guaranteed the Republic's people the right to live and work in the States and even to serve in the American military.

"We couldn't remain a trust territory forever," Milne explained. "So we chose our political status and told the U.S., 'This is what we want.'"

Since then there has been a small but steady exodus to the United States, perhaps made more pronounced as a result of a drought in the islands in March 2007 and a serious energy shortage in 2008. Still, for all the health problems that the Marshallese have endured as a result of both U.S. nuclear-testing policy and their inadequate health care at home, its citizens who come here often suffer from tuberculosis, diabetes, and other ailments but are not eligible for Medicare, nonemergency Medicaid, free health care, or other forms of public assistance.

Its bleak history notwithstanding, the Marshall Islands can be seen today as a Pacific paradise, a Bali H'ai with lush palm trees, blue waters, golden sunrises, and that dark secret past whose poisoned footprint still exists, hidden in its warm oceans, white sands, and cool winds.

A Kwajalein Youth

Milne, who sometimes seems inconsistent about his age, says when pinned down that he was born in November 1943, "during the military time. When I opened my eyes, Americans were there."

One of his great-grandfathers, a Scotsman, married a woman from the neighboring Gilbert Islands and set up an English school on Ebon, where Milne grew up and was a student. The son of a deacon in the Protestant church, he moved to Kwajalein after high school and worked at the missile range there, where his job included taking inventory of government property.

It was on Kwajalein that Milne also met Helena. While he says he was attracted to her from the beginning, their families made the real match, as is the Marshallese custom. Together the couple raised five children and enjoyed what he describes as a good, easy life.

"People just live by the land," he says. "You go pick fruit, and you go fish on the reef. I had my boats, and early in the morning when the tide is right, I just took off and got a lot of fish like red snapper and tuna, which I brought to my house or gave to my friends. Here, it takes a while to get used to river fish, which sometimes smell muddy—I don't really like that."

Ask him about the difference between life in the Pacific and life here in Arkansas, and he will tell you that one good thing about Springdale is the opportunity to get an education. "Also, here, anything you need, you can have it as long as you work hard for it," he says. "Here, I call it 'restless life.' You've got to be on time, or they fire you. Over there, you live in tidal land, and people just go out of their house as soon as the sun comes up. Anytime you want to go to work, it's up to you. You can go swimming or sailing, so you cannot get bored. Or you can go from house to house and talk stories—that's our custom. But here, everybody stays inside; you'll be crazy if you go to [another] house. There, if you stay *inside* the house, you're crazy."

The easy life had its downside, however. In the Marshall Islands, says Milne, depression and alcoholism are both rampant. "I used to be involved in sports and every time we won, we always celebrated and drank," he says. "And I was crazy then. I used to be an alcoholic. I would drink six, seven, eight beers, then go to work early the next morning with a hangover. But then, when I realized that I had to have beer every day, I knew I was in trouble. And so, after ten years of it, I stopped."

....

A born leader, Saimon Milne constantly finds himself in a position to represent the Springdale Marshallese community. At a meeting in a large room in the Jones Center complex, about two hundred people show up to hear the U.S. representative from Washington, D.C. Men in T-shirts and women, young and old, all wearing gaily colored floral muumuus, sit and listen. But nobody from the area speaks—except Milne.

"That's the way the Marshallese are." He shrugs. "People come and listen, but only a few talk. I don't understand it. They're kind of shy or afraid. Me, I'm not. What I've got here"—and he taps the breast-pocket insignia of his security uniform—"I bring out."

Milne sometimes becomes frustrated with compatriots who come to the United States but refuse to Americanize. "I believe what the Bible says. 'You go to Rome, you live like Romans,'" he explains. But Marshallese women who settle here, his wife and daughters among them, cling fast to their language and island traditions. Milne's wife, like so many other older women, barely speaks English and continues to wear the hometown muumuu—"even in winter when you've got snow coming down," he observes, a touch impatiently. "It's silly. And Marshallese women don't go to the beauty salon to cut their hair. They wear it like in the Marshall Islands. But everybody is united globally now—there are fashions of the world." Apparently, for Milne, muumuus are not among them.

This question of how thoroughly to assimilate is one that every immigrant family—Marshallese, Indian, Mexican—confronts almost immediately on arrival. How completely should the women, especially, adapt to American garb and customs, and how firmly should they hold dear to their *hijabs*, their muumuus, their saris? Does the family keep to its religious dietary laws or throw them away? Do newcomers embrace the religious orthodoxy of their homeland, which may included segregated prayer rituals, dating rituals, teen motherhood, and arranged marriages, or do they try on the new clothes and customs of their adopted country? And do they open themselves up to new friendship with those who might inadvertently provide powerful cultural temptations? Such concerns affect both family elders and their children, who are both eager to please their parents and to taste the freedoms of the new world of Northwest Arkansas.

Immigration, Language, and Diversity Challenges

Marshallese who move to Springdale are sometimes frustrated and irritated to discover, on arriving here, that locals often lump them together with the area's Hispanic immigrants, simply because many members of both groups are dark skinned. "Sometimes people treat me as a person who has just crossed the Mexican border and came here to work without proper papers," Milne explains. "They don't know our Compact. They don't get the deal between our two countries."

For the Marshallese, learning to deal within the mostly white, mostly English-speaking community of Northwest Arkansas has been at least as difficult as it is for the Hispanics, although the Marshallese don't have the singular concern of needing legal documentation. But many Marshallese, including children, do not speak English at all. Maribel Childress, the principal of Monitor Elementary School in Springdale, has been teaching Marshallese children for more than a decade and understands why learning English is so difficult for them.

"The Marshallese alphabet is different from the American alphabet," Childress explains. "The Marshallese have letters that we don't have, and we have letters that they don't have. So the sounds that Marshallese children learn to make in speech, and which carry over into reading, are different from ours. The kids are looking at letters they've never seen before and trying to make sounds they've never heard before. And it can be a real challenge, unless, of course, they were exposed to English early on."

At the same time, few, if any, Americans speak Marshallese, which is an Austronesian language. Yet millions of Americans speak some Spanish, and millions more are fluent in it. The language barrier for Marshall Islanders sets up other barriers within the community. For instance, in Springdale there are more than 130 volunteers who help translate Spanish for those who cannot communicate in English; there are only 4 volunteers who are able to do the same for the Marshallese.

The fact that so many Marshallese children have difficulty learning English tends to create even further barriers to assimilation—and to learning itself. A recent report released by Northwest Arkansas Community College noted that while the number of its minority students had increased by 25.5 percent from the spring of 2007 through the spring of 2008, there were no Marshallese high school graduates from either Benton or Washington counties enrolled at any two- or four-year colleges in the area.[1] There is also a substantial dropout rate among local high school students, relegating young Marshallese to the same small circle of unskilled jobs as their parents and preventing their upward mobility within the community.

Albious Latior, a Marshallese immigrant and recent graduate of Springdale High School, now works thirty-three hours a week as an Americorps volunteer at the school, for which he is paid $800 a month. A slight, slim young man with elegant hands, a soft voice, and two gold caps in the front of his mouth, Latior, who came to the United States with his family in 1997 at age ten, acts as an adviser for the high school's Islanders Club. "I try to encourage Micronesian students to complete high school and move on with their lives," he says. He also attempts to get them to assimilate within the larger school community.

But his task is a weighty and frustrating one. Even trying to get the Marshallese students to sit with the non-Marshallese in the lunchroom is impossible. "After five minutes they move back to their old tables and sit alone with each other," he says. "And when I ask them why, they say they are more open when they can speak their own language. They don't feel comfortable with English. They want to be open to Americans, but they are scared."

The only sibling from a large family to have completed high school,

Latior characterizes some of his peers as "lazy" but says that the situation is more complicated than that. Even Marshallese students who grow up here speaking English begin to self-segregate by high school, Latior notes. "When they're younger, they're open to more things," he says. "Later, they drift back to the other Marshallese and close up again."

Latior began studying business at Northwest Arkansas Community College in the fall of 2008 and claims to have friends across the spectrum. "They e-mail or call me," he says, "and I call them." Nevertheless, he, too, holds his own community dear. He talks to Marshallese across the country via an online chat room, cannot imagine marrying a non-Marshallese girl, and when I ask what he likes to do in his free time, he responds quickly: "Go to church." He attends services at the First Marshallese United Church of Christ on Sunday mornings and evenings as well as Wednesday evenings.

Yet he is one of the few who is bridging the chasm between cultures for young Marshallese. "Albious is an inspiration, and the students really follow him," says Al "Papa Rap" Lopez, Springdale High's student coordinator.

"We Marshallese are happy to meet new people, and we have an open mind," Latior tries to reassure me. "But we are very shy inside."

Carmen Chong Gum, the Jones Center's outreach coordinator for the Marshallese people, agrees, noting, "We tend to keep a low profile and stay close together."

This emphatic, almost desperate, cliquishness brings to mind Robert D. Putnam's famous but often misunderstood observation that "in the presence of diversity, we hunker down. We act like turtles. The effect of diversity is worse than had been imagined."[2] By this he means that in diverse communities, we tend to bond and create friendships and social structures with those most like us while developing suspicions and mistrust of those least like us.

Yet Putnam has been quick to repudiate those whom he calls "racists and anti-immigration activists" for interpreting his work as a celebration of insularity and a warning against multiculturalism. Setting the record straight to a reporter for the *Harvard Crimson* in 2006, he explained that while diversity might be seen to shatter community harmony in the short term, over time it can break down old barriers and rebuild a newer, more encompassing sense of community. "In my lifetime, Americans have deconstructed religion as a basis for making decisions," he told *Crimson* reporter William M. Goldsmith. "Why can't we do the same thing with other types of diversity?" As an example, he points to Jewish humor, which in the first half of the twentieth century was geared to and understood only by Jews. Nowadays most of us regard Woody Allen's movies and Jewish-based humor as American, first and foremost.

Traditionally, the Marshallese community and family structure are tight. Many Marshallese who still live on the islands also send their children to school here, and these youngsters live with grandparents, aunts, uncles, and family friends, often referring to them as "Mom" and "Dad."

"Marshallese are family-close nuts," says Milne. What's more, the family's social activities often revolve around Marshallese churches, of which there are more than thirteen in Springdale alone. "In the Marshall Islands people are very religious. In America, you can find people that don't believe in God, but over there you cannot find even one," Milne explains. "*Everybody* believes."

The majority religion of the Marshall Islands is Protestantism, but Milne and his family all joined the Mormon Church shortly before they arrived in this country. "We studied together," he says. "I told the others to do what they believed, but they said, 'You're the one who leads us, and so we follow you.' And my wife says, 'I think you won't lead us in the wrong way.'"

So although Marshallese choose to come to the United States, they also choose, in Putnam's words, to "hunker down" as a unit. This is true for adults, and often their children reflect this behavior. While Milne moved here to give his daughter, Selena, the opportunity for a solid education, she chose not to take advantage of it. While telling me that she liked school— "particularly English," she says—she preferred hanging out with her Marshallese boyfriend. Dropping out to be with him, she soon became pregnant with their first child, a daughter. Now, at age twenty, she is already the mother of three.

Milne, angry with his daughter for lapsing into the familiar behavior of island women who marry early and develop no work skills of their own, nevertheless worried that she and her boyfriend would not be able to manage by themselves. "So when a small apartment in the back of my house became free," he says, "I told the owner that I wanted it for her. So she is back here, along with the boyfriend and the boyfriend's mother."

Only days after the traumatic birth of her twins, this painfully shy young woman, her plastic hospital identification bracelet still encircling her wrist, wanders over to her father's house. Wearing a black muumuu adorned with large pink flowers, and with her hair swept up and back in the Marshallese style, Selena still seems weak and shaky. In some ways she sounds like a typical American teen—she likes pizza, malls, and hip-hop dancing at local clubs. But, as with so many Marshallese transplants, she seems torn between island culture and American culture.

Where would she like her children to grow up?

"Here," she says without hesitation or irony. "So they can get a good education."

And where would she herself prefer to live?

"The islands."

But why, I ask her.

"Because," she replies, "they have nice weather—and the ocean."

A Summer Visitor

The ocean, a glistening turquoise blanket that occasionally turns storm-cloud gray, is key to the Marshallese temperament and culture. Maribel Childress, having worked for eight years as principal of Parson Hills Elementary, which has the largest number of Marshallese students in Springdale, before going over to the newer Monitor Elementary School, became fascinated by the culture and spent the summers of 2005 and 2006 teaching school on Majuro, the largest of the islands.

"I remember my first trip," she says. "When the plane broke through the clouds, I looked down and thought, 'Oh, my God, how did people end up here in the first place? And how is my plane going to land on *that*?'"

That was the tiny speck of an island below her, a small land mass surrounded by water. "Majuro is thirty miles long," she explains, "but width-wise, when you're standing on it, you can see the water on both sides. And the land itself can be between a mere ten yards and one hundred yards wide. It's *very* narrow."

With a common land area that tiny, Childress observes, there are few places for the children to go during lunch hour. "What would seem like a lack of supervision based on what we're used to here in the United States is common there," she says. "Nobody is on duty during recess, and the kids run home or to the store."

What impressed the principal was the generosity and dedication of the island teachers. Because the Marshall Islands are so isolated, the teachers don't have easy access to such staples as paper, pencils, and dry erase boards. "I took supplies with me and left them behind for a few of them," she says. "And the afternoon I left, they divided the material among the entire staff when they could have kept it all for themselves. They want to do everything they can for the students, but they don't even know how limited their resources are, because they don't know any different."

Childress became enamored with the island, its beauty and its customs. At school and at home children and adults alike would leave their shoes at the door Asian style. She began to appreciate the slow pace, the moments when, just as darkness fell, people moved out to their porches or strolled from house to house, visiting one another. "They would fix each other's hair," she says, "or play volleyball or basketball. They also love their own music, singing, and dancing. Evenings, everything else stopped while they spent time with each other. And I kept thinking, How sad is the life we lead here in the States. I can't remember the last time I had a conversation with my neighbor."

More than anything else—"Above work, above being somewhere on time," Childress professes—the Marshallese respect their relationships. "Going through life slowly and paying attention to one another, valuing each other as they do, is very beautiful," she adds.

And yet Childress kept summoning up images of that great divide between island culture and Ozarks culture, and recalling how all Marshallese in the United States are transplanted from a life in which the ocean surrounds them twenty-four hours a day to one where they are in a landlocked suburb and *never* see blue water. "I can't imagine how claustrophic they feel," she says mournfully.

So, are the Marshallese, who cling together here in Springdale, happier in Arkansas than in the Marshall Islands? Some miss the island, says Childress. And others, children who were born here, build up a myth about what it is like back home. "But going back there to live would be a culture shock for them," she observes.

What's more, the price of a round-trip ticket to these off-the-beaten-path islands is sky-high—more than $2,000. Sometimes families work for years to earn the fare back home.

Childress is concerned, too, that the U.S. government does not make reciprocal life easier for the Marshallese. But the truth is that the American government has its own interests, which do not necessarily jibe with those of the Marshall Islands. "And because the Marshallese population isn't very significant, I don't think the people have great advocates for what they deserve," she says. "They struggle internally as well because they are very proud, and it is sometimes hard to know that their existence is thanks to handouts and support from another country."

An Anniversary Celebration

It is barely 9:00 A.M. on Saturday, May 24, 2008. A crowd of Marshallese women in bold muumuus with garlands of white flowers in their hair, accompanied by men in tropical shirts, has flocked to the Jones Center, and, high with anticipation, the group marches into the spacious gymnasium. They are here to open the three-day celebration of Constitution Day, the twenty-ninth anniversary of the 1979 signing of the treaty with the United States, which created an independent Republic of the Marshall Islands. During the next few days, perhaps six thousand to seven thousand Marshallese from all across the United States will gather in the area to eat island barbecue, to visit with families and friends, to browse a health fair set up to give them critical information, and to participate in various sports tournaments. More than sixty teams of children and young people have arrived here to compete in such sports as softball, volleyball, and basketball. In colorful uniforms, team members are now milling around the gym, some carrying team flags.

This Constitution Day is even more special than usual, since the new president of the Marshall Islands, Litokwa Tomeing, who was elected in January, has come here with his wife, Arlin, for the festivities; it is the first time in five years that any Marshallese president has visited Northwest Arkansas.

"It is tradition in the islands [that] when people from different islands get together, they always have games,"[3] explains Tony DeBrum, the foreign minister, who has flown down from Washington, D.C., for the merrymaking—and also to attend his nephew and granddaughter's graduations from local schools. DeBrum goes on to suggest that in the islands those games might be slightly different, since they would include diving, spearfishing, and coconut husking.

At the center of the party, as it turns out, is Saimon Milne, the de facto king of the Jones Center, who thought up the program, along with Chong Gum, the Marshallese outreach coordinator. "I wanted to make the younger generation aware of their folklore," Milne says. "We used to have chants to motivate people when they were canoeing and fighting. So just before the games started, I said I would sing some of these chants, or great oral stories. And I came up to the microphone and explained how these chants were so important to our ancestors."

A childhood friend of Tomeing, Milne, dressed casually in a baseball cap and his gray knit shirt with the SECURITY imprint on the front pocket and across the back, then chants a story from Marshallese mythology about a large rock that the tide washes up onto the sandy beach of an atoll. Eventually, the island's chief springs from this rock the way Hera sprang from Zeus's head; and he fathers so many children that it is necessary to call a meeting and divide them into tribes.

But for all the good fun and camaraderie of the ceremony and the competitions that follow it, a serious undercurrent runs through the proceedings. President Tomeing is here to announce the creation of a Marshallese consulate in Springdale. If the U.S. government approves this, it will be Arkansas's second consulate, the first being the Mexican consulate that opened in Little Rock in 2007. Tomeing and DeBrum both note that this consulate, when established, will help Marshallese deal with issues such as housing, health care, insurance, schools, and even driver's licenses.

"This is a recognition of the importance of the population here," Kathy Birkhead, director of diversity and inclusion at the Jones Center, says after the announcement.

Officials also meet to discuss how to secure government-funded health care for Marshallese who come to the United States with such lifelong health problems as diabetes, congenital heart defects, and thyroid malfunctions, all the legacy of atomic testing. The first step, they say, is that the community will need to conduct a special census count through local Marshallese churches in order to determine the current Marshallese population of the area.

Self-Invention, American Style

A week after Milne has plucked his daughter from the emergency room of Springdale's Northwest Medical Center, he is still smoking with anger. He enlists a friend to write a letter of complaint to the hospital's CEO and hand-delivers it himself to the secretary.

That very evening the CEO phones Milne to apologize. Milne refuses to meet with him, holding yet another grudge because the CEO's secretary had not allowed him to hand off the letter in person.

A few weeks later, however, during an off-site staff meeting at one of the Jones Center's conference rooms, the CEO seeks out Milne. "And he told me that he fired the guy in the emergency room," says Milne. "But I said, 'You don't have to fire him. You just have to tell your staff the difference between an emergency and a sick call.' But the CEO says, 'It's history. He's gone.'"

The following day another apologetic hospital executive calls. "He was even higher up," Milne says as he beams. "And he thanked me for the letter and for telling them about the issue so they could adjust things and make them better."

Finally, Milne feels vindicated.

. . . .

What makes Milne's experience so American is that at an age where most others, especially his island compatriots, would have been long retired, Milne has taken the opportunity to reinvent himself. He prides himself on his work—by the way, the Jones Center lists him as vice president of security—and his local celebrity. Undeniably, the guy makes good copy. But he is also a fearless fighter, as comfortable with non-Marshallese as he is with fellow islanders.

It is striking that Milne and his wife have developed an emphatically American work ethic, something they share with their love of family life, which, he says, is core to most islanders' values.

Consider Helena Milne's schedule, which, during her grandchildren's first year, was perhaps the most grueling of all. While Milne worked days, this woman, who had never held a job in her life, now, in her sixties, worked on the line at Tyson from 9:00 P.M. every evening to 7:00 A.M. Returning home, she made sure that the household was in order, then went to sleep at 9:00 A.M., rising in late afternoon to help her daughter. Her exhaustive pace was like that of so many immigrants who come to the United States and work round the clock in order to grab even a small slice of that increasingly compromised American Dream.

"She's a tough lady. I know she's tough," Milne says of his wife's brutal schedule, using his favorite word to describe her.

In the spring of 2008, Helena took what began as a two-month leave from Tyson for knee-replacement surgery. After receiving a letter from the company asking if she planned to come back, Milne instructed her to return to her job. "If she doesn't like it or cannot do it anymore," he said, "she can always leave." A year later she has yet to return to the poultry line. "She's getting better, but also a little lazy," Milne observes.

Milne worries most about his daughter, who has dashed his dreams for her. "I hope she won't have any more babies, so she can finish her schooling," he says. "But she don't listen to me. She's very spoiled."

After the twins were born, Milne, concerned about Selena's health, says he instructed her boyfriend to quit work and stay home to help. "They fired him anyway," he says. "But if he didn't quit [to help her], I'd kick the guy out."

Who, in the meanwhile, paid their bills?

"I did," he says.

. . . .

A man who savors his role as spokesperson, Milne seems like a natural politician. But ask him if he wants to become the new Springdale consul, and he dismisses the idea.

"It's a big responsibility. I can't work with people who don't want to help themselves," he says. "I know the Marshallese. Remember the story of the cat and the mouse? The mouse hangs a bell around the cat's neck so that every time he moves, the mouse will know. The Marshallese don't want to do the extra mile. Or take that next step."

And what about running for elected office in the Marshallese government?

Milne's skepticism surfaces once again. "Our government is young," he says. "When the Americans liberated us, we were so poor that we made our clothes from bags. And now these people who run for the government want to grab what they can because they don't want their children to be poor like they were. They just travel and have per diems and housing allowances. They don't try to make life better for the people, who can't even buy shoes. I am always surprised when they pass a bill to give themselves raises. But I know this: politics is not bad; *people* make it bad."

Milne also worries that doing government work would rob him of time with his family. "It is my job to make sure that my family's welfare is in good standing," he says. "My wife and all my children. And if I ran for the government, I would have to do the same thing for the people of the islands as I do for my family."

Milne has given plenty of thought to his future. "I'm a dreamer," he says. Right now those dreams include staying in Springdale for two or three more years—in 2009 he moved his family into a much larger apartment that saves him almost two hundred dollars a month—and then flying back home to one of the outer islands of his tainted tropical paradise. There, he hopes to live comfortably off his and his wife's retirement, watch lots of videos, and read lots of books.

"The Marshall Islands is the easiest life," he says. "You live by the land. You don't have to work. No rush, no anything. I'm going to go fishing. I'm going to play the ukelele.

"And every day I'm going to 'talk story.'"

6

Of Buyers and Sellers

....

Ed Clifford's desk looks out, appropriately enough, onto Bentonville Square, which, on this summery, golden day in October 2008, is still in the midst of cosmetic surgery. At the moment, a road on the southwest corner is being widened to accommodate the mob of tourists the town expects after the Crystal Bridges Museum opens in 2011.

"It's Alice Walton's gift to art," says Clifford, the president and CEO of the Bentonville/Bella Vista Chamber of Commerce. "It's *not* a Wal-Mart project. I think we're going to get a lot of tourism, whether the economy is back online or not. And we have the rooms to handle it."

Some would argue that the surgery on the square is being performed on a dying patient. The renovation has taken more than ten months, during which time the town's niche businesses—already in last-gasp mode since the construction of the Pinnacle Mall and various Wal-Mart Supercenters—had been on life support as roads were repaired, lampposts installed, and existing buildings on and around the square spruced up to look the way they had fifty years ago.

Finally, however, Bentonville Square is exhibiting signs of life. New businesses are slowly beginning to move in, among them the Table Mesa Bistro, a tapas restaurant; and School Squared, an upscale school-supplies store. And as the construction of Crystal Bridges moves forward, more and more retailers are, according to Clifford's spin, beginning to see the possibilities of setting up shop here, less than a mile from what will surely be the area's primo bona fide tourist attraction.

A small yellow-haired man who is wearing glasses, a yellow shirt, and brown tweed jacket, Clifford, on this particular day, seems to have had his entire being color coordinated to match the walls of his office, which happen to be painted a warm tan hue. As a former Wal-Mart hardware buyer who retired in 2001, Clifford, like Mayor Bob McCaslin, a one-time Wal-Mart vendor whose office is two blocks down the street, seems a perfect choice—perhaps the better word is *advocate*—to balance the town's economic opportunities with the needs of the company that has been its motor for more than half a century.

Clifford began working with Wal-Mart in 1984, having previously bought hardware for a chain of stores in Oklahoma City and, before that, Saginaw, Michigan. At the time, he says, there were four hundred employees in the home office, 400 stores, and only twenty buyers in all; today, there are 7,390 stores and Sam's Club locations in fourteen markets employing more than two million associates.

Clifford bought for Wal-Mart and Sam's Club through 1990. Then he worked with the group building Retail Link, a software forecasting system that now connects all the suppliers to the Wal-Mart mainframe.

"It was a pretty small thing when we did it," Clifford explains. "Then our information systems department got it and built it into a big thing." For five years he bought all the hardware imports for the company and throughout his entire seventeen years traveled at least once a week—to suppliers for presentations, to hardware shows, and to Asia or, as he calls it, "the Orient." If that exotic and, some say, politically incorrect term conjures up Charlie Chan, Marlene Dietrich, and opium dens in 1930s movies, the truth is that Ed Clifford went there for something much more concrete and mundane—to buy items such as tools, fans, and kerosene lamps.

Climbing up the company ladder, Clifford did what associates do—he put in long hours, packed like sardines with other buyers into small "pods" in the dingy, gray-walled corporate office.

"We worked 6:00 A.M. to 6:00 P.M. or 7:30 A.M. until 10:00 at night," he says. "Then we worked all day Saturdays and Sunday afternoons. But as we brought in systems that did the work, the hours were cut down and so we worked only half days on Saturdays."

How did his wife and children respond to such a rigorous schedule?

"Well," Clifford says matter-of-factly, "I came here late in life. My kids were all grown. And my wife had a life of her own."

No doubt, that was fortunate, since her husband tracked long hours in the home office and traveled at least once a week. Wal-Mart, a company famed for its tightness with a dollar, allowed its buyers a business-class plane ticket and a hotel room of their own only if they were traveling internationally; for domestic travel, he, and everyone else, including the company's CEO, flew economy class and, like kids at camp, shared rooms with colleagues. Wal-Mart's internal thriftiness was such that by 2001, the year that Clifford retired, while Wal-Mart may have been the largest corporation in the world, boasting $219 billion in revenue, it had increased its number of hardware buyers by only one person.

Unwilling to be specific about his compensation for such enormous responsibility and long work hours, Clifford, however, suggests that in the end the company took good care of him.

"It depends on the year," he says vaguely. "But it wasn't all about salary; that was incidental. It was all about stock options and performance. You have to live on the salary, but it was shares of stock that really enriched management." Senior management who made their "numbers," he explains, were granted options to buy shares each year. "It could be five thousand shares or ten thousand shares. The options were based on sales and profits." If management performed to expected levels, they were rewarded with options, Clifford adds. "There isn't anything at Wal-Mart that isn't measurable."

When asked to describe a day at Wal-Mart, Clifford begs off, saying that no day was like any other. What really satisfied him, he says, was "when you alone, with the other associates, can impact a company and see it go from $4 billion to $219 billion. That was what was great about working for Wal-Mart. You go from one year to the next, and it's bigger and bigger and more complicated. And the systems have to keep up with what you are doing."

Of Christianity and Capitalism

Critics of Wal-Mart have characterized its corporate culture as a manipulative mix of Republican conservatism and paternalism. Nelson Lichtenstein, a professor at the University of California at Santa Barbara, who directs the

Center for the Study of Work, Labor, and Democracy, has frequently written about the company and puts it this way:

> Wal-Mart has proven remarkably successful in propagating a distinctive brand of Christian entrepreneurialism and faux egalitarianism well beyond its Arkansas-Missouri roots. The company prides itself on a corporate culture, but the resonance of that ideology arises not from its uniqueness but from the way that Wal-Mart executives have played a systematic role in translating a Reagan-era conservative populism into a set of ideological tropes that work effectively to legitimize Wal-Mart's hierarchical structure and insulate most employees from other calls upon their loyalty.[1]

One example: the well-publicized Wal-Mart entreaty to employees to support John McCain and not Barack Obama; allegedly the traditionally conservative-leaning corporation was concerned that as president, Obama would put into place the Employee Free Choice Act, paving the way for its store associates to more easily vote to unionize.

Lichtenstein, in discussing "the ideological culture projected by Wal-Mart," explains that one of its components is "that of family, community, and a corporate egalitarianism that unites $9-an-hour sales clerks with the millionaires who work out of the Bentonville corporate headquarters."[2] He cites the myth of Sam Walton, with his homey twang, his beat-up red pickup truck, and his overalls as examples of this, and he points out the company lingo—labeling all employees, from the high school dropout who works at the checkout counter of a local store to Mike Duke, the CEO, as "associates"; dubbing the human resources department as the much more user-friendly People Division—as something meant to democratize this egalitarian fantasy "through an adroit shift in the linguistic landscape."[3]

Yet someone like Ed Clifford sees the Wal-Mart culture in a much more black-and-white, nuts-and-bolts way. When asked to describe this culture, he replied: "[It means] you want to buy everything for the lowest possible price. You want to be able to go to market with the customers with the lowest possible retail. And we were totally neutral as far as suppliers were concerned. We didn't take any gifts from them, not even a cup of coffee."

Then there is the matter of the local Christian culture, which so completely defines the Bible Belt and Northwest Arkansas—and, some say, Wal-Mart itself. "Even more important than this faux classlessness," writes

Lichtenstein, "is the Wal-Mart culture of country, faith, and entrepreneurial achievement."[4]

If Sam Walton was inspired to help better his employees' lives by giving them shares of stock and creating what at first was a family of happy associates, if, as a young man, he attended Bentonville's local Presbyterian church and even taught Sunday school, he never relied on Christian dogma; rather, he displayed the core Christian values of thrift and hard work.

"Is Wal-Mart a Christian company? No," Don Soderquist, the former chief operating officer of Wal-Mart and a man of emphatic faith, said at a 2005 prayer breakfast. Then, subtly backtracking, he added, "But the basis of our decisions was the values of the Scriptures."[5]

Indeed, Wal-Mart is restrictive and downright prudish about what it will and will not sell. Sexually explicit magazines such as *Maxim*, *Cosmopolitan*, *Rolling Stone*, and *Vibe* have all been pulled off the shelves, as have books and CDs with provocative cover photos and questionable lyrics. In 2004 the company refused to carry the late comedian George Carlin's book *When Will Jesus Bring the Pork Chops?* because the cover spoofed the Last Supper. In 1996 it would not stock Sheryl Crow's second album because one song, "Love Is a Good Thing," describes children who bought bullets at Wal-Mart.

And most notoriously and seriously, the corporation has refused to carry the Plan B morning-after birth control pills unless ordered to do so by state law. Surely, that is a religious decision above all else.

On the other hand, Wal-Mart sells an excess of one billion dollars' worth of Christian books, music, action figures, and other merchandise each year.[6]

It could be said that the Christian culture is reflected even in the famed Saturday morning meetings, which always begin bright and early—at 7:00 A.M.—and last until 9:00 or 10:00. Until 2008 the company required all associates to attend at least two a month; recently, that number has been pared down to one per month, ostensibly to give family members more downtime with one another, and the venue was changed from the Wal-Mart headquarters on Walton Boulevard to a larger auditorium at Bentonville High School, which has twelve hundred seats and can more comfortably accommodate the numbers who must attend.

The meeting I attend on the week before Christmas is held in the smaller, cozier auditorium of the home office. Paying homage to the season, an unspectacular and even dowdy Christmas tree with silver ornaments sits almost forlornly on the stage. The place is jam-packed with men and women of all ages, most wearing jeans or sweatpants. (Why are they not out doing last-minute shopping for their kids this morning?) The room itself, despite a series of flags representing the nations that host Wal-Mart stores, gives off a tatty, if functional, aura. The deep blue walls are decorated almost like a school gymnasium's, but rather than Go, TIGERS! pennants, black-and-white photos of Mr. Sam and banners emblazoned with excerpts from his famed Ten Rules adorn the place. One counsels: SWIM UPSTREAM. GO THE OTHER WAY. IGNORE THE CONVENTIONAL WISDOM.

A second advises: APPRECIATE EVERYTHING YOUR ASSOCIATES DO FOR THE BUSINESS.

And a third: MAKING PEOPLE WANT TO COME BACK . . . THAT'S WHERE THE PROFITS COME FROM. . . . PEOPLE COMING BACK OVER AND OVER AGAIN.

As for the proceedings themselves, they combine economic news, self-congratulatory corporate back-patting, and folksy shout-outs. On this particular morning, the company's bespectacled CEO at the time, Lee Scott, in a long-sleeved white polo shirt and blue jeans, stands on the stage in front of a giant video screen and discusses the percentages sold the previous week and expectations for the rest of the holiday season. Then he leads the group in singing "Happy Birthday" to the year-old daughter of a lanky associate, who accepts the group's good wishes while the birthday tot teeters on his shoulders. Next we applaud another associate celebrating his twentieth year with the company and watch a clip of him dancing at last year's Christmas party. Finally, we cheer an Iraqi-born manager who is being commended for his twenty-fifth year of service; along with his wife and daughter, he comes forward and with effusive praise tells how she survived cancer, thanks in part to Wal-Mart's medical coverage and in part to emotional support from other associates.

When the testimonials are complete, the congregation—for it *is* a congregation—stands as its ersatz minister, CEO Scott, closes the meeting just as it has begun, with the company hymn, better known as the Wal-Mart Cheer.

"Give me a W," he shouts, and his flock responds, "*W.*"

"Give me an A."

"*A!*"

When he arrives at the hyphen, which was deleted from the new logo in 2008, Scott commands, "Give me a squiggly!" and the brethren wag their fannies, throw up their hands, and yelp in unison, "*Squig-gly!*"

Finally Scott intones, "What have you got?" and the fellowship cheers: "Wal-Mart."

Very summer camp. Very folksy. And very much like a revival meeting. But apparently such a down-home, corny benediction works, communicating to the associates that sense of family, religiosity, "faux egalitarianism," and community that Wal-Mart diehards insist is at the heart of the company.

Still, Ed Clifford, who has been through his share of Saturday morning meetings, firmly dismisses the idea of Wal-Mart as a Christian culture. "I don't think the way Wal-Mart runs its business has anything to do with being white or Baptist," he insists. "They're in sixteen countries. They have associates of every religion and color. And companies all over the world are imitating them as much as possible, no matter what their culture. So why would someone think that this is a white Baptist culture?"

Leaving the Mothership

I ask Clifford why he finally decided to leave the company, and he shrugs. "It was time," he says cryptically. "You wake up one morning, and you just know."

In retirement Clifford remained true to his energetic nature. Six days after he left Wal-Mart, the chamber of commerce offered him its top job, and he jumped at it. "This was a good fit for me," he explains, swiveling in his chair and looking out onto the square. "I also owned a business for a while—a car wash. But I wasn't ready to play golf every day."

From the local statistics that Clifford spouts, he has hardly had time to straighten his tie, let alone visit the local green. As Bentonville has grown, so has the Chamber's membership—from four hundred to fifteen hundred.

"When I first got there, we had a staff of three and a $200,000 budget, and now we have a staff of eight and a million-dollar budget," Clifford tells me. "Not only has the area grown—it has *outgrown* itself. We've built too many houses, commercial spaces, and banks. Now we have to catch up."

Although the recession and subprime mortgage crisis has hit Bentonville just as it has the rest of the nation, Clifford, with deft spin, shrugs it off. "The market's downturn is a signal that Wal-Mart sales are going to pick up," he says. "And they have. When times get really tough, Wal-Mart does better than anybody else. People don't go to Neiman Marcus—they go to Wal-Mart to buy basics. Wal-Mart just bought a significant building in town to move its Sam's Club headquarters into. They're going to stay here, and because of the economy they will probably increase their employment by 3, 4, or 5 percent over the next year or so, which is good for us."

Earlier, Clifford's associate, Rich Davis, the Chamber's vice president of development, had corroborated his boss's point of view, explaining that the town's vacancy rate for commercial real estate in September 2008 had been a whopping 40 percent.

"But Wal-Mart acquired one building with five hundred thousand square feet and that vacancy rate immediately plummeted to 17 percent," Davis said. "They bought that building because of their need to grow."

Clifford figures that this uptick in employment will bring in more associates and suppliers as well. "There are already about 1,250 suppliers here," he says of the employees from such big companies as Schlitz, Sara Lee, IBM, Procter & Gamble, and Ghirardelli Chocolates, who have established offices in Northwest Arkansas and moved hordes of vendors and their families into town to do Wal-Mart's bidding.

The biggest task for Bentonville now, he says, is to create and enhance the infrastructure that will allow Wal-Mart to remain in the area, although it is difficult to imagine the corporate colossus picking up its vast tent and abandoning its roots. Still, Clifford draws a picture of what creating a comfy climate for Wal-Mart means: making sure the water supply and waste water plants are sufficient, the schools remain top-notch—they are currently the best in the state, by far—and the roads and highways are ample enough to help transport associates to work every day without traffic snarls.

"Otherwise people won't move here," says Clifford. "We're all about doing the right things to keep our twenty-nine thousand Wal-Mart associates in Northwest Arkansas." Of those, about fourteen thousand work at the home office on Walton Boulevard.

To further amplify its environment, Wal-Mart has the cash to buy and sell as it likes—and does just that. In 2007 the corporation purchased thirty acres of rundown fairgrounds, complete with decrepit and moldy buildings, where the Benton County Fair had been held every year, which happens to be only a few blocks from the home office. In return, Wal-Mart relocated the fair association to nearly sixty acres in nearby Vaughn, enabling the fair to construct new buildings and add twenty acres of parking to accommodate the thirty-five thousand visitors who attend each year. Similarly, when Wal-Mart decided that it needed the Melvin Ford Park for parking, the corporation purchased fifty acres for the town down the street and paid out four million dollars to transform it into Memorial Park, a newer and better public space featuring two swimming pools; a skate park; four tennis courts; baseball, softball, and soccer fields; and a sand volleyball court.

So here, of course, exists another example that seemingly contradicts the image of the company that America loves to hate—the Big Bad Daddy who has been accused of taking advantage of its poorest associates, as well as underpaying and underpromoting its female employees; the callous monolith, so inattentive to the needs of its stores that three shoppers at various Wal-Mart garden centers have been bitten by pygmy rattlers in the past three years; and the money-hungry corporation, too stingy to put enough crowd control at the front door of a mall during holiday sales.[7] Yet does the community ever disagree with Big Santa Daddy? Has it ever risen to thwart something he might want to do?

"I haven't seen that," Clifford says matter-of-factly. "Remember, a lot of people made a lot of money here from Wal-Mart. They don't want to stand up in front of the truck."

Of Vendors and Vendorville

The world of Wal-Mart's small business vendors differs strikingly from that of its homegrown buyers. Charlie Blaustein, a New York sunglass vendor in his early fifties, worked with the corporation for a little more than ten years and tells a story of partnership and exploitation.[8] He says that he began coming to Bentonville in 1988, when the town was still small and rural, and to get there from New York, buyers had to take two flights, then drive about forty minutes from Fayetteville or fly to Dallas and drive for five hours to Northwest Arkansas. "But we went down there twice a year to try to sell Wal-Mart our product, and they either didn't give us an appointment or gave us a fifteen-minute brush-off," he says.

Finally, in 1994, two years after Sam Walton's death, the Blaustein Sunglass Company began doing business with Wal-Mart. "And at the time," Blaustein says, "all they cared about was Sam's Ten Values or Rules and their relationship with the vendors. And as a vendor, you wanted to do what was best for Wal-Mart, and Wal-Mart wanted to do what was best for the consumer. Every buyer had to have these Ten Values in his office, and copies hung in every one of the vendor conference rooms. They drilled this into your head."

Blaustein, his brown hair close cropped and salt-and-peppery, says that the goal of any salesperson coming of age in the late 1980s or early 1990s was to sell to Wal-Mart. "At the time there were all these regional mass merchants like Bradley's, Caldor's, and Ames, and they were considered large accounts because they were one-hundred- to two-hundred-store chains," he explains. "Then suddenly there was Wal-Mart, with its eighteen hundred stores—and selling to the company was like selling to fifteen Bradley's chains."

Doing whatever it took to work with Wal-Mart meant attending at least six Saturday morning meetings a year. It meant, for Blaustein and other New York Jews in the apparel and accessories trade, working during the High Holy Days, because, he says, "there was little sensitivity about the Jewish religion. Wal-Mart didn't care whether you were religious or not. They would schedule appointments on Rosh Hashanah, and even if they were coming to New York, they wanted you to be there."

Isn't the company more diversity-sensitive today, however? Blaustein acknowledges that possibility. Still, as recently as Rosh Hashanah 2008, Wal-Mart representatives wanted to meet with his wife, an apparel buyer, in New York City; although she said she was unable to attend the meeting because of the High Holy Days, the company refused to change the date. "And so," he says, "she sent her assistant, who is Asian." (On the other hand, Sheldon Hirsch made the point that the Bentonville home office *was* willing to shift the date when he protested a High Holy Days meeting in 2008.)

Blaustein's own story is extraordinary. In 1995 his company started out furnishing sunglasses to fifty Wal-Mart stores on a test basis. Over the years he built an enormous business with the company and eventually vendor-managed its eyewear and sunglasses program, being responsible for replenishment and even choosing what Wal-Mart selected from other vendors. "On average, we grew between 15 and 20 percent a year," he says. "Our Wal-Mart business went from $200,000 in revenues in 1995 to $55 million at our high point in 2003—approximately a third of my business. Everybody was thrilled."

Wal-Mart seemed so thrilled that, according to Blaustein, they pushed him to build a $15 million, three-hundred-thousand-square-foot state-of-the-art distribution center for them. "Still, they said, 'We want you to deliver to every one of our stores twenty-four hours from the time we get the order.' So their operations people helped us plan it." But Wal-Mart did not contribute a penny to the facility.

Subtly, however, Blaustein's business relationship with the company began to change. Around 2002, Wal-Mart was beginning to build its own direct imports business, and the top brass told Blaustein that on his next trip overseas, company representatives would come along. "Their disguise was that they wanted to make sure there were no child-labor abuses and that the factories were stand-up factories," he remembers. In reality, a team of Wal-Mart people living in Hong Kong, China, and Taiwan "would come to our factory towns, and we would introduce them to the owners who we had used to manufacture all our products." Before long, the Wal-Mart representatives were establishing direct relationships with the factory owners and excluding Blaustein from the meetings, although he says he was forced to educate the company representatives on the specifics of his business. It was only a matter of time before he, his eyewear, and his distribution center would become completely irrelevant.

By the time that Lee Scott had become the corporation's CEO, he began the push to increase its percentage of direct imports, Blaustein says: "So by now we were competing with Wal-Mart. And if we sold sunglasses for $2 a pair, they suddenly said, 'Why should we buy these from you when we can buy them from the factory for $1.20? You guys have to be competitive.'"

Blaustein tried to explain that a price so pared down—a nickel more than what he was paying the factory—left no margin for returns or fixtures. But his Wal-Mart counterparts did not care. "They told me, 'We have to do what's in the best interest of the Wal-Mart customer.' And suddenly, where we represented six hundred styles in 2002, the next year our orders were cut by 75 percent. Our business went from $50 million to roughly $20 million. The next year it spiraled down to $7 million. And they put us into Chapter 11."

Blaustein subsequently gave up his business. Today he works as a consultant to other companies and says, "The whole thing is aggravating."

As trying as it was, Blaustein's experience typifies that of other vendors—both the independents and those with major companies—who have had to relocate to Bentonville over the past decade. When Wal-Mart said, "Jump!" he jumped. When Wal-Mart told him to show up at department meetings and Saturday meetings, to work during his holidays, to do the company cheer at the beginning and end of every meeting, and to wiggle his tush each and every time, he obeyed.

"Wal-Mart was a cult," he says. "But if you wanted to do business with the company, you tried to do what they asked."

During Sam Walton's reign, Blaustein points out, the kind of mistreatment that he endured would have been far less likely to happen. "Sam Walton built that business on the vendors he had developed as partners," he says. "*Everything* was a vendor partnership."

When David Glass took over after Walton died in 1992, Blaustein explains, "Glass drove the company forward and emulated Sam. It was truly an open-door policy. Whatever issues you had, a guy like David Glass would listen; he cared about making sure that Wal-Mart was doing right by their consumers and respecting the vendor partnership as well."

Under Lee Scott's guidance, the Wal-Mart dynamic changed. "He began driving the company's message. But to be fair, the retail climate has also changed, and he has diversified worldwide. He was under enormous pressure," explains Blaustein.

Yet as the historian Nelson Lichtenstein has observed, "The power of Wal-Mart is such, it's reversed a hundred-year history in which the manufacturer was powerful and the retailer was sort of the vassal. . . . It turned that around entirely."[9]

Blaustein can still appreciate the positives of his business relationship with the corporation. "When things are going well, it's great to do business with Wal-Mart," he says. "But if they threaten or pressure you, you find yourself in a tailspin."

....

Mel Cantor, a New York apparel buyer who sold to Wal-Mart for twenty-five years, suffered an end similar to Blaustein's but remains more loyal and philosophical about the company.[10]

Cantor recalls the morning, early in his relationship with Wal-Mart, when Walton himself phoned him. "I was on my kitchen floor playing with my two-year-old son. And Mr. Sam got on the phone and says, 'Your items are bestsellers, and how quickly can you get reorders to us?' And he extolled his philosophy of how vendors or suppliers became his partners and how he relied on our expertise to build his firm. And after that I did a very nice business with him for twenty-five years, although I never actually met him."

What impressed Cantor was Walton's respect for his vendors. "Many years ago I had a friend in the apparel business who Mr. Sam wanted to honor at an awards dinner in Bentonville," he recalls. "My friend is a Holocaust survivor and an observant Jew, and he declined, saying, 'I'd like to attend, but I keep kosher.' And Mr. Sam told him, 'Please don't worry about that.'" As it turned out, Walton had a full kosher meal flown into Bentonville from Little Rock so that this Orthodox buyer could participate in the dinner.

As a retailer during the 1980s, Cantor sold to K-Mart as well as Wal-Mart until K-Mart insisted he choose between the two companies. "I told them I'd get back to them, but I never spoke to them again," he says. "Mind you, Wal-Mart never gave me such an ultimatum."

When Wal-Mart opened up its own product development department and began producing exactly the kinds of goods that Cantor himself had been making, he says, "I closed my doors. But I do not consider that Wal-Mart bankrupted me. I made a wonderful living from the company. And Mr. Sam made me a better businessman by teaching me how to build a better mousetrap, so to speak, by driving down costs while maintaining quality and integrity in the product."

Cantor believes that Wal-Mart gets an unfair rap from critics who claim that by bringing the manufacture of goods offshore, it hastened the closing of American sewing factories.

"The facts are different," he insists. "The American workforce did not want to sew anymore. I owned a factory in the South. I had 350 sewing machines, and the area had 30 percent unemployment. But I could only find fifty sewers. No one wanted to sew anymore. So I set up factories in Jamaica, Haiti, and other Central American countries. At one time I had one thousand workers sewing in four different factories."

Cantor agrees with Blaustein that Wal-Mart's partnership with its suppliers began to change after Walton's death. But that, he says, is to be expected. "When the founding titular head of the business dies, other people come in who don't share his philosophy," he says. "And it soon starts to erode."

But he misses working with the company. "Sam and his crew were very honest," he says. "Whenever they gave you business, their word was their bond."

Today Cantor works as a real estate broker in Manhattan but bears Wal-Mart no bitterness. In fact, he says, "If they called me up tomorrow and said they wanted to work with me again, I'd immediately put my money on the table."

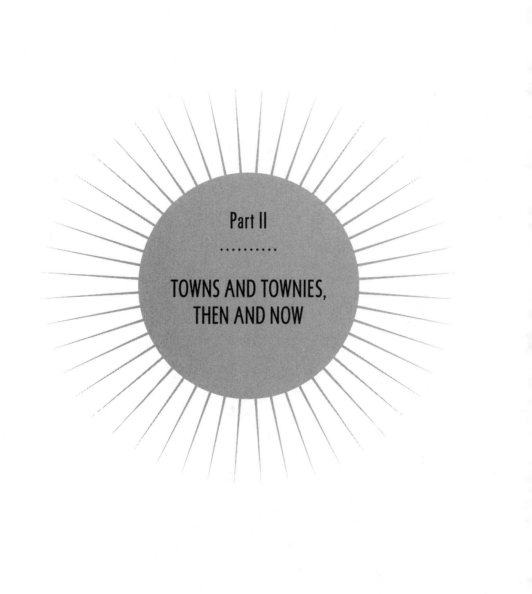

Part II

. . . .

TOWNS AND TOWNIES, THEN AND NOW

7

Bentonville's Ex-Mayor, the Boom Town, and the Daughters of the Dust Bowl

....

"This is my street," says Terry Black Coberly, Bentonville's hometown girl and ex-mayor, as we drive down Twenty-eighth Street, a broad suburban road dotted with small homes, which under her twelve-year administration was paved and widened to accommodate the burgeoning traffic and which, like many others built during her term, stretches clear to Rogers. "Actually, these are *all* my streets," she adds as she laughs with a touch of self-effacement.

On a dark and scowling January afternoon, Coberly is showing me around her Bentonville in her red Volkswagen convertible. Snub nosed and with the blond good looks of an ex–prom queen, she manages to defy the weather and look chic and cheery in a black-and-white checkered coat punctuated by a bright red wool scarf, which she has swathed around her neck.

As we pass the massive fire station that is being built, she points it out with pride. "I was instrumental in its planning," she says. "But the new mayor didn't invite me to the groundbreaking." More than a year after her defeat by former city councilman Bob McCaslin, the loss still smarts.

Even so, Coberly takes comfort in her mayoral accomplishments. "We did so much during my administration," she says. "And nobody can take that away from me."

Indeed, she counts among her achievements a new water line and water contract for Bentonville; an independent electric contract "written in stone," she says; the purchase of 130 acres of park property; and the most extensive street construction in the town's history in order to improve the infrastructure and relieve a brand-new problem—rush-hour traffic.

"I'm very proud of the roadwork," she says. "The growth happened so fast. When I was in office, I saw it all on paper, yet even I was shocked when I saw it on the ground. Bentonville has changed so quickly."

The first female mayor of Bentonville, Coberly, a former and current schoolteacher, guided the town during its most significant growth spurt, from 1994 to 2006, the same period when Wal-Mart staked out its identity as a corporate colossus. In 1995 the company did $93.6 billion in sales and began a major push at recruiting middle- and upper-management employees from cities such as New York, Chicago, and Dallas and from such countries as Pakistan, India, Brazil, and Indonesia. By 2005, Wal-Mart ended the year with $312.4 billion in sales in its ever-swelling worldwide market.

Just as Wal-Mart exploded, so did Bentonville's population. In 1990, the town had grown to 11,257 inhabitants; by 1995, Coberly's first year as mayor, there were 15,363. Ten years later, the population had nearly doubled, to more than 27,000. Make no mistake, says Coberly, "We *are* Wal-Mart. And we have enjoyed the benefits of its growth."

Growing Up in the Jailhouse

And nobody can understand that growth better than a native of the area. When Terry Coberly looks back on her Bentonville childhood, she remembers it as ideal—riding her bike to elementary school little more than a block away from her family's Craftsman home on Central Avenue; going to classes with Sam Walton's son Jim and to Brownie day camp on the Walton property because Sam's wife, Helen, was the troop leader. She also played kick-the-can and sold lemonade with her sister on the square, right across the street from Walton's 5 & 10. A self-proclaimed tomboy, Coberly explains, "What was wonderful was that there was not much difference between the haves and the have-nots. It was a small town—Mayberry, but in a good way." (Mayberry, of course, refers to the fictional small southern town that was the setting for CBS's *The Andy Griffith Show* in 1960 and its 1968 spin-off, *Mayberry R.F.D.*)

Coberly, in fact, comes by her mayoral mantle with some legitimacy. Born in 1948, she is the daughter of Hugh "Tater" Black, one of the town's towering characters, who served six terms—that is, twelve years—as Benton County sheriff.

"I never heard anybody say anything bad about him. He was a likable guy with a really good sense of humor," says former Benton County sheriff Andy Lee, who served seven terms from 1988 to 2002. "In fact, here's a humorous story about Tater. He was a staunch Democrat, and I fell in line more with Republican politics. When I won my last term, he came in one day and sat down, and I said, 'Tater, are you having a bad day or what?' And he stared and stared and finally said, 'You know, I'm mad at you, Andy. I don't mind that you won another term and served longer than I did and beat my record. What I *do* mind is that you were a damned old Republican.'"

Tater Black was sufficiently beloved and had enough influence for Bentonville to name a street after him—the Hugh Tater Black Memorial Road. After a brief career playing on the Merchants, a local baseball team, he traded his bat for a billy club, starting at the local level—as a beat cop. Every evening, when he walked through town, it was part of his job to routinely check the doors of various storefronts to make sure they were locked, then to visit the local hatchery to turn the eggs. When he became Benton County sheriff, the family had to live in the downstairs quarters of the town jail, a two-story red brick building half a block north of Bentonville Square.

"The sheriff's wife was supposed to cook for the prisoners, but my momma, who worked as a secretary at the high school, put her foot down and said no, she would not do that," Coberly remembers. "So we hired a woman to cook for them and for us as well. Mama Becky, we called her. And we all ate the same food."

Life on the ground floor of the jailhouse may have been exotic, but it did not cramp Coberly's childhood one whit. "I'd play badminton and croquet in the backyard with my little sister, Toni, and the prisoners would always cheer for us," she says. "Since I was the oldest, I made up the rules and bossed her around."

One can only imagine the local drunks and ne'er-do-wells who might be confined in the town's jail, peering out the barred windows, entertained, at the very least, by the lithe seventh grader and her little sister in pedal pushers or jeans, scrambling around their tiny backyard, rackets in hand, short blond hair flying.

For Coberly, the high point of life in the town jail took place one day when a pair of jailbirds decided to use a crowbar to bend the bars on their second-floor window and escape. "My father had been told about it in advance, and so my sister and I sat at our windows, watching the men shinny down a sheet, just like in the movies. Then they were captured, of course," she says. "You know, it never occurred to us that we were any different from anyone else. It was such a happy-go-lucky, innocent time. Bentonville was an excellent place to grow up."

Rejecting That Old-Time Religion

Coberly drives me through the streets of Bentonville. As was the case in Springdale and Rogers, I am struck by the sheer number of churches on every corner, many clustered together in twos and threes, some no bigger than Cape Cod bungalows and with one-off names such as the Cowboy Church of Northwest Arkansas or Radiant Life Church. The *Morning News* lists no fewer than 494 houses of worship, excluding mosques and Hindu temples, in its Sunday church directory for all Northwest Arkansas—as many churches on each street as, it seems, there are nail salons in Manhattan.

Speaking of her own religious convictions, Coberly explains that while she was born a Baptist, as she grew up, she was shocked to learn that her church frowned on dancing. This may be why, as an adult, she converted to Methodism. Even so, she is wary of the local obsession with faith. "What they have here is religion, religion, religion, and religion," Coberly sighs with refreshing irreverence. "We are Bible Belt. And sometimes I think we all have been drugged. I just don't get the religious fervor."

In fact, the current mayor, McCaslin, speaking to me from behind his spotless desk a few weeks after taking office, underscored the power of his own religious conviction. "I am a man of faith. It's not about me, it's about me allowing God to work through me," he said. "I'm a Christian. From the time I wake up until the time I go to bed, I ask for wisdom like Solomon. I think you can have the greatest impact on mankind if you can ask for God's wisdom in every decision you make, be it large or small."

. . . .

As Coberly guides her car down Central Avenue, which crosses Bentonville Square, we pass an elegant mansion just east of the square, at number 606. It is a two-story white clapboard house with tall pillars, and it is set well back from the street on five acres of property surrounded by a wrought-iron-and-brick gate. Coberly tells me that the home, unlike any other in town, was built by A. B. Greenwood, her great-great-great grandfather, who had been a lawyer and congressman. At one point James "Bud" Walton, Sam's profligate brother, lived there—he was something of an anomaly in the Walton family, which, at least according to local mythology, appreciated humility and simple living. Today, a local builder occupies this grand estate.

All the other homes lining Central Avenue today are considerably more modest, although many have charm and are of historic interest. A few are refurbished Victorians; others are stone-and-wood Craftsman bungalows, like the one in which the Black family lived prior to the jailhouse, and like the home across the street in which Coberly and her second husband, Jody, live today. That house, built in 1870, was, between the years 1937 and 1940, home to the well-known aviatrix Louise Thaden, a local heroine. In 1936, Thaden and her copilot, Blanche Noyes, were the first female team to win the Bendix Transcontinental Air Race.

As we pass the square itself, Coberly points to a spot on the south side. "Crow's Drugstore used to be right there," she says. "After school, we'd all go to Crow's for cherry Cokes."

Further down the street is the Old High School, an imposing brick-and-stone building with five arches marking the entrance. In 1928 it housed the town's elementary and high school; by the early 1960s, when Coberly was a student, it held seventh through twelfth grades. Today it is one of Bentonville's nine elementary schools. In addition, there are three middle schools, two junior highs, and one high school, which holds more than three thousand students in two sprawling brick buildings.

We head past what Coberly used to call "the four-way stop," which is now the red-light turn for Walton Boulevard. "In the fifties, when I was a kid, we didn't lock our doors," she says. "We were outside all the time. These days we hardly let our grandkids outside at all."

By the time she got to high school, there were dances every Friday night at the Presbyterian church down the road—the same church the Waltons attended. Says Coberly, "We did the Push, where you twist under and around; the Twist, and the Mashed Potatoes. And everybody danced."

Turning right again, we zip up Highway 71 toward Bella Vista, with its lakes and mountainous terrain. In the years before air conditioning, Bella Vista emerged as the Catskill Mountains of the Ozarks, with summer resorts such as the Sunset Hotel and woodsy cabins whose screened porches helped families escape the stifling August heat.

Pretty Lake Bella Vista, punctuated by a storybook footbridge, comes up, again on our right. "We had our senior prom here," Coberly says. Now, on an acre-and-a-half site just beside the lake, the snazzy if ostentatious Veterans' Wall of Honor pays tribute to thirty-five hundred veterans whose names are carved in granite, and a series of flags and plaques surrounding it recount U.S. history. The town swimming pool, with three progressively higher diving boards, including one called "The Tower," used to be here, she says. The old pool house is now, appropriately, a local VFW and American Legion post. "Nearby," she recalls, "there used to be the Hill and Dale Restaurant, with a roller skating rink on the second floor." That is gone, too.

In some ways Coberly lived the kind of girlhood that most teens dream of, and she just may be the only mayor in the United States whose resume includes having been a high school cheerleader and a member of Bentonville High's Homecoming Court.

Terry Black, as she was then known, loved her Bentonville life so much that when her dad was appointed deputy U.S. marshal, requiring the family to move to Fort Smith, sixty-nine miles away, she was beside herself with disappointment. A junior in high school, she spent six months in Fort Smith, then struck a deal with her family, who allowed her to move back to Bentonville to finish school. "First I stayed with my uncle, and then with Mama Becky, who had cooked for us at the jail. I remember how she sure could stretch a dollar. Sam [Walton] should have hired her."

From Cheerleader to Mayor

Coberly, who began her career teaching special education to migrant workers' children, has often contended that teaching is the best training for public office. "Each day," she has said, "you never know what you will be dealing with, and you deal with people from all walks of life."

(above) Walton's first variety store, on Bentonville Square, is now a museum.
Photo by Marjorie Rosen.

(left) Baseball team, Bentonville, Arkansas, around 1912. The team was part of a regional African American league that covered the area from Fort Smith, Arkansas, to Joplin, Missouri. Back, from left: Thad Wayne, Marion "Sonny" Finney, and Lloyd Trout. Front, from left: Yates Claypool, Virge Black, and John Barker.
Courtesy Shiloh Museum of Ozark History/Elizabeth Robertson Collection (S-95-7-42).

The Confederate soldier on Bentonville Square, 1913, looking south.
Courtesy Johnny Haney.

Bentonville Square in the mid-1920s.
Courtesy Johnny Haney.

Strawberry market on Emma Avenue, Springdale, Arkansas, about 1935.
Mr. Davis, photographer. Courtesy Shiloh Museum of Ozark History/Famous Hardware Co. Collection (S-82-193-19).

Leghorn chickens in yard, Northwest Arkansas, 1930s.
Courtesy Shiloh Museum of Ozark History/Roy Watson Collection (S-83-250-13B).

Workers at Keeshan Poultry in Rogers, circa 1940s.
Courtesy the Rogers Historical Museum.

Sam and Helen Walton Appreciation Day, Bentonville, Arkansas, October 8, 1983.
Brenda Blagg, photographer, Springdale News. *Courtesy Shiloh Museum of Ozark History/Springdale News Collection (SN 10-8-1983).*

Bentonville Square and the Confederate soldier, nowadays called "'Feddy."
Photo by Larry Ash.

The synagogue Etz Chaim, a former Hispanic Assemblies of God church.
Photo by Marjorie Rosen.

The Church at Pinnacle
Hills, with its 165-foot-
high crosses and seating
for twenty-four hundred
people.

Photo at right by Larry Ash.
Photo below by Marjorie Rosen.

(left) Chanukah on Bentonville Square.
Photo by Marjorie Rosen.

(below) Fadil Bayyari in front of his construction project, Temple Shalom.
Photo by Marjorie Rosen.

Papa Rap and Ana Hart at Ferncliff Diversity Camp.

Photo by Marjorie Rosen.

Diversity mural at Springdale High School.
Photo by Marjorie Rosen.

(above) Coleman and Shirley "Peaches" Peterson.
Courtesy Coleman and Shirley Peterson.

(right) Carl Stewart, at home with his mother, Gloria, in November 2008.
Photo by Larry Ash.

Fadil Bayyari with his family at Christmas, 2008.
Photo by Kimberlea Bass.

Chabad rabbi Mendel "Mendy" Greisman at home.
Photo by Larry Ash.

Murthy and Padmaja Kolluru and their daughters, Varsha (left) and Soumya.
Photo by Marjorie Rosen.

Ajaydev Nallur and (from left) his daughters Saranya and Varenya and wife Subha in front of the photo of "the Hugging Mother."
Photo by Marjorie Rosen.

The Springdale truckers' coffee klatch. From left: Bobby Eldridge, Lenny Brobst, Floyd Collins, Homer Smith, Roy Anderson, and Carroll Crisler.
Photo by Marjorie Rosen.

Saimon Milne, at home with his daughter, Selena.
Photo by Marjorie Rosen.

Homer Smith shows off his Elvis decanters.
Photo by Larry Ash.

The Bonilla family in their kitchen on a summer Sunday. From left, Eric, Sal, Ruth, Daisy, and Krist.

Photo by Marjorie Rosen.

Former Tyson chicken plant worker Ahidee Noriega with her son Noel.

Photo by Marjorie Rosen.

The Vargas Family at home. Clockwise, from left: Cesar, Frank, Andrew Deeter, Nataly, and Esther.

Photo by Larry Ash.

Tater Black's daughter decided to enter her first mayoral race in 1994. A high school teacher, she had been a part-time city clerk and poll worker before throwing her proverbial hat into the ring. She duked it out with five other candidates but in the end was victorious.

Some say that Coberly won by promising to do battle with the Arkansas Department of Pollution Control and Ecology, which had cited severe sewage treatment problems in the town, namely that sewage was leaking into storm drains; as a result, the department had threatened to place the town under a construction moratorium. Once she was sworn in, Coberly videotaped sewers throughout the community, documenting how she had had the leaks repaired. In the end, she was victorious and the moratorium was never declared.

Coberly's first term coincided with the first wave of explosive growth in town, and she handled it with striking efficiency. Then she won reelection to a second term, unopposed, and beat out two opponents for her third term.

But in 2006, campaigning with the slogan "Serving the Citizens of Bentonville with Vision, Leadership, Pride," Coberly lost. Suggesting that the mayor had been vanquished simply because she had been in office for so long, one local woman said with a shrug, "People thought it was time for a change."

Another explained cryptically, "Certain people control certain things in this town, and they put people in power who they think can be helpful to them."

"They elected someone who sells cheese," Coberly says bitterly, referring to the fact that Bob McCaslin, the current mayor, is a one-time Wal-Mart vendor for Kraft Foods; as such, she suggests, he has a close relationship with the Walton family.

Does this mean that McCaslin is in their pocket and will favor their whims and wants? On the other hand, who in power in this town would not? Some say that Coberly went down simply because it was time for a change; others maintain that she was on the wrong side of a controversial bond issue that would help pay for massive improvements in the infrastructure. The town had been using a pay-as-you-go model, which brought in between $5.5 million and $6 million annually for that purpose—a mere pittance as Bentonville grew larger and needed more work.

"There are many reasons why people voted for McCaslin," says Rich Davis of the chamber of commerce. "Bob went door-to-door and asked residents what they thought, what they needed and expected, and he just

listened. He wanted to carry out his constituents' mandate regarding quality of life and place."

Yet the broader truth is that Bentonville is a Republican town, and the
lengthy reign of Coberly, a Democrat's daughter and a Democrat herself,
was an anomaly.

"Terry is a hometown person, and her heart and soul were and still are
in Bentonville," adds Davis. "But that election really became a matter of
keeping abreast of how the environment has changed, and how the *political* environment has also changed."

Today Coberly has returned to teaching, first as a substitute, and then
as a full-timer teaching special education at Bentonville High. In 2008 her
husband, Jody, who works in the county assessor's office, ran for a seat on
the city council—and lost.

The Long Shadow of Wal-Mart

If the ex-mayor speaks frankly about her religious beliefs and her disappointment that the Walton boys, her childhood friends, did not support
her candidacy this time round, she is a good deal more careful discussing
Sam Walton, dead since 1992 but still the pillar of the Bentonville community and a force whose muscular shadow hovers over the entire town.

Asked what kind of man Walton was, Coberly quickly replies, "Driven.
He gets credit for being so caring, but he had people do his dirty work—
you know what I mean? Generally, the Walton family has a fine reputation.
But even in his book, Sam said that when the company was growing, he
didn't always take good care of his employees. My first husband worked
in one of the Wal-Mart stores back in the 1970s. He worked ninety-two
hours a week and grossed $140. It wasn't even minimum wage. He finally
quit, but it was before we could benefit from it." Coberly remembers with
some bitterness when Wal-Mart's stock went public in 1970, the same year
that her son, Lance, was born. "You had to be an employee to buy it [for
an inside price]," she says with a wry laugh, "but by the time the buying
opportunity trickled down to assistant managers, it was all sold out. And
so my husband and I didn't get any."

Yes, but so many of the original managers made small fortunes from
their Wal-Mart stock. "They stayed with it longer," she says. "The stock
didn't do well for a real long time."

But in the end, it was not only the managers who did well. Coberly's aunt, Maxine, a saleswoman at the Walton 5 & 10 on the square, "earned slave wages, but she had profit sharing and eventually became a millionaire," says Coberly. "So many of these associates didn't expect much and got a lot."

....

Coberly has lived in Bentonville long enough to remember when making a living in the area was difficult. "When I was growing up here, before the boom," she says, "you had to leave to succeed. But I'm thankful that people can now stay in Bentonville and make a good living in many different fields."

Refusing to take credit for the area's enormous growth, Coberly believes it can be attributed to the vendor community living here—"which," she says, "is definitely a result of Wal-Mart's 'suggestion' [read: insistence] that vendors have a presence in town."

She reiterates: "We *are* Wal-Mart. There is no getting around it. And there's no doubt as to whether it's a good thing or a bad thing—it's a good thing."

The bottom line is that Wal-Mart means jobs. Interestingly, since its expansion into what is essentially a global Godzilla, Northwest Arkansas, even with its huge population of undocumented immigrants, is now so wealthy that it provides one-third of the income for the entire state.

A Town Is Born

What is today known as Bentonville began life not as an idyllic small town but as a rugged frontier outpost populated largely by Osage Indians. It had been part of territory that the United States acquired with the Louisiana Purchase in 1803, and its first white settlers arrived in the early 1800s. The town itself was established in 1837, a year after Arkansas became a state. Both the town and the county were named for Missouri senator Thomas Hart Benton, who helped persuade Congress to admit Arkansas to the Union; Benton also happened to be the grand-uncle of the well-known twentieth-century painter Thomas Hart Benton, whose 1934 work *Ploughing It Under,* depicting the hardship of Depression-era farm life, will be part of the Crystal Bridges Museum of American Art's permanent collection.

By the 1880s, Bentonville had become the county seat. Yet the local soil was poor to middling and not especially conducive to growing most crops, so the area never attracted a plantation culture or slave population. In fact, during the Civil War, when the Battle of Pea Ridge was fought about twelve miles up the road, Bentonville, that unfortunate crossroad, was torched by both Union and Confederate armies; at the war's end, barely a dozen buildings remained, and the town needed to be completely rebuilt.

Bentonville received another body blow in 1881 when the St. Louis and San Francisco Railroad, known as the Frisco, built a line through Benton County but missed Bentonville by six miles. As one story goes, when discussions about the railroad were held, the town's then-mayor antagonized the railroad's top executives, who, as payback, chose to bypass Bentonville and build the depot far away. Another story suggests that the Bentonville brass refused to pay a $15,000 fee to the railroad. Either way, the town of Rogers was born—out of spite—and named after Captain C. W. Rogers, the railroad's manager. Two years later, a track was laid between Rogers and Bentonville, but the county seat had already lost its cachet—and its power.

In a difficult-to-reach area and with a spotty local economy, the town enjoyed brief success with tobacco crops until prices failed in the 1890s. As a result, Bentonville, like its more fertile, slightly more southern neighbors Springdale and Rogers, turned to fruit production. Its apple orchards became the core of the area's economy until the late 1920s, when such diseases as apple scabs, worms, moths, San Jose scabs, and Phoma spots fatally weakened the crop. Today Bentonville has no orchards at all.

The square was always the center of town activity. When the monument honoring the Confederate soldier was unveiled on August 8, 1908, crowds of people, including war veterans, came from as far away as Fayetteville and the Missouri border towns to watch the parade of floats, to listen to the speeches, to hear the band play "Dixie" and "Bonnie Blue Flag," and then to enjoy a basket picnic, which was followed by a concert on the square.[1] The sturdy square was also, for years, the site of the Benton County Fair, which featured a Ferris wheel, food, canning competitions, and minstrel shows. (Gloria Stewart, whose son Carl integrated the Bentonville schools, told me that her sister had danced in them as a young woman.)

Daughters of the Dust Bowl

The temperature has fallen to a rude seventeen degrees on a January morning in 2008, but since 8:00 A.M. an elite sorority of women—those who came of age here during the Depression—have been stopping by for their weekly visit to Shear Beauty, a no-nonsense hair salon in the small shopping center that Jim Walton owns right behind Bentonville Square. Here, these women, who grew up without airs and grew old without benefit of Botox, hair dye, or cosmetic surgery, come for a cut, curl, and comb-out, and sometimes a hearty complaint or a dose of local gossip.

Geneva Mason, a delicate-featured woman of eighty-seven, has been living on a fixed income since her husband's death, and she worries about soaring taxes, big-city prices, and traffic. "If Sam were here today, it wouldn't be like it is," she says. "Wal-Mart wouldn't, either. He wouldn't have let Bentonville get out of control like it is now."

The women here at Shear Beauty resist change. Frugality and caution are in their blood, as are memories of their tough Dust Bowl girlhoods. "I was born on a farm four miles south of Bentonville. In the late 1920s there were difficult times," says the majestic and hard-bitten Marie Buell, who at ninety-six still manages to look remarkably spry. "After the banks all closed, a dime looked like a million dollars."

The Great Depression hit Northwest Arkansas hard and early, beginning with the Flood of 1927, the worst natural disaster in the United States prior to Hurricane Katrina. Arriving in late spring, the flood ruined the state's agricultural economy and destroyed bridges, homes, and railroad line across more than six hundred thousand acres. Even before Arkansas could recover, it was enveloped by the severe drought that created the Dust Bowl and signaled the beginning of the Depression. In Bentonville proper, the banks shut their doors on December 6, 1930, and remained shut for more than a year. Soon small dry goods companies and other local businesses followed. Springdale was hit so hard that its schools had to close down.

Peggy Banks, giggly and good-natured, is having her short, snow-white hair cut and permed today. Neither the chilly weather nor her need for a walker and portable oxygen tank dampens her disposition. Born in 1921, Banks remembers the beauty of the area during her girlhood—more than two million apple trees blossomed every spring and wove a floral blanket from Bentonville to Springdale. But soon the coddling moth, a type of worm, invaded the orchards. "They sprayed with lime. I know because I rode the spray rig on our farm," she says. "But it didn't help." Eventually the apples rotted and the orchards died.

The Depression, says Banks, was "horrible. My grandparents had their life savings in the bank, and a woman who worked there told my grandfather, who was a barber, 'You'd better get your money out because it's going to go broke.' But he didn't think she knew anything. Eventually they turned off our electricity and the phone. People didn't have enough to eat. Nobody had money to buy sugar or even to can goods, which is how families usually managed during the winters."

But small pleasures offered sustenance. Banks was in high school when *Gone with the Wind* came to town—a major event. "Why, they turned out school so everybody could go see the movie," she says. "And I loved it."

Geneva Mason walks to Shear Beauty every week from her home a few blocks away. On this chilly day, she looks immaculate in gray wool slacks, rimless eyeglasses, and an apple-red car coat. "It was pretty rough," she says of her own Depression-era youth on a farm in nearby Pea Ridge. "By about 1936, the third year of the drought, people had to sell their livestock. There was no grass, no feed for cattle. Nobody had water because the wells ran dry. Eventually, the government bought the cattle for eight or nine dollars a head and slaughtered them."

But without refrigeration in the area, locals were unable to buy and eat the meat. Says Mason, "Don't forget, we didn't have electricity or bathrooms until REA—that is, Rural Electric—put in the lines. That was around 1937."

With farms coming up dust, farmers headed west to make ends meet. "First they'd go to California and pick the fruit, then to Idaho for the potatoes," Mason recalls. "That's how they survived the winter." She was lucky; her grandmother had a spinning wheel and harvested wool from their sheep to make clothes for her family. They also stored apples and potatoes in cellars underneath the house. "So we had most of what we needed," she says.

World War II made things even more difficult. "We rationed everything—gasoline, sugar," she says. "They gave us food stamps, and you had to be careful not to use them all the first day."

The war also dried up jobs in town. Once again, young men and women headed west, this time to work in California arms factories. Others, said Mason, went to towns such as Wichita where work was also available. She herself had married in 1940, a week after her eighteenth birthday, but kept it secret because she wanted to graduate high school. Staying in Bentonville, Mason, along with other women, headed to City Hall on Bentonville Square every week and wrapped bandages to send abroad.

For decades, the women at Shear Beauty recall, Bentonville life centered on the square. There were three five and dimes, three drugstores, grocery stores, and fruit stands, as well as Black's Ready-to-Wear and Putnam's Ladies and Men's Clothing stores. The square also boasted a number of family restaurants, the most popular of which was the Horseshoe Café. "You could go to town and get whatever you wanted then," said Mason. "Now you have to go to Wal-Mart."

"Remember what Zelma Nichols used to say? That on Saturday night you wore your red shoes to town," says Carol Girth as she combs out Mason's hair. Girth, who, with her round face and blond hair, looks like a modern version of the thirties movie star Joan Blondell, has owned Shear Beauty for twenty-seven years.

In pre-Wal-Mart days, people from the country drove into town every Saturday at around 5:00 P.M. and parked their cars as close to the square as they could manage. They did their weekly shopping, then during the warm weather sat around until 10:00 P.M. to hear the band concerts.

Bentonville boasted four theaters back then—the Royal on the north side of the square, the Park, and the Cozy; and down the street, across from the Massey Hotel, which is owned by the Waltons, was the Plaza, the town's most popular movie house. When Nadine Hitt, an energetic, gray-haired woman, and her husband moved here in 1952, they bought the Plaza, which had recently been the site of a mini-tragedy. "There had been a fire in the projection booth," she says. "The girl in the booth had been badly burned, and she died. Nobody ever really knew what happened."

. . . .

Ask the Shear Beauty crowd how the town has changed since Sam Walton brought his 5 & 10 to Bentonville Square in 1951, and it is as if someone has turned on a high-voltage switch. The women immediately become animated and opinionated and angry.

"It got too damned big!" insists Hitt. "Everything has changed."

"The population, oh, now it's overflowing," adds Mason.

Back in the day, they insist, Bentonville was quiet and manageable. Like most of small-town America, nobody locked the doors, and there was no unwelcome traffic, no foreigners, and no "jacked-up prices." But the women don't blame their friend, Walton.

"The town liked Sam. He was a common man, very down-to-earth, and so was Helen," Mason observes.

"If Sam were alive today, Wal-Mart would not be like it is," adds Girth. "Sam didn't want you to flaunt what you had. When the powers-that-be came in, it was push, push, push. Sam didn't like that."

The women appreciated the folksy nature of the Waltons. Sam may have looked like a movie star, but he favored overalls, plain talk, and his now-iconic dusty old red pickup truck; Helen, too, preferred simple outfits and an unassuming lifestyle. "I once saw her squat down and pick weeds in a dress she had just worn to a business meeting," says Girth, noting that Sam's wife usually wore her hair in a braid curled on top of her head or, occasionally, in two long pigtails.

"She wasn't into fixing her hair," she adds.

Mistakenly or not, these daughters of Old Bentonville insist that the Waltons' direct and down-home style would have extended to Sam's business practices if he had lived. As an example, Mason complains that real estate agents have twice attempted to buy her home because it is situated so near the future Crystal Bridges Museum of American Art; she believes that these people represent the Waltons, although they have not identified themselves as such. "That family owns so much land in Bentonville that nobody even knows about," she says. "But if Sam had wanted to buy something, he wouldn't have done it that way. He would have been open, and he would have come and talked to you."

These women also hold dear the notion that Walton would have or could have held down local prices and taxes connected with the construction and operation of new schools and the expansion of roads and waste management facilities.

"The town grew, but your money situation didn't grow like it should have," says Girth.

In fact, prices are so inflated these days that a simple sandwich at the only remaining cafe on the town square—a second sandwich shop recently went out of business—costs between $6 and $8. Wal-Mart managers can afford such prices, but the old-timers, many of them widows living on fixed incomes, cannot.

Mason, for one, laments the fact that she lost part of her annuity check when her husband died. "And it's just a lot harder to live here now. People are losing their homes because the taxes are high," she points out. "And they're talking about building more schools, which will increase taxes even more."

· · · · · · · · · ·

Certainly, one fact of small-town life across America is the decimation of the town square. As with Emma Avenue in Springdale and First Street in Rogers, both of which sprang up around railroad depots, Bentonville's downtown hub has all but disappeared. Today, the businesses that border the square include an Arvest Bank (owned by the Waltons); a local jewelry shop; a brand new gift shop; and the Station Café, a malt shop that sells greasy burgers at big-city prices.

At the moment they are struggling to stay open. Despite all the current work of the chamber of commerce, and the opening of a handful of new businesses, the revitalization of the square has yet to happen. Roy's Office Solutions, a stationery story that had been in business since 1948, closed in the summer of 2007, one of many mom-and-pop shops unable to compete with Wal-Mart. Bentonville, like so many rural towns, has become a bustling sprawl with no center—a series of malls, traffic arteries, churches, and box stores, usually megastores with vast square footage that are part of a retail chains—whose square sometimes feels like a ghost town.

Suddenly Out of Season

Debbie Matteri definitely had held her finger to the wind. When, on July 25, 2008, she closed her women's apparel shop, In Season, which occupied a choice spot at the entrance to the Midtown Shopping Center, right above the square, she already felt the tsunami that was about to take down the global economy the following fall.

"It has really hit us here as far as the housing market goes," says Matteri, a rosy-cheeked, ruddy-complexioned brunet in her mid-forties who can charm the Peter Pan collar off a blouse. "So many people were building such big homes, which are sitting empty. There's a lot of empty commercial space, too."

For sixteen years Matteri had nurtured her small, pleasant shop, and as the area grew richer, her inventory grew more sophisticated and expensive. By 2008 she was selling jeans for $160 to $190 and blazers and jackets for between $250 and $300—New York prices, some would say.

But foot traffic into the shop, which had been a staple of the shopping center since 1994, had substantially slowed down, and Matteri feared that she would order $150,000 worth of merchandise for the fall season and then get stuck with it. So she held back on her purchasing, phoned her customers, and, as she says, "I sold off my merchandise without having to have a big going-out-of-business sale."

A few months after shutting her doors, she observed: "The hardest part of not doing the business is not getting the opportunity to meet and greet and talk to people. The friendships, the connections—it was all invaluable."

Sing a Song of Sam's Clubs

Matteri began her life in retail at Wal-Mart's Sam's Club in 1986. She was twenty-four, two years out of college, and recently married. "Back then, I had just moved here, and Bentonville had only nine thousand people; now there are twenty-eight thousand," she says. "And Sam's Club was known as Sam's *Wholesale* Club at the time. They only had three stores [nationwide], which they called warehouses. Ours was an old converted skating rink. And a group of young, high-energy, creative people was running things."

Matteri started out by greeting people at the door and acting as a receptionist. Soon she was promoted to merchandising, where she worked as an assistant to the woman who bought cigarettes, tobacco, beer, wine and liquor, and soft drinks for all the Sam's Clubs (Benton County, a dry county, could not carry wine and liquor in its local stores). Matteri was one of three young women who helped negotiate prices. "At the time Sam's Clubs were growing, and by the time I left in 1990, there were maybe seventy-five stores that we bought for," she says.

Although Matteri worked for four years at Sam's Club, she remained a nonmanagement employee being paid hourly wages. "I started at $5 an hour and ended at $10—very fair wages at the time," she says, and worked from eight to five, with a lunch break. But she says that she was not terribly ambitious and so never took advantage of the company's Buyer Program, instead working full-time until she gave birth to her older daughter. "Then they told me I could work four days a week and keep my wages and benefits," she says. She did that for a year. "They were very good. They also offered a fitness program, which cost $2 per paycheck, and a stock purchase program."

Matteri left in 1990. "Taking advantage of career opportunities there would have meant working longer hours and traveling," she says. "And I wanted to be home with my young family. At the time, my husband, Greg, traveled a lot with his job."

By that time, she says, she had accumulated somewhere between three hundred and four hundred shares of company stock, which she promptly sold to remodel her home, a lovely 1916 William Morris bungalow with three bedrooms in the center of town. The next year, she decided, with her sister, to open In Season. They rented space from the Midtown Shopping Center, using seed money that their parents had given them. "When I opened the store, I never had to put my daughters into day care," she explains. "They went to work with me. And I saw that as a great opportunity, that I could have an income and still be with my kids." A few years later and thriving, she moved into a larger two-thousand-square-foot space in the shopping center, which she occupied until she closed the store.

"Working at Sam's Club taught me how to deal with people and how to negotiate things that you want, maybe free shipping or extra dating on your invoices. My experience there was really great," Matteri says in her inimitably cheery way, "I loved it—I *loved* it. It really was a good company to work for. And I'm still in touch with many of the people I worked with back then."

For sixteen years Matteri ran her highly successful store. Women knew they would get good value for mid- to upper-range apparel. Loyal customers, in fact, often came to town with empty suitcases, bought enough outfits to fill them up, and then returned home with new wardrobes. In addition, with her easygoing and welcoming personality, Matteri presided over a mini-salon. Her customers always knew they could drop by and receive a warm hello and a friendly dollop of local gossip.

Living Her Faith, Living Her Goodness

Not only does Matteri, a bedrock Republican, reflect the kind of sunny southern disposition that is almost a cliche by now, but also she embraces the deep-rooted religiosity that defines people in the South, and particularly here in the Bible Belt. Although raised nondenominationally, she says, she and her family belong to a small denomination Church of Christ group that consists of perhaps 150 people. Called the Bentonville Church of Christ, it is located on Walton Boulevard, about a five-minute drive from her home. "We just try to read the Bible and follow what the Bible says," she explains.

One difference that separates her Church of Christ from most organized religions is its rejection of instrumental music. "Everything is a cappella," she says. "We think you should worship with your heart, so we don't have man-made instruments—no organs, drums, or pianos. It's very beautiful."

Matteri and her husband, Greg, who sells corrugated boxes for a manufacturer in Fort Smith, Arkansas, about an hour and a half southwest of Bentonville, along with their youngest daughter, who is in high school, attend worship services on Sundays; additionally, on both Sunday and Wednesday evenings they participate in a Bible study group at one of their congregation members' home. (Their eldest child attends Harding University, a Church of Christ Christian college in Searcy, a three-and-a-half-hour drive from Bentonville.) Although Matteri herself was baptized at age twelve, she says that Greg had been raised Catholic but joined Matteri's church after they married.

Since closing her shop, Matteri has been pondering her work future. Returning to Wal-Mart as an apparel buyer is a possibility; working for one of the town's numerous vendors is another. "Since I have been home, friends and contacts have been phoning, telling me to give them a call when I'm ready to go back to work," she says.

There is also the possibility, she admits, that she might want to return to the women's apparel business when the Crystal Bridges Museum opens in 2011. "In order to survive these days, small towns need to compete," she says. "You've got to have something that brings people to you, that makes you different from all the other towns. So I think we in Bentonville are working really hard to break through to that art culture. People who will be traveling to see it will bring money with them—and a whole new touristy clientele."

A woman who takes her faith and her philosophy of goodness seriously, Matteri concludes our conversation by asking delicately, "I haven't said anything negative or ugly, have I?"

No, I assure her.

"I hope not, because, you know, everything in the world nowadays is . . ."

Her voice fades for a moment. "I keep telling myself it's easier to be nice. It's such a short journey we are on, but I want it to be a good one for myself and my kids. A smile, a kind word, they go a long way."

Taking Care of (Town) Business

The median household income in Bentonville in 2008 was $78,000.[2] (By comparison, the U.S. median gross income was $61,500.)[3] Here, longtime residents are competing with a newer generation of higher-paid men and women, usually transplants with more discretionary income.

"Sure, there will be a clash of cultures," Rich Davis acknowledges. "But at the same time, although some people may want Bentonville to remain Mayberry, that's not going to happen. Everyone is benefiting from the new economy in Northwest Arkansas, and everyone is paying a price somewhere down the line."

As in most of Arkansas, Bentonville's property taxes, currently frozen at 20 percent of the assessed value, are used to build its schools. Property taxes, despite old timers' complaints, remain fairly reasonable. Owners of a home valued at $100,000 are taxed on $20,000 of that, a figure that comes to between $1,200 and $1,800 a year, according to Davis.

Sales tax dollars go toward improving the infrastructure, which is in constant flux as a result of the area's recent growth. In fact, the Bentonville sales tax turns out to be higher than that of New York City. It includes the Arkansas state sales tax (6 percent) and the city sales tax (2 percent). In 2004, during Coberly's reign, an additional 1 percent county sales tax was initiated, the revenue of which goes solely to improving the infrastructure. That means that one penny for every dollar spent helps to pay down the expansion of roads, sewage plants, and water system. Do the simple math: today the sales tax in Bentonville and all of Benton County adds up to a whopping 9 percent.

In addition, the town raised a $110 million bond package in 2007 to cover five specific areas, with $86 million set aside to address the infrastructure and the remainder divided between improving the parks, expanding and upgrading the police and fire departments, and updating the municipal airport.

Part of the bond package included the renovation of the square, from work on the water system and roadwork to brick-paved sidewalks and energy-efficient, Victorian-style street lights, which will hopefully retain the area's historic aura.

"Here, too, Mayor McCaslin brought a new view to city government," says Davis, explaining that to complete the renovation expeditiously—within

210 days—the town offered the contractor a cash bonus of up to $4,000 per day for every day, up to 30 days, that he finished before the deadline.

As for the current recessionary climate, Davis, an erudite former fire-fighter and fire chief, says the town has been slow to feel it. "We experienced stratospheric growth between 2000 and 2004," he explains. "Every month during that period, we added 1,250 people and created 560 new jobs. Today that has slowed down to between 150 and 200 jobs a month. So some who've experienced the explosive level of growth a few years ago are saying, 'There's something wrong.' But Northwest Arkansas's growth is pretty good compared to that of the rest of the country. While others are seeing negative job losses, we are still creating jobs and seeing an influx of new people. The available houses on the market are being absorbed, although perhaps more slowly than they used to be."

As of the third quarter of 2008, the town had 4.4 percent unemployment, the highest in the six years since Davis has been here. But still it is not of great concern, he says: "Usually a statistic of less than 3.5 percent is considered full employment." (Others consider between 4.5 and 5 percent to be full employment.)

Some in the construction and real estate business beg to differ with Davis. "Of course, there has been a slowdown," says the builder Fadil Bayyari, who claims that the shaky economy has already brought down the price of goods, labor, and homes.

In fact, there were indicators that all was not completely well as far back as January 2008, when home sales in Benton and Washington counties fell more than 35 percent from the same period the previous year and pushed the state's monthly average to a three-year low.[4] By June the value of local residential construction permits had plummeted by almost 50 percent from the same time in 2007, leading the *Morning News* to speculate that "the five-year Northwest Arkansas building boom has ended." The newspaper explained, "Bentonville issued 14 new housing permits totaling $3.25 million compared to 36 issued last May, with a value of $5.31 million."[5] Economist Kathy Deck, the director of the University of Arkansas's Center for Business and Economic Research, noted that at the peak of the boom, July 2006, more than 13,000 people in Benton and Washington counties worked in construction jobs, whereas by December 2008, that number had shrunk to 11,000.[6]

As for home prices in Benton County, for a long time it seemed that they, too, might defy the reality of our economy and be recession-proof. However, between January and March 2009, prices slid 5.6 percent and home sales revenues were down a whopping 34.6 percent from 2008. (Whereas 401 homes were sold in 2008, only 332 were sold in 2009.) The recession, it seemed, had finally taken hold.[7]

Although Deck has warned that the weakness of the housing market would, in all probability, continue deep into 2009, the decline in prices has been clearly related to a recent upturn in sales.[8] "Folks are in there looking for deals," she said. "Basically the market is testing itself. The test of when things are going to look a little bit better is when folks go into the market and say, 'I have to buy this now. This is a great deal.' Some of that is going on right now."[9]

Will Culture Save the Day?

Local spin aside, the town fathers, its merchants, and its chamber of commerce and city council all seem determined to make Bentonville proper into something more than a destination point for Wal-Mart suppliers. The linchpin for the future is Crystal Bridges, the museum that Alice Walton, Sam's daughter, conceived of and the Israeli-born artist Moshe Safdie designed, allegedly to celebrate nature; it will contain more than twenty-five thousand feet of gallery space, sculpture gardens, a theater, and public areas for outdoor concerts. But primarily it will be a showcase for American art, and already Walton has bought up works by Winslow Homer, Thomas Eakins, Asher B. Durand, Charles Willson Peale, and Marsden Hartley in a frenzy of spending that seems as extravagant as her father was frugal.

In fact, in August 2008 the *Arkansas Democrat-Gazette* reported that, all in all, Alice Walton, who is personally worth $16 billion (as are each of her brothers); her family; and their foundation have donated $317 million to the museum, "which has nearly half a billion dollars in assets. . . ."[10]

That is not all. Clearly, Bentonville's movers and shakers, among them the Waltons, harbor huge ambitions for the town. A citizens' group has already formed and is planning the creation of a children's museum, a science and technology museum, and a local performing arts center that will be twice the size of the multi-million-dollar Walton Arts Center in downtown Fayetteville. In March 2008, the tentatively titled Northwest Arkansas Children's Museum received a $370,000 exploratory grant from the Walton Family Foundation; in March 2009, a local "Dancing with the Stars" fund-raiser brought in $50,000 for the project. "No, there is no building yet," explains Davis, "but we have already created a board and incorporated. At the moment it looks like the museum will be built in the economic footprint of Crystal Bridges—that is, somewhere within its property. If we were in a totally down economy, that simply wouldn't be happening."

And for those who suspect that the area may be trying to become too artsy, too haute culture, an antidote exists—the brand new Arvest Ballpark in nearby Springdale. Home to the Northwest Arkansas Naturals, the minor league team that is an affiliate of the Kansas City Royals, the state-of-the-art stadium, with seating for seventy-five hundred, is owned by Arvest, the Walton family bank, and was built for $50 million by the same company that constructed the new Yankee Stadium in the Bronx. Arvest Ballpark opened on April 10, 2008, and the good news is that, unlike the "House That Ruth Built," the stadium that Sam and his boys bequeathed to the Ozarks sells seats for between $6 and $12 a game.

Some, however, such as those Dust Bowl daughters Geneva Mason and Nadine Hitt, are less than thrilled by the prospect of so many tourists in town, even if a more vital square is a happy by-product.

Mason pauses and ponders the possibility, then frowns. "That's what I'm afraid of," she says bluntly. "They'll probably have a walking tour that goes right in front of or behind my house."

And Hitt, whooping with laughter, chimes in: "Well, I hope I don't live to see it."

8

A Trucker in "Chickendale"

· · · · · · · · · ·

Back in the twenties and thirties, a wide dirt road named East Emma Avenue pierced the heart of Springdale. Here, on the town's main thoroughfare, farmers set up a daily market for the seasonal fruit that they could not sell locally—mostly apples, strawberries, tomatoes, and green beans.

"They'd all bring it to Emma Avenue, and somebody would buy it and haul it off," remembers Homer Smith, a self-described "ridge runner," or "redneck," who was born in 1924 and has lived in Northwest Arkansas long enough to see it grow from a rugged rural outback with a virtually all-white population of 2,952 into a thriving multicultural boom town of 60,000. Back in the day when Homer was hauling produce across the country by truck, the area was fragrant with fruit blossoms. "Even Welch had a plant here," he says of the grape juice king. "It was paradise. We used to say, 'If you come to Northwest Arkansas, bring everything you own, because you won't want to leave.' And that was true."

But the coddling moths eventually attacked the apples. And chickens, heartier than fruit, came along. By the mid-1930s everything else went by

the wayside, says Homer, because these meaty new "broilers" were rak-
ing in the money. "At one point six or seven chicken houses running halfway down the mountain contained twenty-five thousand chicks apiece,"
he says. People complained that East Emma smelled of chickens. "And
word was out that poultry feathers were all over town. Springdale became
known as Chickendale—a dirty place."

It is something of an irony, however, that East Emma, like the town centers in Bentonville and Rogers, flourished back when the population was
sparse and primarily white. Today, with modest suburban tracts and glam-
ourless industrial malls spiraling out from the dusty center, the town's old
railroad tracks, on which trains began rolling through the area in 1881, no
longer carry either people or produce, except for tourists shuttling back
and forth through the Ozarks between Springdale and Van Buren. Still, a
token railway car, which no longer rides those rails, sits empty at a cross
stop, an unabashed tribute to Springdale's past. While a paltry array of
small businesses—a hairdressing academy, a shabby flea market, a two-
story "department" store, and the run-down remnant of an ice-cream
shop—continue to line Emma, the street now feels like an abandoned
small-town road whose sole inhabitants are ghosts.

And if the ghosts could talk, they would acknowledge that Springdale,
with its fresh springs and good hunting, was, back in the early 1800s, an
area where local Choctaw, Shawnee, Delaware, and Osage tribes settled.
The Cherokee Treaty of 1828 enabled whites to move safely into the area,
and within a decade there was enough cross-country traffic for a settlement, including an inn called Fitzgerald's Station; four years later the
fledgling community built a church, the Shiloh Primitive Baptist Church,
which became a cornerstone of this new town, called, appropriately, Shiloh. But when Shiloh applied to build a post office in 1872, another community had already claimed the name, and so residents decided to call their
settlement Springdale after the clear waters nearby.

Today Springdale is a town in flux, counting Hispanics, both legal and
undocumented, as between 35 and 40 percent of its population. The area's
huge appetite for unskilled laborers who can feed the meatpacking plants
is also part of the reason that the nation's largest population of immigrants
from the Marshall Islands, currently estimated at more than 8,000, have
moved here.

An Unlikely Coffee Klatch

Early on a cold morning in January 2008, Homer Smith sits at a table at the local Burger King with five or six other men, all between sixty-three and eighty-six, all wearing baseball caps and Windbreakers, and all former truck drivers during the area's rural heyday. These longtime buddies, with their hardscrabble Arkansas upbringing, come here every Wednesday at 8:00 A.M. to drink the free coffee that the fast-food chain brews for them and to ride the roads of memory.

On this brisk but sunny morning, the men savor shooting the southern breeze with each other as much as they enjoy their coffee. They have all endured similar childhoods, growing up as poor as cornpones, mostly on small local farms and in big families. Floyd Collins had eleven brothers and sisters; as tough as it was for the family, his father lived until the age of 101. Bobby Eldridge was one of seven kids living with their parents in two rooms without electricity.

"We barely made it," says Eldridge, who recalls how canned goods saved the family from starvation during the Dust Bowl years. "About three or four of us slept in a bed together," he adds. "And our house had cracks in the floor. You could see chickens under the house."

Electricity did not come to rural Springdale until 1941, and as for toilets and running water, "The only running water was a kid running with a bucket," jokes Homer.

Buddies with limited educations, these men have lived good, simple lives, committed to love for their parents, their wives, their Christian religion, and outdoor pleasures such as fishing and quail hunting. But it was through trucking that they, like so many young men in the area in the 1930s and '40s, made their livelihoods.

"Transportation—old trucks. *That's* what built this part of the country," Homer, a lanky fellow with a jovial personality, a drawl, and a prominent, veined, W. C. Fields–type of nose, says adamantly. "That's what everybody got into."

During the 1920s, truckers moved produce out of the area, everything from beans to tomatoes, from berries to grapes. What the railroads didn't carry, the truckers did. But eventually, as disease began weakening the crops of Northwest Arkansas, chickens came to rule the economy. Small farmers had begun raising broilers in the twenties, but poultry did not come to the fore as the area's major economic force for at least another decade.

"Here they bred the chickens to grow quicker," says Carroll Crisler, the oldest member of the coffee klatch, whose only nod to age is his deteriorating hearing and booming voice. "In the forties it took fourteen or fifteen weeks to grow a two- to five-pound chicken. Now it takes only forty-one days to raise a three- or four-pounder."

"With big breasts. Like Marilyn Monroe," says Homer slyly. He knows whereof he speaks, since he happens to own a collection of Monroe memorabilia, which he keeps under lock and key in a small cabinet at home.

Soon the chicken industry took root, with such companies as George's, Armour, and Tyson's growing fast and strong. And many of the men who started by hauling produce made fortunes transporting chickens across the country. Among them were Willis Shaw, who founded Willis Shaw Express Frozen and Refrigerated Trucking; John Tyson, Tyson Foods; Lester Lindley, Lindley Truck Lines; and Joe Robinson, Joe Robinson's Trucking. And Johnnie Bryan Hunt built J. B. Hunt Trucking. Another startling success was Harvey Jones, who hitched up his first team of mules and wagon in 1918 at age eighteen to start a version of Jones Truck Lines (JTL), and in 1980 sold it to Sun Oil for $900 million, becoming one of the area's most impressive philanthropists. Today, more than twenty-six trucking companies still exist in the area.

Crisler, a nephew of Harvey Jones's wife, Bernice, grew up five miles from the heart of Springdale and, with the exception of a stint in the air force during World War II, lived at home with his parents until he married. Crisler had the distinction of being related to Bernice, who eventually made possible the extraordinary community facility the Jones Center. "Bernice!" he says. "To me, she was always that lady who would say, 'Watch your manners!'"

. . . .

Trucking and poultry plants transformed Springdale into a viable working-class community. But the town did not really change until Sam Walton moved to Northwest Arkansas and by 1962 established Wal-Mart.

"Wal-Mart started in this area because everybody here had a little money year-round," says Homer. "There were enough people here doing stuff and creating jobs for people, and Sam Walton understood that."

"I'd say it was the poultry industry and Wal-Mart that changed the area," booms Crisler. "Wal-Mart killed the downtown area in all the small towns. Wal-Mart killed Emma—there's no doubt about it."

Walton's retail experiment affected the local economies both negatively and positively, says Crisler. "Wal-Mart was a bad influence on small towns all over this nation. Yet it helped people. They could buy cheaper. And it created a lot of jobs in Springdale and throughout this country. Still, if I had a store here, they would have put me out of business."

The two multimillionaires Harvey Jones and Sam Walton shared their poor-boy backgrounds, their penchant for saving, and their refusal to put on airs. Homer likes to tell a story about them that may be apocryphal. "Harvey and Sam, who both wore bib overalls, were standing by a restaurant one afternoon," he says, adding that they looked less like a pair of millionaires than farmers who needed a handout. "And Artie Banks walks by and mistakes Harvey for a bum. 'Hey,' he says to him, 'get yourself something to eat.' And Harvey takes the coin, puts it in his pocket, and never says a word."

The truckers chuckle like men who have heard this one before.

Trucking—and being local guys in a small community on the way up—helped some of these men make small fortunes as well. Both Crisler and Eldridge began investing in Wal-Mart from the beginning; that alone would make them wealthy men today (a hundred shares bought in 1970 for $16.50 a share, and adjusted for splits, would have accrued to about $10.5 million today).[1] Both also bought Wal-Mart's Mexican stock, which originally went on sale for a dollar a share in the early 1990s. Now, Crisler says, the Mexican stock "has hit $40-something—not a bad return."

"I have so much of it that I cannot sell because of taxes," says Eldridge, who lives simply these days. Since his wife died, he has moved into a local senior citizens' center, where, he says, there are 400 seniors, 350 being women. With more money than he can ever use, he owns up to having bought a car for himself and another for his granddaughter as a graduation gift. As for his bundles of stock, he shrugs, "I'll probably give it all to her and let her sell it."

"I don't spend any more than I ever did," says ever-thrifty Crisler. "Going through the Depression, you learned to save."

Collins, a robust man in jeans and a blue-striped shirt, suggests that it took less to make their generation happy.

Homer Smith had his opportunities to make a fortune, too. The very same Artie Banks who threw the nickel at Harvey Jones wanted to sell Homer seven acres and a house right off Emma for $700. "I'm sure it's worth $3 or $4 million right now," he says with a small smile. "But what would I do with $3 or $4 million? People would have drove me nuts. 'Can

I have $2?' Now I don't have any money, but I'm not obligated to anything. These guys"—and he gestures to his pals—"have got to work and worry all day about others taking advantage of them."

Surviving the Hobo Jungles

Homer, whose family moved west to Lincoln, Arkansas, when he was eight, lost both his parents at eleven and developed a serious stutter. "I couldn't talk," he said. "I was considered 'afflicted,' and nobody wanted me around. But I didn't want to go to the reform school, so I got out. I caught a train out of Fayetteville and wound up down in the hobo jungles in Van Buren."

Homer's Great Depression boyhood could well have inspired the photographs of Walker Evans or Dorothea Lange. "A lot of people had a rough time back then. It wasn't very pretty," he says. The hobo jungles he lived in were, he recalls, surprisingly clean. "And they'd boil whatever they could put in the pot for stew."

So at the age of thirteen, gangly, stuttering Homer was riding the rails and trying to stay alive. "I'd go around to people's back doors and set there, and because of the stutter, it took me maybe five minutes to tell them what I was doing. Sometimes, I think, they'd give me something to eat just to get rid of me."

After Homer took an odd job helping a woman bring stove wood from her yard into her house, other hobos chastised him, saying, "You can't work *and* be a hobo." "So I said, 'The hell with the railroad.' And so me and another guy named Harry got on the highway. He taught me to hitchhike, and he also taught me to talk by making me read out loud the road maps and billboard signs between here and California." By the time Homer reached the West Coast, he knew the capital of every state and, for the first time, could hold a conversation without stuttering.

While his pal, Harry, proved to be something of a lady's man, young Homer, whenever they pulled into a town, would get acquainted with the waitress at the local hotel where they stayed, and she would get him a job in the kitchen. "There were always a couple of prostitutes and a bootlegger who ate in the kitchen, too," he says. "And the only time people knew what they did was when the sheriff raided the place. And they'd give me advice. They told me to be honest and nice to people because you might meet them later in another way."

In 1942, Homer Smith finally rode a bus back to Springdale and decided to settle there. He was eighteen and felt safe now. "Everyone who had wanted me to go to reform school was now in the war," he says. He tried to join the army, too, but was rejected. Luckily for him, manpower was scarce. So, having learned to harvest wheat in Enid, Oklahoma, he took a job working in a local feed mill. "And I tried to do a good job," he says.

In Springdale the young truckers who were just getting started also helped the hard-working teen get work as a driver. "And it was great for me," Homer says. He shared a room at the Arcade Hotel on the east side of town with eight other drivers and recalls how, with four or five beds to a room, they staggered work shifts. And for $6 a week, he got not only a bed but also a woman who would wash his underclothes a few times each week. Downstairs at a beer joint called the Blue Castle, where Ryan's Department Store is today, "They served the best hamburgers you ever ate," Homer recalls. Occasionally, the big drinkers would go into the alley behind the Blue Castle and fight it out, while everybody else would hang out of their windows to watch the impromptu boxing match.

Homer started off hauling produce—back in the 1940s a sixty-acre farm was considered big. "But then chickens came along," he said. "And soon everything else went by the wayside because chickens made more money." He remembers how the chicken litter was used as manure for grass that the cattle would eat. "The chickens brought the cows," he says. "Now they're trying to say that the chicken litter is ruining the streams."

By the mid-1940s poultry was boosting the local wartime economy. "They soon found that a chicken killed in this part of the country was better than a chicken hauled to Chicago and then killed," he explains. "Chickens are 98 percent water. By the time you got one to where it was going, it would be dried out and wouldn't weigh much. So there were a lot of processing plants here because of the humidity."

The Chickens Come Home to Roost

Unquestionably, trucking helped define the Springdale community and encourage growth in the poultry industry. But chickens would eventually emerge as something more—a business that would eventually go global and transform Northwest Arkansas emphatically and in ways that, back in 1945, were simply unimaginable.

In fact, in 1935, John Tyson began to build his empire as a simple trucker, transporting chickens from Arkansas to Kansas City and Chicago. Quickly, however, he realized that incubating chicks from birth, selling them to local growers, and milling his own feed were ways to grow his company. By 1943 he had purchased his first broiler farm here in Springdale and discovered that crossbreeding different types of birds yielded a meatier product. By 1950 he was processing ninety-six thousand broilers a week; the chicken business had already become huge in Northwest Arkansas, with twenty-nine other companies competing with Tyson.[2] By the end of the decade, working with his forward-thinking son, Don, Tyson built the first processing plant in the area, allowing his own company total control and the ability to breed, feed, kill, cut, package, and ship birds across the country.

Tyson went public in 1963, officially changing its name to Tyson Foods, Inc., in 1971. By that time it was producing more than 72 million broilers annually. Chickens were fast becoming an American food staple. As the decade wound down, Tyson produced 234 million birds a year—an increase of 325 percent from the beginning of the decade.

Since then, Tyson has grown into "the world's largest processor and marketer of chicken, beef, and pork, and the second largest food production company in the Fortune 500," distributing its product throughout the United States and to more than eighty countries.[3] In 2001 the company acquired IBP, the largest beef processor in the country. The deal, according to the *New York Times*, "created a $20 billion company that dominates the meat counter at supermarkets and is a leading supplier to fast-food restaurants like McDonald's and Burger King."[4]

By 2000 the United States was exporting 2.5 million tons of chicken a year, with China and Russia emerging as the two biggest international consumers of American poultry.[5] In Russia chicken thighs and legs, the country's favorite import, were referred to as "Bush legs," after the first President George Bush helped alleviate the country's food shortage in the early 1990s by arranging for the inexpensive import of these poultry parts.[6]

As Tyson grew into a chicken titan, the company, like others in the area, needed to hire manpower to run its hometown processing plants in Springdale, as well as subsidiaries around the country. The work—hanging up, then stunning and disemboweling live chickens and cutting them up on an assembly line—is dirty and disgusting; even worse, it is dangerous. One in five workers is hurt on the job, with injuries ranging from repetitive stress to lacerations and amputations.[7] Health insurance is often inadequate or nonexistent, and wages are as low as companies can get away with. Who would be available to do such a task?

The answer was simple: Hispanic immigrants—unskilled, and often undocumented, workers who are desperate to make a living. For many, jobs at these poultry-processing plants paid better than fieldwork in Southern California, where most immigrants had migrated up until the mid-1990s. In addition, the cost of living here in Northwest Arkansas was substantially less. And so the great Arkansas migration began.

Stories abound that describe how Tyson Foods would send buses to the Mexican border to transport newly arrived illegal immigrants to Northwest Arkansas, where they would be provided with identification numbers and put to work immediately. In fact, in 2001 the government, after a thirty-month investigation, brought a thirty-six-count indictment against the company, accusing six employees of conspiring to smuggle illegal immigrants across the border to work in more than fifteen processing plants in nine states.[8] The charges were made more serious because Tyson had been on probation since 1997 after pleading guilty to giving illegal gifts to then-secretary of agriculture Mike Espy.

The government, in its suit, also said that Tyson officials had contacted local smugglers to help recruit newbie workers. One such was Amador Anchondo-Rascon, a U.S. citizen and Mexican resident who first came here in 1979 and had once been employed at Tyson's plant in Shelbyville, Tennessee. Amador told authorities that he had originally begun to sell fake Social Security cards in a small grocery he owned in Shelbyville. But in 1997 the Immigration and Naturalization Service (INS) confronted and co-opted him. So when a Tyson manager asked him to smuggle in two thousand Guatemalan workers, offering a recruitment fee of $200 a head, he agreed. Despite the fact that he was in cahoots with the INS, Amador was doing so well by 2000 that he owned five homes, two stores, and a number of cars.

A little background: In 1986 the Immigration Reform and Control Act had made it a crime for an employer to *knowingly* hire illegal aliens. There was a loophole or two, however—as long as the company was unknowing and as long as these employees could show matching identification cards, employers were protected from prosecution. "Widely considered unenforceable," said author Joseph Rosenbloom, "the law has had the perverse effect of fueling the black market in counterfeit documents."[9] Tyson enacted a policy of its own in 1999, specifying that all its employees must follow immigration law and proclaiming "zero tolerance" for any violations of same. It also signed up for an INS program that would check and authenticate employee Social Security cards.

Eventually the INS indicted not only Tyson Food but also two Tyson executives and four former company managers. The corporation distanced itself from responsibility by explaining that these executives were rogues working on their own. "No one in the corporate offices knew of this," Barry Hirsch, a Tyson attorney, insisted to the *New York Times*.

Apparently Tyson's legal team, aided by three of the executives who admitted their own guilt—another manager under indictment committed suicide—was able to convince the jury that the corporation was blameless and, in fact, a victim of overambitious employees. On March 26, 2003, the jury voted that Tyson was not guilty.

At the time, Tyson said that it considered its Hispanic workers integral to its American operations and argued that Hispanics were not taking jobs away from Americans. A company spokesman, Ed Nicholson, noted, "The Latino workforce is not competing with the local available workforce; they're augmenting it. Anybody who wants to work can work."[10]

As for Amador, he spent two years in prison for his role as the recruiter. Even in the midst of his ordeal, he paid tribute to his adopted country, which allowed him to live the American Dream—and, to some extent, the American Nightmare: "I think America is the greatest country in the world," he told BNET Business Network reporter Melinda Ammann. "We have to work seven days a week ten hours a day, but that's okay—as long as we have a good future for our family."

A Redneck in a Dollhouse

Walking into the Smith home on a side street off Emma is a little bit like walking into a dollhouse. The wood-paneled living room is small and filled with knickknacks. Tiny porcelain dolls, originally designed by Maud Humphrey, Humphrey Bogart's mother, fill curio cabinets and tabletops. Pristine white lace curtains set off a deep floral wallpaper in both the dining room, with its pretty crystal chandelier, and the small kitchen. Even the laundry room is wallpapered and lacy.

Dorothy Smith met and married Homer more than sixty years ago when she was a young girl working in the Monarch, her mother's Springdale restaurant. Today she is wearing a white floral vest over a white turtleneck and an immaculately coiffed bouffant hairdo. The couple graciously shows off a surfeit of surprising memorabilia that includes Homer's collection of Marilyn Monroe plates, statues, and photos, all picked up on the road. These share space in a corner cabinet with his model cars—an elaborate miniature yellow Duesenberg that replicates an auto once belonging to the actor Jimmy Stewart and two silver cars that are copies of others made for Clark Gable and Gary Cooper.

Homer, who gave up his truck routes in 1990 when he was sixty-seven, owned a liquor store for nineteen years, and he takes me on a tour of the upstairs bedroom that once belonged to his son but now houses his collection of Elvis Presley decanters. At least a dozen wacky Elvises take over closets and shelves. Some are porcelain, others, ceramic; many, at least three feet tall with wax seals, sit on support pedestals. There is Elvis in his studded white Vegas outfit; Elvis in army duds; Elvis decked out in an outfit from *Blue Hawaii*. Homer says he got first crack at the new decanters every time they were produced—and couldn't resist. "If someone offered me $5,000 for one today, I'd turn him down," this unlikely collector assures me.

Also on display in the room are a number of trophies that look like the kind that high school kids win at track meets. But no, these, he tells me, are for showing his prize possession: a 1964 Bentley, which, Homer says, "is now valued at $70,000 at least. I bought that car on credit. The banker almost fainted when I phoned him about getting a loan."

Homer invites me downstairs to his garage to view his pièce de résistance, a shiny black sedan with blue leather upholstery, an exquisite silver figurehead on the hood, and a beautifully cut crystal wineglass thrown casually in the backseat for show.

"I retired without having a hobby and just about went nuts," says Homer. But the open road still called. "So I bought the Bentley."

Quick to define his country-boy values, lest I get the wrong idea about his splurge, Homer, who attends the First Christian Church most Sunday mornings, says, "I don't love that Bentley. No, I love family, God, and country. But I sure *enjoy* that car. I drive it to car shows. I took it on old Route 66. I went from here to Chicago and back and from here to Santa Monica. Then, I turned at the Santa Monica pier and went home."

Did he take Dorothy with him on this long haul? No way, he says with a laugh. "She's a perfect housewife and a perfectionist about her surroundings. But that's not her cup of tea."

A Time of Transition

On a hot August afternoon, Homer has just come in from mowing his lawn. "We've got a good-sized lawn, and I tried to clean it up, mowing and trimming," he says with his usual amicability. "It's got a motor on it, but I still push it. That's pretty good exercise for a lazy old guy."

How does Homer feel about the changes in the Springdale population during the last decade?

"Well, we don't like it," he says. "It's overpopulated. And it has taken everything that we've got to try to fix our structure, our sewers and water system. We thought we had everything fixed until we got overpopulated. And all at once they were *all* here. Now we're flooded with Mexicans."

Homer particularly dislikes the fact that so few immigrants speak English. "Our schools try to teach the younger people English. But if you can't hear English from any of the families, it's hard to teach the young ones a language that they don't hear except at school. And us that have been here, we don't understand why the newcomers are taking all our benefits but they don't want to learn our language. I'm part Indian because my grandmother was Cherokee. And in those days, if they talked Cherokee at school, the school expelled them. And there's enough of us who remember that."

The common perception, he says, is that half the immigrants who arrive in Northwest Arkansas immediately go on welfare. "They know all the ins and outs," he adds.

Still he feels compassion for the hourly wage workers in today's economic climate of cutbacks and uncertainty. When gasoline was $4 a gallon, he points out, immigrants working for $7 or $8 an hour on the poultry lines at Tyson's and George's, or in the Wal-Mart Supercenters, and living twenty miles away from their jobs found themselves—with virtually no public transportation system in Northwest Arkansas—having little choice but to pay out a small fortune in daily transportation costs. "It's either that or quit working," says Homer.

"Luckily," he adds, "old cronies like me and the other guys, we don't have to go anywhere. We just have to stay home and eat hot dogs—which is OK by me. Anyway, I'll stick around here. For me, it's a paradise."

9

The Mayor of Rogers Takes on Undocumented Workers

· · · · · · · · · ·

Steve Womack is the kind of man who seems to revel in his own polarizing personality. Swaggering with self-confidence, the mayor of Rogers has led the charge to make life more difficult for illegal immigrants in Northwest Arkansas. "I'm a law-and-order guy," he boasts when I arrive at the antiseptically modern Rogers City Hall to hear him out in January 2008. "I believe that one of the things about the genius of America is the rule of law. I am also concerned when somebody, to improve his station in life, violates employment laws by producing fraudulent documentation to suggest he is someone who he is really not."

And so it is with good reason that Womack, the mayor who presides over the community directly south of Bentonville, has earned the reputation as Public Enemy Number One among the Hispanics of Northwest Arkansas. During the past decade, the Latino population of the town, and of neighboring Springdale as well, has mushroomed to more than 35 percent, and almost half of those workers are undocumented. The origins of this wave of immigration corresponded to Womack's arrival at Rogers City Hall in January 1999 for the first of his three mayoral terms.

Now, surrounded by family photos, sports mementos, and a large wooden signature nameplate, his tough pink face implacable above his well-tailored gray suit, the tall, silver-haired mayor sits in his neat office and ponders how Rogers has changed since he first took office in 1998—"a demographic change," he says, "that made a lot of people anxious."

That change, said Womack, was the introduction of a non-English-speaking, unskilled, and uneducated workforce into the peaceful, white, Christian community of more than fifty thousand.

"Ostensibly, these people were taking jobs that others wouldn't do for the same kind of money—you know, for $7 an hour," he says. "They eviscerated chickens for Tyson and other food processors in the area and had fraudulent documents. This clashing of cultures was and is today, in my judgment, a concern to many in the traditional population."

Unafraid to ruffle the Latino community's feathers, Womack bluntly complains about what he believes are its cultural norms and how they conflict with the local sense of propriety. "The Hispanics think it's OK for three or four families to live in one house," he says. "They have multiple cars parked all over the grass, which is just not acceptable. They play loud music and have loud, wild-colored homes—pastel colors, purples, and weird greens—that are atypical and unacceptable. It just degrades the neighborhood."

Bold in his style-and-lifestyle critique, the mayor goes on to ask how a Hispanic working on the line for between $7 and $9 an hour at, say, Tyson Foods or George's, another prominent chicken-processing plant in the area, can possibly provide for a wife and three or four children. "In our society, while there are exceptions, most people have the number of kids that they can reasonably support," he says. "And people in our community wonder. After all, these kids are going to our public schools. They are going to be on free lunches."

Of equal concern, he points out, is that children of uneducated, non-English-speaking parents have more academic problems than those from middle-class, English-speaking homes. "And then your public education system starts being degraded. These problems upset the social balance of the community."

After a moment—is it a split second of remorse or an attempt to pass the buck?—Womack offers an apologia. "Forgive me if I sound like I'm stereotyping," he says. "I'm certainly not. I am just repeating what a lot of people say to me."

Yet the bottom line for Womack, a self-described hard-liner, is a harsh one. "To me, it has been proven that many people who sneak into the country do other illegal things and contribute to the degradation of society," he says, reworking one of his favorite words—*degradation*.

The Womack Solution

For a long while Womack had been searching for a way to check the population of undocumented Hispanic workers moving into Northwest Arkansas. As far as he and many other local residents were concerned, it was not just daunting—it was out of control. Indeed, a 2007 Winthrop Rockefeller Foundation study produced by the Urban Institute announced some astonishing findings: between 1990 and 2000 the state had the nation's fourth-fastest-growing immigrant population (196 percent). Even more dramatic was the fact that between 2000 and 2005, the population of Arkansas grew 48 percent—a figure that surpassed that of any other state—with 51 percent of the state's immigrants, as of 2005, undocumented (whereas the national percentage was 29 percent). Researchers went on to explain that this growth occurred as "a form of labor replacement" for an aging native-born population, with most immigrants settling in Northwest Arkansas, particularly Rogers, Springdale, Fayetteville, and, about forty-five minutes south, Fort Smith.[1]

The Rockefeller study also went to great lengths to explain the economic advantages that this boom of largely unskilled Hispanic laborers has brought to the area. For instance, immigrants positively impacted the economy to the tune of almost $3 billion, and while they cost the state $237 million in 2004 for education, health services, and corrections, this figure was offset by the Hispanic community's tax contributions of $257 million, resulting in a net surplus to the state budge of $19 million—or approximately $158 per immigrant. The study projected that if trends continued in the same direction, by 2010 the positive impact of immigrant spending on the economy could be as high as $5.2 billion.

Still, the general population seems unmoved by—and possibly unaware of—these figures, which underscore how much more robust the local economies have become as a result of this immigration influx. Randy Capps, a researcher with the Urban Institute who has been studying immigration issues in Northwest Arkansas, points out that the Rogers and Bentonville area residents have had to digest major demographic change "virtually overnight." Fifteen or twenty years ago very few rural areas had many immigrants or much diversity. "They had a black-white divide. There was long-standing segregation and other race issues that were partially resolved or not resolved at all," he says. "The demographic was consistent—and almost entirely white. This was true of Northwest Arkansas. But with Wal-Mart bringing vendors in from all over the world and a blue-collar workforce arriving in the area that is mostly Latino, changes were occurring almost overnight. Within ten years, a school district goes from 5 percent to 40 percent Latino, or something like that. And different places respond differently. Sometimes they overreact. Sometimes they are more hostile, other times more open."

Yet as Capps points out, during the height of the economic boom three years ago, there was general recognition that this wave of immigration was connected with the prosperity. "People may not have liked it culturally, but everyone was profiting from it," he says. "I don't know if it's a coincidence, but a lot of this backlash started two years ago at the same time that the economic downturn began."

Mayor Womack had been open about his hostility to undocumented workers and his impatience with the Bush administration for refusing to enact serious legislation to seal this country's borders. Then, serendipitously, a friend in Miami law enforcement e-mailed him information about the Immigration and Customs Enforcement (ICE) program known as 287(g). This federal program, passed by Congress and little known back then, gives local agencies the authority to get involved in ICE matters. "And it was my Booyah moment," he says, referencing the favorite mantra of CNBC's manic host of *Mad Money*, Jim Cramer.

As a result, in November 2006, Womack contacted Department of Homeland Security (DHS) assistant secretary Julie Myers, asking that Rogers be allowed to participate in 287(g). In short order, Bentonville and Springdale climbed on the bandwagon, although Bentonville had evidenced no real criminal issues involving undocumented workers, nor was its Hispanic population of a similar consequence to that of the other communities.

The following August, five police officers from Rogers, five from Springdale, and four from Bentonville traveled to Boston to participate in the five-week program. By October 2007, 287(g) was up and running in Northwest Arkansas, and Rogers has since trained a sixth man. By early 2009, sixty-seven towns and cities in twenty-three states had trained more than 950 officers with the program, and more are on a waiting list. The ICE Web site claims that it has identified more than 79,000 people suspected of being in this country illegally.[2]

As a result of their participation in 287(g), local authorities can now tap immediately into DHS databases to check the immigration status and documentation of people they pick up who are suspected of even minor infractions of the law, such as running a traffic light or littering, and to speedily remand those with fraudulent papers into federal hands for deportation. This has met with significant local resistance. Already, the ACLU has requisitioned all correspondence between local authorities and the DHS concerning ICE, and the Mexican consul in Little Rock has vigorously protested the ICE program.

"The stated purpose of many of the local leaders who signed on to 287(g) is to create a significant deterrent—to make the risk of prison worse— so that undocumented people will voluntarily leave the area before they get caught," says Randy Capps of the Urban Institute. "The way 287(g) is implemented, you give local people some power and they stretch it. They are under pressure from the public, who would like to see a reduction in unauthorized immigration, to respond to the Hispanic population. That's how politics works."

For Womack, 287(g) has from the first seemed like a perfect law-enforcement response. "And I felt, 'My gosh, if you get sued for that, there's no hope,'" he says, "and you might as well accept the reality of the fact that if a federal program passed by Congress didn't work, what more can you do? At that moment I would lose optimism." In the first six months after 287(g) became a fact of life in Rogers, Womack points out, seventy-five people had been set for deportation—"mostly criminal aliens with backgrounds."

On reflection, Womack's commitment and continued fearlessness seem both appalling and refreshing. When we first spoke in January 2007 just after he had applied for 287(g) but before Rogers had been accepted into that program, he had seemed edgier, more defiant, when, almost as a dare, he had told me, "You can write anything you want about me. I don't care."

Now, with 287(g) well under way, the mayor walks with quiet conviction. The chip on his shoulder has shrunken (but not disappeared). While Womack seems even more self-confident, if possible, he is less hostile. He invites me to join him at various meetings, though my schedule makes that impossible, and insists on personally showing me around the Rogers Adult Wellness Center the next morning.

This is thoughtful and also smart, I think. What single thing could better humanize the game of this steely and glibly articulate mayor? And what could be further afield of his immigration position than a big, warm embrace of—and by—the community elders?

Keeping Up with the Joneses—or, at Least, the Jones Center

"Howdy, Mr. Mayor. Good to see you."

"Bless you, Mayor."

Steve Womack may have earned an antagonistic reputation among the Hispanics of Northwest Arkansas, but as he strides through the Rogers Adult Wellness Center—the $7 million, fifty-five-thousand-square-foot facility that he built as a promise to the city's senior citizens—the mostly white, mostly male patrons who are spending the morning here greet him like a conquering hero.

And why not? Thanks to Womack, anyone over fifty who lives in Rogers can, for $25 a year, spend the day at this spanking-new facility, swimming either in its lap pool or thermal pool, which is kept at a beneficial joint-healing 90 degrees; exercising on state-of-the-art equipment; or just finding a card game. "It is revolutionary in terms of how we look at, care for, and accommodate our senior population," Womack tells me as he shows me around, looking sharply elegant in a black suit, pale yellow shirt, and black-and-yellow-striped tie. "It's partly about wellness and partly about stimulating the emotional and social well-being of our seniors."

What is revolutionary about the center? Womack insists that no senior facility like it exists in Arkansas, although in some ways—the sparkling clean, good-sized pools, state-of-the-art fitness equipment, and almost absurd affordability—it seems competitive with the Jones Center in Springdale, the equally impressive, if larger and more complete, facility that inspired it, whether Womack wants to admit it or not. The Jones Center is open to families, children, and the fifty-plus crowd at no charge. But the Wellness Center seems more compact and easier for seniors to negotiate.

"People think of senior citizen centers as places where people come in on walkers and in wheelchairs," Womack says. "And where they eat a low-cost meal, play some pinochle, and drool on themselves. That's not what I had in mind. I wanted a place where seniors could go to do arts and crafts or listen to a speech on Medicare in one end of the building, and then do the physical part in the other. Here they can get into the warm-water therapy pool or lap pool, walk on the track, or use the weight machines. And when they leave, they are better off emotionally, socially, and physically than when they walked in."

"It's an absolutely fantastic facility," says John Swearingen, a local octogenarian and retired broker.

Yet as bright and shiny as the facility is, one demographic seems conspicuously absent. Hispanics may make up almost one-third of the town's population, but on this nippy January morning they are nowhere to be seen at the Wellness Center.

The Land of the Big Red Apple

Rogers, directly to the south of Bentonville and a ten-minute car ride from the Wal-Mart home office on Walton Boulevard, virtually sprang into existence in 1881 as the area depot for the Frisco Railroad. If railway personnel had not decided to bypass Bentonville, six miles away, Rogers would not exist today.

For many years the town, which became a central clearinghouse for the area's apple crops and their byproducts, including jams, jellies, and brandies, was called the Apple Capitol of the World, and Northwest Arkansas became known as the Land of the Big Red Apple. It was home to the largest apple-cider vinegar plant in the world and to acres and acres of farmland stretching across Benton and Washington counties. These orchards produced Jonathan apples, which were used to make apple-cider vinegar, and also Winesaps, Old Fashioneds, red and yellow Delicious apples, and the famed Arkansas Blacks, whose fine flavor and tough skin made them a perfect choice for cold storage in winter. In 1901, Benton County became the leading apple-producing county in the country, and that year the state lawmakers, for good reason, chose the pink-and-white apple blossom as its flower.

By 1919—a peak year—Northwest Arkansas was selling five million bushels of apples at $1 apiece. In 1923 a local orchard owner with a penchant for publicity helped organize the first annual Apple Blossom Festival, featuring a parade of floats decorated with crepe paper blossoms and pretty young girls in gossamer dresses—a modest forerunner, perhaps, of today's Rose Bowl Parade. For months local shopgirls made blossoms from tissue paper by hand and stored them in cartons under their desks until the townsfolk were ready to build their individual floats.[3] The event, spotlighting an Apple Blossom Queen, her court, a flock of apple blossom fairies, and other young people costumed as "Ozark Breezes," "Sunshine Girls," butterflies, trees, and flowers, attracted as many as thirty-five thousand people to the area, some of whom came by rail and were dropped off in the center of town.

But such variables as weather, insect infestation, and blight quickly took their toll on the Ozark apple industry—and its annual celebration. In 1927, the year of the Arkansas floods, the festival was permanently suspended. The drought of 1930 hit the area hard as well, and what remained of the orchards fell into disarray. As farmlands were sold off, the hardier chickens began upstaging apples as an economic force.

John Swearingen, the son of a Rogers country schoolteacher, was born in 1920 and still vividly remembers the Depression. "My grandfather had a little money and some rental property," he says. "We had our own gardens, where we grew beans and potatoes, and we canned goods. We also had a cow, so we sold milk and cheese and scraped by by the skin of our teeth."

Now retired from A. G. Edwards, the brokerage firm, Swearingen recalls the tightness of money back then. By the mid-1930s, he was in high school and worked part-time at a local vinegar plant, pressing apples and bottling vinegar. "We were at the tail end of the apple orchard business," he says. "And I made fifteen cents an hour and considered it a good-paying job. By the way, it was hard work."

Down on First Street, not far from the railway depot, Gary Townzen's grandfather opened Townzen's Barber Shop in 1930 and during the Depression years cut hair for ten cents a head. The average wage was a dollar a day for a ten-hour day, and Gary, now the third generation to operate Townzen's, recalls how hard the family, and the townsfolk, worked to get by. Every Friday and Saturday, the latter of which was known as Grocery Day, Townzen's was open from 7:00 A.M. until midnight. People would drive in from their farms early in the morning, park, and shop, then spend the rest of the day sitting on the hoods of their cars and visiting with friends. After grabbing a bite at the Candy Kitchen, they would come into the barber shop and get a haircut for church the next day.

"And at night," says Townzen, who was born in 1950 but spent years absorbing the stories that his father and grandfather shared with customers, "we'd go down the street to the picture show at the Victory Theater."

On Second Street, the Victory, with rich red velvet curtains, a dazzling lobby chandelier, and ample seating for 750 (in a town of a mere 3,554), opened in 1927. By the 1960s, as box-office receipts tumbled, the movie house, designed by Rogers's most prominent local architect, A. O. Clarke, fell on hard times, and by 1977 it housed a local flea market. Happily, the Victory was restored in recent years and, bolstered by a $150,000 grant from the Walton Family Foundation, among others, was transformed into the Rogers Little Theater. Here, local productions of plays such as Neil Simon's *Brighton Beach Memoirs* and Lerner and Loewe's *My Fair Lady* receive showcases throughout the year.

But during the harsh days of the Depression, the Victory, offering up Hollywood escapism for a dime, flourished while a number of businesses, among them two of Rogers's three banks, failed. To lure customers, local shop owners dreamed up the ploy of offering shoppers tickets for a drawing that took place every Saturday in the town square. All the downtown stores contributed money, and the top prize was a whopping $5—but you had to be on hand to collect it.

"And so there would be so many people there, you couldn't move," says Townzen, a local historian who every year publishes a town calendar for the Feed the Children charity, using historical Rogers photographs from his own collection.

Despite hard times, a number of businesses found their way to Rogers during the Depression era. Tyson Foods was established in Rogers in 1934, and in short order such companies as Pet and Carnation Milk established branches there; the Harris Baking Company and Munsingwear followed.

Throughout the next two decades the town began to move away from agriculture and food and toward industry. But the biggest local boost came in July 1958, four years before the opening of the first Wal-Mart, when Daisy Manufacturing moved to Rogers from Plymouth, Michigan, along with a hundred of its Michigan employees. Daisy immediately hired more than four hundred locals to manufacture the famed Daisy air rifle and BB guns; in the end, the company boosted the local economy enormously.

"The Daisy BB gun factory had as much to do as anything else with this town getting going," says Womack. "In 1958 we didn't have a lot of industry. And Daisy came in here and represented some pretty serious change as to how we were going to look at job recruitment. In fact, we just brought them back home because they were doing their assembly in Mississippi."

Nothing has immortalized Daisy quite as memorably as the 1983 classic movie *A Christmas Story*, based on a memoir by the humorist Jean Shepherd, which revolves around how desperately a boy, Ralphie, covets a Daisy Red Ryder 200-shot carbine-action gun with a compass—a gun he describes as "as cool and deadly a weapon as I had ever laid eyes on." The company still courts significant nostalgic value today, judging by the fact that the Daisy Airgun Museum in downtown Rogers remains one of its most popular tourist attractions. It's interesting, too, that the Rogers City Hall memorializes Daisy's heyday with a striking black-and-white poster of a clean-cut and scrubbed-looking young American boy, all smiles, clutching his Red Ryder.

A Balanced Kind of Guy

When Mayor Womack talks about his childhood in Moberly, Missouri, he is quick to make one thing clear: "A number of my best friends were African American kids." The way he describes it, he and these four black pals were inseparable. "When I had a sleepover, those kids were there. We played ball together, we hung out together, we shared something in common, mainly in sports—we were just friends. Now I can't tell you where these guys are today, but when I was ten, eleven, and twelve, they were just like me. And so I'm at peace knowing that the attitudes that I bring to the table right now about demographic change in our community have nothing to do with prejudice or bias. I'm not a sociologist, I just happen to be a balanced person—a balanced human being."

Womack moved to Rogers in the fall of 1979, after graduating from Arkansas Tech University, in order to get into the broadcasting business. With his father, he established KURM Radio in Rogers, one of the most conservative stations in the area, and dabbled in sales and on-air broadcasting; he also managed the station until 1990, when he left to work with the Army National Guard at the University of Arkansas. At the same time he served as executive officer of the University of Arkansas ROTC program for six years. He left to work as a financial consultant at Merrill Lynch in 1997, serving twice on the Rogers City Council before running for mayor and promising to crack down on undocumented workers. After the 9/11 attack on the Twin Towers, Womack interrupted his term and returned to the military when the reserve unit he commanded, the Second Battalion, 153rd Infantry Regiment of Arkansas's 39th Infantry Brigade, was called to active duty in the Sinai. This marked the first time in the brigade's thirty-five-year history that it was mobilized for overseas duty.

The people of Rogers clearly viewed Womack's patriotism and his commitment to military service as twin assets. In 2002 he ran again for mayor, this time unopposed—and won. He was elected to a third term in 2006.

It's the (Rogers) Economy, Stupid!

When pushed to choose the most important change in Rogers since 1999, when he was first sworn in as mayor, Womack says that it has nothing to do with 287(g) or the increase in the Hispanic population to about a third of the general population of the town.

"No," he says, "the most dynamic change in the community has been totally unrelated to diversity. It has been about economic development."

One way to measure the well-being of a town may be whether or not it can support the ambitions of its young people. John Swearingen, echoing the sentiments of former Bentonville mayor Terry Coberly, notes that the most critical upshot of the Northwest Arkansas boom of the past decades has been this: jobs, good jobs, for perhaps the first time.

"We have two boys who are architects," Swearingen says. "And quite frankly, they wouldn't be living here if we didn't have the increased population that creates business."

For years, Womack explains, most of Northwest Arkansas was considered, first and foremost, a bedroom community of Fayetteville. "A bedroom community means that's where you sleep. But if you want to eat a good meal or go to the theater or shop, you need to leave town and go somewhere else. When I moved out here, we had Waffle Hut and little else."

In fact, folks in Northwest Arkansas used to drive down what they called "the Pig Trail" on their way to Fayetteville or Joplin, Missouri, for good shopping or a first-run movie. Now, Womack says with pride, that is not necessary because Rogers itself has become an upscale destination point, thanks to the Pinnacle Promenade, built right off Exit 83 and open for business in October 2006. It features Dillard's, a large midpriced department store; dozens of smaller specialty shops such as Coach, Sephora, Nine West, and Ann Taylor Loft; and five national sit-down restaurants, including the upscale Chinese chain P. F. Chang's China Bistro. There is also a twelve-screen Malco Theatre, a food court, and across the highway, the

John Q. Hammons Convention Center, an Embassy Suites Hotel, and a series of even more upscale shops. The truth is that this is the kind of mall that is familiar across the United States, from the suburbs of New Haven to the San Fernando Valley and back. There is little about it that reflects the Ozarks region, but in practical terms it enables people in all the small neighboring towns to enjoy the same kind of shopping that exists in every suburb and city in America.

Womack regards the Pinnacle Promenade as not just a convenience for shoppers but also as a revenue stream. "When I took office, my number-one objective was, and remains to this day, to make sure that Rogers is in a position to resource its needs. And that means expanding," he says, the words pouring out precisely and rapidly, as though he has given this speech a thousand times. There are two ways to expand, he says—to raise taxes or to grow the town's tax base. "And I'm an anti-tax guy. I think our taxes are high enough."

The hefty 9 percent sales tax in Rogers, charged to citizens and visitors alike, is, to his way of thinking, something else entirely—desirable and necessary. And so the Pinnacle, now a frequent destination point for shoppers, has emerged as a perfect way to increase the town's tax base. "In Arkansas we live and die by the collection of the sales tax," explains Womack. "That's what funds so many of our operations. And because we're such a growth area, there are demands for things that cost money.

"I am trying to position our city for its future, which was clearly reliant on the expansion of our retail base," says Womack, pointing out that an extra benefit is that while many people visit the Pinnacle every day, it is far enough away so that they don't "necessarily intrude on this side of town— our quiet, quaint, and traditional community." All the action and revenue gathering, even the suddenly congested rush hours and weekend traffic at the Pinnacle intersection, happily occur three miles east and one interstate exit south of the heart of town.

The Hispanics Push Back

Ask people in the Hispanic community, and they will tell you that what 287(g) allows the Rogers Police Department to do is, quite simply, to intimidate both undocumented workers *and* the documented members of their families. Since the program's implementation, Hispanics all now live in

fear that they will be picked up for no reason at all, and their family structure, not to mention their incomes, will be shattered by the deportation of
loved ones.

Jim Miranda, a Hispanic activist and founding member of the Arkansas Friendship Coalition, is no fan of the Rogers mayor. This salesman for
the Dow Chemical Corporation, who is self-educated in the law, thinks
and talks like an attorney. He moved to Northwest Arkansas in 2006 after
traveling to the area and falling in love with it; and he says that he first
became aware of Womack and his perceived hostility toward Hispanics
soon afterward.

"It was in October of 2006 that I first heard him accusing immigrants,
especially undocumented immigrants, of being 'responsible,' as he put it,
for a disproportionate percentage of the crime in Northwest Arkansas. It
piqued my interest. And what really jumped out at me is that he said that
he was not willing to be painted into corners with percentages—and that
he was not willing to defend his words. And I thought, 'Wait a minute,
what is he, royalty?' Since when do elected officials not have to defend their
positions? Of course, he has to."

Womack told me in April 2007 that his police department had, at the end
of the previous year, offered up "numbers" that were pretty astounding:
"Over 50 percent of our most serious drug problems involved illegal immigrants. That 55-plus percent—or something along those lines—participated
in the crime called 'possession with intent to deliver.'" He also noted that
of fifty-seven drug arrests, more than 50 percent involved drug trafficking.

Miranda, deciding not to let Womack's comments slide, started
researching the statistics. "And I was very surprised to learn that not only
was what he was claiming completely *not* true, but also the statistics did
not bear out that any segment of the Hispanic population was responsible
for a disproportionate percentage of crime."

But nobody challenged Womack, says Miranda, until he himself did. He
began chatting up reporters, wrote opinion pieces for local newspapers,
and confronted Womack at a city council meeting on November 14, 2006.

"I stood up and read a twenty-minute speech in which I completely dis-
counted everything he had said, and I cited statistics," says Miranda. "I told
the mayor that good leaders did not govern with anecdotal evidence. I was
polite and respectful, but it was very much a confrontation."

At the time, Miranda, using Rogers's own crime statistics, noted that
78 percent of all arrests in Rogers did not even involve Hispanics. Using

numbers that the Rogers Police Department itself had gathered in 2005, he pointed out that of the 6,946 total arrests that year, only 1,535 were Hispanic, and only 8 of the 50 arrests for narcotics were Hispanic. Considering that the Hispanic population of the town had hit 30 percent, the number of arrests of Hispanics relative to the size of the population was only 22 percent, a figure proportionally lower than for whites.

And how did the mayor respond to Miranda's challenge?

"With silence," Miranda recalls. "And with complete and utter shock. He had not done his homework. To date, he has not done any of his homework. Even so, he was very angry. He told the press, 'He is not even from Rogers. He has no business dealing with Rogers. He needs to stay out of what is going on in this area.' I was surprised that the mayor would take that position. I thought, 'Wait a minute, what are you talking about?' I live in Northwest Arkansas. I do business in Rogers, I shop in Rogers, and everything that goes on in Rogers goes on in my world."

Racism Revisited?

Whatever personal animus Miranda has toward Womack, he does not stand alone in his belief that the crime statistics that Womack touts are seriously distorted. Ray Hernandez, a retired twenty-year member of the Marine Corps who has lived in Northwest Arkansas for almost that long and now teaches English as a second language at Northwest Arkansas Community College, agrees with Miranda. A member of the short-lived Rogers Anti-Gang Task Force, Hernandez says, "The mayor made some public statements saying that the Hispanics were responsible for the rise in crime and that illegal immigrants were the majority of the people in jail. And when we looked at the facts, they did not support any of the statements he was making. And yet he used that fear to push through the 287(g) memorandum with ICE."

The implementation of 287(g) in the fall of 2007 brought with it heightened feelings of persecution and fear among the Latino population of Northwest Arkansas. "We have not had a mass exodus," Jim Miranda says, "but restaurants and other businesses are seeing a serious drop-off in patronage—somewhere between 20 and 30 percent. One reason is that people are afraid to go outside and risk being in public."

Miranda tells the story of one local Hispanic woman who was bitten by a pit bull and lost partial use of her wrist. "But she was afraid to report it," he explains, "for fear that the hospital would report *her* to the police."

Another woman, a permanent resident, took her baby to the hospital and was pulled over for not having a taillight. The traffic police officer asked both her and her male passenger for proof of residency. Because the man did not have papers on him, authorities warned him to be ready to leave the area within four days. Although the passenger was, in fact, undocumented, a decision in the Eighth Circuit Court deemed it unlawful to ask for documentation in a situation such as this. Still, there are repercussions.

"Now this woman doesn't want to go out of the house," Miranda says. "It's a real climate of fear."

In a speech at the University of Arkansas Clinton School of Public Service on May 22, 2008, Miranda publicly discussed ICE abuses as a result of 287(g) and connected the entire immigration debate with what he called "a reawakening of racism." The issue, he suggested, gives the Ku Klux Klan and a number of other white supremacist organizations, all located just forty-five minutes away in the infamous Harrison, "a new sense of legitimacy." As an example, Miranda pointed to a measure proposed by the group Secure Arkansas to limit illegal immigrants' access to public benefits and discussed the history of Rogers. Like Springdale, the town is notorious as one of the former sundown towns that "Negroes" were required to leave by nightfall or fear for their lives.

Gary Townzen, who, as a boy, occasionally sneaked downtown to Klan rallies and hid in the bushes to see if any of his neighbors were in attendance (only once was he able to identify one), also remembers that the nearby resort area, Monte Ne, which was destroyed by floods and no longer exists, used to feature minstrel shows with black performers who were always required to get out of the area before dark.

Additionally, Townzen still keeps in his barber shop a 1932 Rogers phone directory, which offers up a brief history of the town. "And it says in there, 'With a population of 4,637, Rogers can *boast* an all-white community,'" he says.

While the Klan has been largely inactive in Rogers, it organized a rally in nearby Siloam Springs in August 2000. Its target? Not surprisingly, the growing Hispanic population.

These days, as Miranda points out, "The rhetoric once reserved for blacks and Jews is almost exclusively Latino oriented."

Of course, the issue is not just about rhetoric. It is about how punitive and sometimes neglectful the interpretation of the new law, 287(g), has become toward illegal immigrants, especially Hispanics.

Take, for instance, the case of the undocumented Mexican worker Adriana Flores-Torres, thirty-eight, who was arrested on a Friday in March 2008 and thrown into a holding cell for selling pirated CDs at a local flea market (three of her colleagues, who pleaded guilty, were sent home; she pleaded not guilty, however, and was placed in confinement in a Washington County cell). Apparently, nobody at the jailhouse remembered that Flores-Torres, a mother of three who has been in the United States for nineteen years, had been locked up, and after the bailiff left for the weekend, she spent four days in a nine-feet-by-ten-feet cell without food, water, or a bathroom. To survive, she used her shoe for a pillow and drank her own urine. The bailiff found her barely conscious on Monday and sent her to the hospital. When asked what had happened, Jay Cantrell, the chief deputy of the Washington County Sheriff's Department, replied, "[The bailiff] just flat forgot about her. It was just a horrible mistake."

Eventually the pirating charges were dropped, Flores-Torres's lawyer, Charles Kester, said, adding that she is now undergoing treatment for the residual effects of psychological post-traumatic stress disorder. She is also still fighting deportation.

Today Townzen, among the many whites in town who remain resolutely positive about the Hispanic explosion in the area, refuses to be drawn into the fray.

"It has been an issue to a lot of people," he says. "But to tell the truth, I don't see the problem. I'm just not like that. I look at it differently. I've been to Mexico, and I'll be honest with you, [if I were Mexican] I'd do whatever it took to get here. And hey, the Hispanics spend money, too. And they work hard. They love their children just like I do. All they're trying to do is better themselves."

But John Swearingen has more ambivalent feelings about the town's newcomers. "I enjoy their being here and taking over construction and roofing, because they are doing work cheaper for us," he says. "But I don't like the fact that maybe four families live in one house and park their cars everywhere—all around the yard and on the street. So that's a negative effect."

Swearingen, like so many other whites who avail themselves of inexpensive immigrant labor, seems either unaware of, or unwilling to comprehend, the reality of so many immigrants. Surely, it is because they work for lower wages and can barely afford to get by that they share housing—and parking. Surely, in the best of all possible worlds they would luxuriate in their own homes which would feature private bedrooms, multiple baths, and three-car garages.

And the way the community's Hispanics live is not all that bothers Swearingen. "Go to Wal-Mart now, particularly on Sundays, and it's just filled with Hispanic people," he says. "They are quite at home, and their kids are pretty loud, and they have a good time. But we don't go to Wal-Mart on Sunday."

Creating a Climate of Fear

Almost every Latino whom I spoke with in Northwest Arkansas during the winter of 2008 possessed at least one story about the harassment of friends, family, or colleagues—men and women who are being stopped in grocery stores or pulled over on the road, or who must deal with police officers showing up at homes and apartments and entering illegally to make arrests. Although some Hispanics are leaving the community, it is difficult to determine how much that decision is related to intimidation and fear and how much is simply a result of the recent economic downturn in the housing-construction industry.

The repercussions of this climate of fear are endless, says Miranda, who tells of one Hispanic man with a false driver's license whose insurance is now going up because a police officer rammed into the back of his car but, on discovering that the man was undocumented, blamed him for the crash.

"This undocumented Hispanic called me and said, 'It wasn't my fault, but now my insurance is going up. What should I do?'" says Miranda. "As much as my heart pained me to hear this tale, there was basically nothing he *could* do. Without a proper driver's license, he is at risk. It's a trade-off."

Miranda wrote an op-ed piece not long ago about a young Latino mother facing ten to fifteen years in prison—extreme punishment—for possessing fake identification. "And the question I posed is this: Will the University of Arkansas be attacked now? Are the authorities going to throw all those white kids in prison for having false licenses that they can use to go drinking?"

Miranda is convinced that Womack has hitched his career to the issue of illegals because he plans to run for Congress. "Recently, when I voiced my concerns to him," says Miranda, "he agreed that what I said had merit but that there's something called collateral damage. He was telling me that innocent people would be caught up in the mess and their civil liberties compromised. Anyone like that doesn't respect the U.S. Constitution and what it was founded on. How can you argue with that mentality?"

A Man with a Mission

Womack, for his part, denies reports of illegal police searches and frightened families abandoning homes and leaving town before their undocumented loved ones can be picked up and deported. He seems deliberately unfazed by the chaos and terror that 287(g) has unleashed within the Hispanic community.

Like many hard-liners, he also believes that the immigration issue boils down to what kinds of compromise this country can make. "It's futile to think you can accomplish anything meaningful without doing two things," he says. "First, we must secure the border, and second, we need to cut off benefits for people who are undocumented."

Womack refuses to be seduced by the notion of "anchor babies"—children born here to undocumented workers who, by virtue of their birth on U.S. shores, immediately become American citizens. Does Womack seriously think that undocumented workers deliberately give birth in the United States as a means of getting an immigration foothold?

"I don't think that. I *know* that," he says emphatically. "That's why somebody coined the term *anchor babies.*"

The parents' illegality, he believes, should trump any responsibility this country has toward their babies—from bestowing on them citizenship to giving them an education and medical benefits. "The best circumstance is for the kids to be with the parents and for the parents to go back where they came from, taking the kids with them," he says bluntly, adding that if the parents believe that life in the United States is such a precious gift to their offspring, worthy of the sacrifice of separation, then obviously the United States has a constitutional obligation to provide for their education and benefits. "I disagree totally with the concept of anchor babies, period," says Womack. "I don't think this is what the Founding Fathers had in mind—that if you come to the United States of America and have a child, then you're going to be given some automatic right to be here."

And how has Wal-Mart, the motor of the community, responded to the issue?

"I'll answer it this way. I have not had good or bad vibes, one way or the other, from the corporate office," Womack says carefully. "They have not called and said, 'You shouldn't.' They've not called and said, 'We're supporting you.' But I've had key executives at Wal-Mart pat me on the back and encourage me to stay in the fight."

The importance of Wal-Mart to all Northwest Arkansas, including the Rogers community, cannot be underestimated, if you ask Womack, who says, quite simply, that the company has helped put the area on the map, thanks to talented leaders who give of their time and resources. "No better example than Bentonville, where they've given money to the libraries and schools, and they've done a swap for some land and built the town a beautiful park," he says. "And they've done a few things here. They've helped me expand my activity center for kids, and they've pumped money into other worthwhile projects on a year-to-year basis—everything from $2,500 grants for the Little Theater to $250,000 for buying a rescue truck for our airport fire station."

Wal-Mart has also provided seed money for the Rogers Community Support Center, an attempt to help newcomers assimilate. "For instance, we put out a brochure, *Friendly Facts,* in English and Spanish," says Womack, adding that he asked Tyson, a leading local employer of Hispanics, for help but did not get much of a response.

Disappointed by the Bush administration's refusal to even attempt a solution to illegal immigration, Womack knows that tough decisions lie ahead. Yet he does not expect much from the Obama administration either. "I'm totally against blanket amnesty because that just rewards the perpetrator," he says. "And I don't think it is reasonable to assume that we can load up twenty million illegal people and fly them out of the country today. I'll be the first to tell you, if they've got any criminal activity going on whatsoever—if they've been stealing identities or gangbanging or doing drive-by shootings—they have to be dealt with swiftly and effectively. After all, another function of my job is to protect the public peace, health, safety, and welfare of the people that I'm charged with representing."

The mayor says he has a bagful of mail supporting his point of view, and this even from immigrants who believe that everyone else who wants to come here should do as they did—wait in line and do everything legally.

"I can't tell you how many people tell me that they enjoy newcomers coming into the area," says the mayor. "But if these people are trying to escape another culture and do something better for themselves, please don't bring that culture with you, because it creates conflict for us. If you're trying to get away from something, then *why* are you so adamant about re-creating that culture here?"

In a world of grays, this mayor's vision is resolutely black and white. But give the man credit. While most political figures would happily sweep the immigration issue into someone else's office, he is one who is facing the problem head-on and with relish.

"It's all about behavior," he says with sharp chiaroscuro conviction. "If you have to sneak into this country, you shouldn't be here."

On a subject this complicated, the man's self-assurance and bravado seem almost absurd, and yet bizarrely refreshing. At least he tells you what he is thinking. "These people came here one at a time, and they are probably going to have to be escorted out of here one at a time," he insists. "But I'm not a defeatist. I think that we can still make a difference and restore sense to our immigration program. And so that's where I am right now."

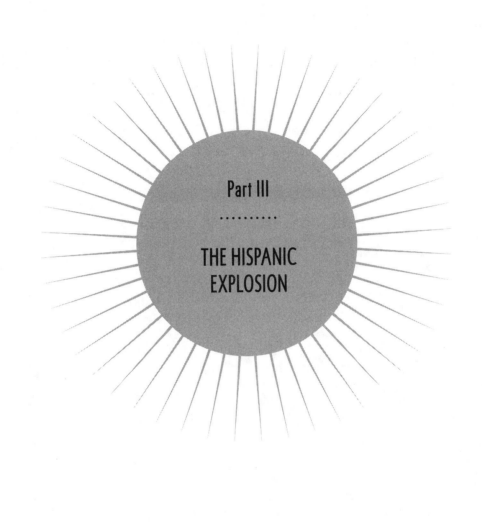

Part III

· · · · · · · · · ·

THE HISPANIC
EXPLOSION

10

Incident at
Bentonville High

....

Ruth and Salvador Bonilla left their home and families in El Salvador
twenty-nine years ago to escape a civil war and gang violence. The couple—good looking and hardworking—remade their life in Los Angeles, but
in 2005, when gangs started seriously to threaten the quality of local public
schools, Sal, a truck driver for a concrete company, moved his family from
the San Fernando Valley to Bentonville. With their three teenagers and two
dogs, they settled into a small but pretty two-story home in a lovely middle-
class, mostly white neighborhood in the northern part of town.

And so it is something of an irony that on a wintry afternoon at the end
of January 2007, the Bonillas' version of the American Dream clouded over
when Bentonville High School authorities accused their son, Krist (pronounced Chris), of participating in a "jump-in," or gang initiation, after he
was found horsing around with six other Hispanic kids in a school stairwell right before classes began. "At his school in California he never, *ever*
got into trouble," Ruth, a petite certified nurse's assistant who works at a
local day care center, says in her small, sweet voice. Sitting at the table in

her cool, pristine kitchen on a sticky August afternoon eight months after
the incident, her eyes, behind thin, gold-rimmed glasses, well up as she
recalls what happened.

Krist, fifteen at the time, stands about five feet ten inches with a burly
frame and the soft, full-lipped face of a cherub. He repeatedly claimed he
barely knew the other boys he was roughhousing with. It didn't matter to
the authorities. Although he had never had a discipline problem at school,
school personnel did not bother to call his parents in to discuss the situation before deciding his fate. Instead, administrators suspended him and
the other kids that very afternoon and then scheduled a formal expulsion
hearing.

Now, between trips back and forth to the barbecue on the family's
back porch, where he is helping his mother grill steaks, Krist, looking
like Everyteen in a white tee and baggy blue jeans, speaks shyly about
the events, which, he feels, marked him as a pariah at Bentonville High.
The ordeal began on a cold Friday morning, he says, when the school bus
dropped him off and he headed to the library, where he usually meets up
with friends. This time they weren't there.

"So when some other kids said, 'Hey, you want to hang out?' I went
with them to the stairwell," Krist recalls. "And we started to play around
and to push and shove like in World Wrestling. Then Officer Steve Vera,
the school's resource officer, came by and said, 'Hey guys, what are you
doing?' And we said, 'Nothing.' The bell for classes was about to ring, so
he let us go."

Krist did not think about the encounter again until that afternoon,
when he was pulled out of his sixth-period class and sent to assistant principal James Swim's office. "And he showed me this videotape of us in the
stairwell, and he was saying, 'Your friends already confessed to me that
this was gang-related activity.' And I was like, 'I don't know what they're
talking about. We were just messing around.' And he started getting mad
because he thought I was lying."

Then Swim began questioning why Krist had been wearing gloves—
this despite the fact that it was an icy January day marked by snow flurries.
"'What's up with the gloves?' he asks me," says Krist. "'I see a lot of Hispanics with gloves.' And I say, 'It doesn't mean anything to me. My mother
bought them for me—it's cold out.'"

"I bought them for him two days before the incident," says Ruth. "At
Wal-Mart."

"If it was a white person or black person wearing the gloves, they would mean nothing," Krist says, assuming, naively, that black students never suffer racism.

The assistant principal eventually allowed him to return to class but later that afternoon informed him that he had been suspended for "gang-related activity." "All in one day," Krist observes wryly.

When Ruth picked her son up from school that afternoon, as she always does, authorities had not yet notified her. Krist explained what had happened, and an hour later school personnel finally phoned, saying that they had a tape of this jump-in and would review it before deciding whether to let the students return to classes; they then asked the Bonillas to come to school on Monday for an expulsion hearing.

"They said one student had told them that it was a gang initiation, but they never said which student it was," Ruth remembers, adding that the principal, Steve Jacoby, was requesting of Gary Compton, the superintendent of schools, that all six Hispanic boys, as well as one girl who had been sitting on the steps watching them, be expelled (the school accused her of being the lookout).

That is when the distraught Bonillas consulted their next-door neighbors, Susie Hoeller, then a Wal-Mart attorney, and her husband, Ted Hoeller, cofounders of the American Center for International Policy Studies.

"The only reason that this expulsion got challenged is that we were there to help them," Susie says. "The school seemed to be saying, 'These people are Hispanic, their English isn't perfect, and so they can be pushed around.'"

In fact, Susie, a tall, slender blond very much in the Scandinavian mold, says that when she walked into the hearing along with another white woman, Lynn Gordy, president of the local homeowners' association in the development where they both lived, the Bentonville High contingent was visibly taken aback. "Jacoby, Officer Vera, and two women were sitting high up—like on a dais—when we came into the room," says Susie. "And they flipped out. They were surprised to see white people."

The Bonillas had brought in their pastor and one of Krist's teachers to testify on his behalf. "And she said to him, 'Can I give you a hug?'" Ruth offers plaintively. "When I asked her, 'Do you think he's a bad kid?' she said, 'No, no, it's a misunderstanding.'"

School authorities, however, were unmoved. At the hearing, they refused to show the families the allegedly incriminating videotape. Two hours after the meeting's conclusion, a spokesman phoned the Bonillas to confirm Krist's one-semester suspension. "There was no due process at all," Ted Hoeller reports.

The situation raised a red flag for the area community at large and for the Hispanic community specifically. It is possible, as well, that an alleged jump-in at Rogers High School in December of 2006, about six weeks before the incident in the stairwell, had helped to create a particularly sensitive and explosive environment. In that case, a teenage girl was reported to have accused a seventeen-year-old Hispanic boy of beating her up as part of an initiation into a gang called the Southside Devils. Authorities at Bentonville High also insisted that Krist and the other boys had fought, but none had been bruised or scratched, and the videotape did not support the story of the punch-up.

The encounter was further complicated when a gang expert from California was called in to express his opinion that the "devil" insignia on one of the Bentonville boys' backpacks unequivocally connected him to a Mexican gang. However, nobody could come up with any criminal acts that either Krist or the other boys (and the girl) were either doing or planning. Nevertheless, local TV stations led with the jump-in story and newspapers made it front-page news. It was as though the fracas had been the rumble in *West Side Story*. (In fact, Sergeant Kelley Cradduck, the Rogers Police Department's gang liaison officer, announced that the boys called themselves the West Side gang or the Westies—a claim that Krist still emphatically denies.)

Jim Miranda, the activist, became involved with the incident only after receiving assurances from Gary Compton, Bentonville's school superintendent, that it was "nothing but horseplay." "That is why I took the public position I did on this incident," says Miranda. "This guy told me, 'You know, Jim, I was raised in the Eight-Mile district of Detroit. I've seen gang activity, and I can assure you there are no gangs in Bentonville and no gangs in the high school. These kids don't have a name; they are not affiliated with anyone, not even a loose-knit group. They are just buds engaging in horseplay.' If they had been a group of white football students with long hair, ripped jeans, and Hollister T-shirts, I guarantee that they would have used the word *hazing* rather than something as nasty as *jump-in*. And it would never have gone past the 'horseplay' stage."

Susie Hoeller makes a similar point by underscoring Bentonville High School's major legal problem: "Its definition of gangs was so vague," she says, "that if white girls had been caught in the stairwell, the incident could have been called a sorority meeting." (As a result of this case, the school has subsequently rewritten its gang policy.)[1]

The Hoellers contacted an ACLU lawyer in Fayetteville and pressured Bentonville High authorities to conduct an open hearing. But two hours before it was set to begin, administrators, finally admitting that the video captured no gang activity, struck a deal with the families. The school agreed to remove the accusation of "gang-related" activities from the students' records and publicly branded the incident "a misunderstanding." In addition, the year-long expulsion for the six other teens was reduced to six months; however, Krist's initial six-month suspension remained as is, for no reason that his family could fathom; nor did the school offer up an explanation. Perhaps administering the same punishment to all the students was more about simplifying the bookkeeping than doling out justice.

Finally, instead of returning to Bentonville High, all seven youngsters were required to attend a special school at a Regional Educational Alternative Program in Rogers, better known as the REAP Academy, for the rest of the spring semester. "'During the period of this expulsion, Krist is not to attend any Bentonville High School sponsored activities nor is the student to be on campus for any reason," Principal Jacoby wrote to the Bonillas on February 13, 2007.

"Even the teachers at REAP said they didn't understand why I was supposed to be a Crip," Krist remembers. "We were all quiet [kids], and they were wondering why we got kicked out."

The REAP regiment, he reports, was "weird" and like a military academy, with a strict dress code that required either white or gray shirts and forbade earrings. "Instructors would scream at you and try to get you to talk back to them so they could make you come back the next semester," Krist says. "And at lunch you have no privileges, and you have to stand up and wait for everybody else to eat before you can."

It says something about the exclusivity of Bentonville High School that Krist came to appreciate REAP. Despite the abundance of rules, he said that here he did not feel as much like an outsider. Also, the class size was small—five kids per class rather than thirty. "And they taught us good," he says. While he still had trouble with geometry, he earned passing grades in his other classes.

Still, as the semester drew to a close and Krist awaited a return to Bentonville High for the fall 2007 semester, it was unclear what credits he would receive from REAP and when, or if, he would be able to graduate.

Stigmatized!

Almost a year after the fact, some, such as Officer Steve Vera, the high school's resource officer, still considered Krist Bonilla part of a "wannabe" gang. But what does that really mean? In a school society where Hispanic boys were made to feel like outsiders and misfits, it seems reasonable that Krist and a few Hispanic friends, including two with whom he bonded after they were all involved in the alleged jump-in, got together. "They formed a clique and gave themselves a name," Daisy, Krist's older sister, told me. "And they wore baggy clothes. But they were not a gang. No way."

What made these boys wannabes as opposed to a clique, a club, a fraternity, or simply a group of friends? Did they plan to make trouble? To destroy property? To paint graffiti on the town square? Since there were no guns, no drug activity, and no plans to participate in anything illegal, what kind of wannabes were they?

Lieutenant Mike Johnson, the public relations liaison in the Rogers Police Department, says that to be considered a wannabe, a teenager must be wearing gang insignias and be involved in petty vandalism such as breaking and entering. "I'd say that 25 percent of our breaking and entering crimes involve young gang members," he says.

Yet the bottom line, as Susie Hoeller expressed it, was this: "The high school's definition of 'gang-related' activity was vague; the offense was not clearly defined; and the evidence was flimsy to nonexistent. Finally the penalty for Krist and the other kids—a semester at what is basically a reform school—was unduly severe."

Perhaps, given the lopsided demographics—only 10 percent of Bentonville's 3,117 students are Hispanic—it is not surprising that the school's Latino students wanted to band together in a clique and have had more trouble assimilating than those in either Rogers or Springdale, which are each between 30 and 40 percent Hispanic. It is also interesting that at Bentonville High, the number of African American students is even smaller—74 in 2009, a mere 2 percent of the student population. (By contrast, Springdale High School has paid tribute to its emphatically multicultural population with a colorful student-painted mural in its corridor, created during a diversity seminar. Entitled *Diversity*, it features drawings of people of all ages, colors, and ethnic backgrounds, some sporting *hijabs*, others turbans and colorful native dress. One figure even wears a kilt and is playing the bagpipes.) In fact, when Jim Miranda interviewed Krist and the five other Latino students involved in the supposed jump-in, all who happen to be American citizens, one boy complained about trying to join a school basketball game but being rebuffed by white kids who said bluntly, "No, you're not one of us." Another resisted taunts such as "Hey, kid, you can't come into our classroom unless you show us your green card."

Krist's anguished father, Sal, after examining the chain of events that his son had been swept up in, concluded, "He was in the wrong place at the wrong time."

Up until this point, the family seemed to have been living the best scenario possible for an American immigrant family. Ruth and Sal understandably wanted to give their kids the education that they did not have. Their eldest, Daisy, graduated in June 2008 from the University of California, Riverside, with a bachelor's degree in history and film and is now back in Los Angeles, working and planning to enroll at a local school for her master's to study advertising and marketing. The couple hope that their sons will choose similar paths, although Daisy, who had developed stronger verbal, academic, and social skills than the boys, seems to have had an easier time integrating into the multicultural world.

In Bentonville, Sal and Ruth experienced a certain cultural displacement, having moved from a familiar primarily Latino environment in Los Angeles to a neighborhood in a town that is much whiter and more isolating. It has taken them time to make friends, and they have not completely understood the way Bentonville High School works, in part because the couple are still not completely fluent in English and in part because the Bentonville community itself has yet to figure out how to successfully communicate with its Latino families and how to integrate their children into its cliquish, mostly white, and sometimes cruel high school environment.

Still, it is telling that after a trip to L.A. for Daisy's graduation, the first time in two years that the Bonilla family had returned to its old hometown, Ruth had difficulty getting on the plane to return to Bentonville and leave her old friends and family. But Sal and the boys couldn't wait to return.

"It was 115 degrees in the San Fernando Valley. It was too hot," Sal said, laughing. Krist, his travails notwithstanding, had clearly grown roots in Northwest Arkansas, too, and displayed a spark of resilience. Besides, he had just gotten his driver's license and wanted to use it.

A Rush to Northwest Arkansas—and a Rush to Judgment

In Northwest Arkansas, which up until a decade ago was an insulated, white, Christian society, locals are finding the extraordinary recent growth of the Hispanic population daunting. "The people here have never really been exposed to folks who are different from them," observes Susie Hoeller. "Some don't even like the Wal-Mart people. There's a resentment factor among these small-scrabble farmers and the average white people who were living here before Wal-Mart and Tyson arrived. There's a real undercurrent of xenophobia among them."

Begrudging the immigrant population clearly makes it easier to blame them for other problems—such as gangs. "Rogers has some serious gang problems with Hispanics and illegals," says Ted Hoeller. "So they want to keep all immigrants out of Bentonville and paint everyone with the same brush."

The alleged jump-in, the Hoellers believe, stems from an unspoken desire in Bentonville to discourage Hispanic families from moving into its community, which has a significantly smaller Latino population—it was 8.5 percent, according to a special 2005 U.S. Census, and probably has grown since then—than either Springdale or Rogers. Bentonville, Ted believes, wants to keep that differential intact.

The high school's insistence on punishing the seven Latino teens so severely for this "misunderstanding" in the stairwell seems, on one hand, curiously out of synch with Bentonville's diversity efforts both at the home office and in terms of the yearly Multicultural Fair and the religious sensitivity that the town had been displaying during the holidays. Was the suspension of these boys just a way of saving face? Or a means of placating white families alarmed by incendiary local newspaper headlines suggesting that gangs had infiltrated the school?

For Compton, the issue has less to do with prejudice and more with the social status that money bestows. "The playing field needs to be flattened," he admits. "One out of every four children in this district comes from poverty—and that means a family of four earning less than $21,000 a year. When all your white people are rich and all your Hispanics are poor, you are going to have some issues. Most of those are driven by economics. 'You can wear that; I can't afford it.' 'You drive that car; I've got to drive this.' Remember, in this town, if you want to make money, it's there to be made." In other words, money, not color or creed, is the great equalizer—exactly the observation that Rana Peterson made about her own high school class in 1994 and 1995.

Compton pauses for a moment. "I think the Hispanic population in our community wants to succeed," he says. "They're here to become successful. In public schools, by the way, the illegal immigration issue is a nonfactor. If you show up at our door, I don't care who you are, we educate you."

Yet teens whose parents earn hourly wages on assembly lines or in construction generally find the playing field that Compton talks about to be bumpy and rutted. "The girl involved in the altercation at Bentonville High was being called a 'trashpicker' by the white girls at school," says Susie Hoeller. And this was despite the fact that Bentonville High had already instituted a Multicultural Club. ("They just make posters and say the Pledge of Allegiance in Spanish and Laotian," says Krist derisively.) The school also regularly holds diversity seminars for students.

Even so, the teens self-segregate at lunch, with the Hispanics, African Americans, Marshallese, Laotians, and whites all, for the most part, sitting separately. (When asked whom he was most angry with, Krist said without any hesitation, "Officer Vera, because in the lunchroom at school, all the whites are *here*, and in *this* little corner are the Spanish. And the place where Officer Vera stands is right here by the Spanish." Whether or not Krist had misperceived and misinterpreted Vera's actions, the boy felt certain that the resource officer had been looking to find fault with the Latinos.)

Jim Miranda says that he, too, has discovered prejudice in a most disturbing and unexpected place—at home. "My own child reminds me of it. Her mother is white—Norwegian and Greek—and both my parents were full-blooded Mexican," he says. "She has come home and told me, 'Dad, I *hate* those Mexicans at my school. They're all nothing but gangsters.' 'All of them?' I asked. 'Do you know that they're *all* Mexican? And *all* gangsters?' 'Well, who cares? What's the difference where they're from?' she replied. This is my *own* child who has grown up in a home where we talk about these things—where skin color and civil liberties are discussed around the dinner table. I'm glad she comes to me to dispel this mythology, but it breaks my heart to hear that this is her perception."

And when Miranda reminds his daughter that she is half-Mexican, she tells him that she does not have a problem with it. What she dislikes are "those Mexican kids *at school* who all hang around together." Miranda then takes her through the reasons why that may be. "I ask her, 'Do you think some of them may feel uncomfortable?' 'Yes,' she answers and adds, 'A lot of my friends make bad jokes about them being beaners.' And then I ask, 'Don't you think they hang out together because they don't want to feel different? They don't want to hear those labels?' Then she says, 'Yes, Dad, I guess you're right.'"

In this otherwise harmonious community, why should students generally prefer separation—and segregation? Does it have to do with the simple comfort factor—the birds-of-a-feather syndrome? Or, rather, with the growing polarization in the community over how to handle undocumented Hispanic workers? Is it general intolerance of students who are slow to assimilate? Perhaps, as Superintendent Compton suggests, it is really about prejudice by those who are "cool" (read: well off) against others who wear the wrong clothes and whose mothers chauffeur them to school because the family owns only one car. Or could students be taking their cues from the examples set by the schools themselves—from the attitudes of resource officers such as Steve Vera (who are, in fact, employed by the local police departments) all the way up to the principal?

The Gang's All Here—or Is It?

Bentonville is not alone in its increasing anxiety about gangs. The new ethnic diversity across the United States has created numerous alienated subcultures in nonmetropolitan America. "Many small towns and rural areas are experiencing gang problems for the first time," say James C. Howell and Arlen Egley Jr. in their piece "Gangs in Small Towns and Rural Counties," published in the *National Youth Gang Center Bulletin* in June 2005.

In his seminal work *Bowling Alone*, the sociologist Robert D. Putnam discusses the importance of what he calls "social capital." "Researchers have come to believe that social capital—individuals connected to one another through trusting networks and common values—allows for the enforcement of positive standards for youths and offers them access to mentors, role models, educational sponsors, and job contacts outside the neighborhood," Putnam writes. "By contrast, the absence of positive norms, community associations, and informal adult friendship and kin networks leaves kids to their own devices. It is in such settings that youths are most likely to act on shortsighted or self-destructive impulses." He then adds, "It is in such settings too that youths are most prone to create their own social capital in the form of gangs or neighborhood 'crews.'"[2]

Still, Howell and Egley Jr. caution community leaders not to jump to conclusions or misjudge their teen populations. "Even if local youths are displaying gang symbols such as the colors of big city gangs, this alone does not necessarily signify a genuine gang problem. Local groups of youths often imitate big city gangs, generally in an attempt to enhance their self-image or to seek popularity and acceptance among their peers. Furthermore, although community officials and/or residents may encounter episodic or solitary signs of gang activity in an area (e.g., graffiti, arrest of a nonlocal gang member, and other isolated incidents), absent further conclusive and ongoing evidence, this is not necessarily indicative of an 'emerging' gang problem that is likely to persist."

Yet law enforcement authorities of Northwest Arkansas have embraced the notion that gangs are infiltrating the towns—and especially their Hispanic communities. The Rogers Police Department's Lieutenant Mike Johnson sets forth two typical incidents. First, a gang in June of 2008 broke into more than thirty cars in a middle-income housing subdivision on a single evening, stealing stereos and whatever valuables they could carry off. During the next two days, the perpetrators followed up with similar activity.

The second incident involved the same teenager who, Johnson says, had beaten up the girl in the Rogers jump-in. In 2007 the boy had guided a crew of six guys and girls who vandalized local schools and businesses, doing about $30,000 worth of damage in one evening. Then in July 2008 the police picked him up for painting Southside Devils tags on local buildings. Will this send him to jail? "He's still under provision of the juvenile court," says Johnson. "But our guys are keeping their eyes on him."

Recently Wes McBride, the executive director of the California Gang Investigators Association, told the *Morning News* that a former partner of his during his career as a police officer had retired here and informed him about local gang activity. "When you see these small towns with poultry industry," said McBride, "they bring cheap labor in the form of immigrants. [Mara Salvatrucha] follows the cheap labor market." ("Mara Salvatrucha" is the umbrella term for a network of loosely connected gangs that originated in L.A., spread throughout Central America and the United States, and are involved in activities from drug smuggling to contract killings.) "You don't notice at first, but then they start fighting, in particular the Salvadorans and Mexicans." McBride claims that this kind of rivalry, which has also infested Los Angeles, "goes beyond fistfights. Gangs are criminal entities, and they will destroy a neighborhood."

In early 2007, at about the same time that the Bentonville "jump-in" created community buzz and gave local parents anxious palpitations, the Rogers Police Department resurrected its Crime Suppression Unit and made sure that all its officers attended gang training programs with police departments in Dallas, Oklahoma City, and Tulsa. Since then, law enforcement has been searching out gang members with the same kind of ferocity that pigs sniff out truffles. "Recently two men came back from Chicago and others went to Indianapolis," says Lieutenant Johnson. "I don't want our guys to just read books. I want them to go into the trenches; that's where they'll learn."

In fact, Rogers has been tracking suspected gang members through a database since 2005. By 2007, according to this database, more than 300 crimes were tied to gangs, and more than 40 gangs and 49 subsets or hybrids had been identified.[3] In March 2008, local agents estimated that Rogers included about 200 people in its database while Springdale had 150, with almost all major national gangs represented—long-familiar names such as the Crips, Bloods, Aryan Brotherhood, and Latin Kings, and others such as MS-13, Folk Nation, Mexicans Causing Panic, and Sureno 13. All ethnic types are represented as well, from white supremacists (including Ku Klux Klanners) to Asians, from Hispanics to blacks.

Road Rage or Gang Rage?

A local murder case, at first reported as road rage, also fanned gang suspicions and racist fears in the area. Three Hispanic perpetrators, while driving through the nearby town of Lowell in May 2006, pulled a pistol on a white man in a truck and shot him to death. Soon authorities began calling it a gang initiation, giving as evidence the fact that the man in the front seat, Manuel "Smokey" Camacho, a Mexican, had tattoos on his arms, which they took to indicate that he was part of the gang called Sureno 13; what's more, because he handed the pistol to Serafin Sandoval-Vega, age twenty-one, the accused shooter in the backseat, who had no tattoos, it was assumed that Sandoval-Vega was committing the murder to prove himself.

Feelings within the community were so inflamed by the news reports that when attorneys began interviewing prospective jurors in July 2008, the defense team could find no more than two people who were not yet certain of the men's guilt. The attorneys renewed motions for a change of venue but feared that the court might seat some of these jurors who had already formed opinions.

Meanwhile, Roxana Hernandez, a young woman who had been in the car with Camacho and Sandoval-Vega—and who, according to the *Morning News*, was "known to police as mouthy and disrespectful"—had agreed to testify for the prosecution in exchange for leniency.[4] Among the points she had agreed to make was that Camacho had wanted to unify all Latino gang members throughout the state.

Although Hernandez hardly sounds like the most trustworthy witness, the men's attorneys, fearing that under Arkansas statutes their clients could be convicted and sentenced to death, entered a plea bargain, and on July 11, Camacho and Sandoval-Vega tearfully pleaded guilty to the charge of capital murder. Both were immediately sentenced to life in prison without parole. The following day police released Hernandez and dropped all charges against her. "She sounded happy, but I am concerned for her safety," said her defense attorney, Reggie Koch.[5]

After the fact, Camacho's lead defense attorney, Kent McLemore, said, "Tim [Buckley, his colleague] and I are more convinced than ever this was not a gang-related act. It certainly was not a gang initiation."

Whatever the truth of this incident, as headline news for months it trumpeted the imminent presence of gangs, as though Northwest Arkansas were East L.A. The case also helped to deepen already-existing animosity toward the area's expanding Hispanic population. "The bad thing about Northwest Arkansas is that, when a Hispanic commits a crime, people assume all Hispanics are criminals," said Hilda Gomez, a third-generation American who has lived in Northwest Arkansas for more than a decade and is president of the local chapter of the League of United Latin American Citizens.[6] "Around here, we have to be thrown in one bucket no matter who we are."

Ask any ten community leaders in Northwest Arkansas about gang activity in the area, and you will receive ten wildly different and sometimes contradictory responses. Gomez is one who is seriously concerned. She believes that gang members are migrating here from California and that kids who are not being given enough family, school, or community attention may be drawn to the notion of a gang community.

Ray Hernandez says that when the Rogers Anti-Gang Task Force was active, the group had two mandates. The first was to dispel a local myth that gangs were only Hispanic, because, as he says, "There are some Laotian gangs and black gangs in the area." (Still, the Rogers Police Department claimed that 68 percent of reported gang members are Latino and most of these are Mexican.) And the second mandate was to educate people in the community about the difference between serious gang activity and mere hoodlumism.

"I think it's, in part, about the level of organization," Hernandez says. "When you're talking about gangs that are nationwide or international, they have a high level of organization and recruiting practices that are better than our military's. Also, they have initiations that are very violent. Neighborhood hoodlums, on the other hand, are young people who take advantage of criminal activity that happens to come along, rather than being more purposeful about it."[7]

Hernandez owns his own company, Ray Hernandez Marketing, which consults with local businesses about how to market to Hispanic consumers. He says that in Northwest Arkansas authorities have already seen what they call "tags"—signage that gangs leave behind, including letters or symbols with which they allegedly wink at or send messages to each other. "We suspect that some families may have relocated here from California or New York to get their children out of gang activity, but when they come here, the kids tag because they're still identified with their group. Or sometimes kids just tag with their friends. And some of our gang experts who were very knowledgeable about the differences between real gang members and 'wannabes' tried to pass that on to local authorities in order to set aside some of the community's fears and be truthful about what gang activity really was."

So what kind of gang activity exists in Northwest Arkansas? Hernandez says that people in their mid-twenties and thirties are the primary source of drug activity but that data and anecdotal evidence both suggest that gangs are taking advantage of high school dropouts and others who fail to find work or integrate into society. "One effort of the task force was to figure out a way to help the school systems embrace these kids and their ethnicity," he says. "And to get the Boys Club, the YMCA, and other organizations in the area involved in offering the kinds of activities that would give them something to do so that getting involved in gangs wouldn't be nearly as intriguing as it might be otherwise."

Meanwhile, the area's police are instituting the Gang Resistance Education and Training program (GREAT) in the public schools. In March 2008 the Benton County sheriff's office began teaching it at Old High, a middle school in Bentonville. Springdale police are bringing GREAT into its middle schools as well.

Kathy O'Kelley, the Springdale police chief, has suggested that authorities need to direct their programs to children as young as twelve and in the sixth or seventh grade. "Schools are key," O'Kelley has said. "We need to distract these kids, teach them life skills. How do you say no, when you are wanting to look like your friends?" She pointed out that school officials may shy away from calling kids gang members for fear that they may simply be trying to copy hip-hop culture.

The Clothes Doth Proclaim the Man—or So Say the Cops

Since the alleged jump-in that originally sent Krist Bonilla's life into a tailspin, local authorities have come to view certain student attire as an important gang tip-off. "They said that the clothes my friends have on, like the South Pole label, have something to do with gangs," says Krist with a shrug and a half-amused smile. Pants that are too baggy and backpacks bearing devil insignias also are taken as gang signs.

Then there is the matter of Bentonville High School's glove policy, which sounds like the stuff of a *Saturday Night Live* sketch. "A friend walking with us only had one glove on because he had lost the other," Krist offers. "And they were trying hard to kick him out, saying it was a gang style. Now they've changed the color of the gloves you're allowed to wear—you can't wear black or blue. Another friend bought gloves with all different stripes—rainbow gloves. She got in trouble, too."

On the other hand, everyone concerned with gang activities issues the caveat that copying gang or hip-hop culture by wearing gloves, painting gang graffiti signage, or getting tattoos does *not* necessarily signify gang membership; just as likely, these kids are desperate to belong, to find a group of their own in which they will have social capital. Still, such externals seemed to play a powerful role as to why Bentonville High School went forward with its jump-in case.

Sergeant Cradduck, who has set himself up as the local gang expert, says that gang researchers are sensitive to cultural mimicry. They, in fact,

call the line between crime and the cultural attraction of rap and gang par-
aphernalia "the tipping point." "Kids realize that together 'we are strong,
we have influence,' and they turn that corner to being a full-fledged criminal," Cradduck said.[8] "Gangs are not simple. It's a convoluted, confused,
complex dynamic."

And yet every generation, it seems, has its own bad boys—boys wearing
motorcycle jackets and riding Harleys; boys wearing zoot suits; or boys,
influenced by rap styles, wearing do-rags, tattoos, and piercings. By the
definition that Bentonville High uses, thousands of innocent teens across
the country would be charged with "gang activity" when their only crime
just might be bad fashion sense.

Rapping for a Fair Shake

Al "Papa Rap" Lopez, one of the area's most visible activists, has for years
served as a conciliatory presence in Northwest Arkansas. In January 2008,
he dismissed the notion of serious gang activity among middle school and
high school students in Northwest Arkansas, suggesting that the issue was
merely a scare tactic by authorities who were beginning to bear down on the
immigrant population; however, by June he had changed his mind. In five
months ganglike activity had increased, subtly but markedly, among kids.
But he says, "Gangs aren't arriving here. They are being *created* here—by us."

Lopez, during his earlier tenure as student relations coordinator for the
Rogers school system and, now, for Springdale, has emerged something of
a walking, talking antigang antidote. This stocky, goateed bear of a man,
who moved here from Puerto Rico in 1994, is—with his thick dark glasses,
wild print shirts, and all manner of geeky hats, from porkpie to baseball to
do-rag—almost as well known for his fashion idiosyncrasies and rap songs
as for his inside work on behalf of the Hispanic community. (Over the
years he has sat on numerous boards and consulted with Wal-Mart, Tyson
Foods, the Governor's Office on Minority Affairs, the Department of Education, and a wide array of local organizations such as Just Communities,
the Hispanic Women's Organization, and the Jones Center.)

But most of all, Lopez, exuding a jolly, trusting presence, has earned the
ear of students, Hispanic and otherwise. Give him a conga drum, a bagful
of percussion instruments, and a group of angry or scared kids of all colors,

and within minutes he has them dancing, kissing, and hugging one another and singing his signature rap-lite ditty "Que Pasa?"—or "What's Up?"

Perhaps because of his ability to create multicultural lovefests wherever he goes, Lopez has, since 1994, been working with kids of every size and ethnic stripe on a series of local public service announcements (PSAs) concerning the dangers of drinking, reckless driving, and smoking, and on the benefits of diversity and extending friendships across ethnic, religious, and color lines. Eventually the PSAs became the substance of his signature syndicated TV show, *Que Pasa*. "I guess it could be seen as a giant fun bilingual PSA," he says, "targeting parents and kids with a positive message of acceptance and celebration of diversity."

Recently he has been teaching children a rap song with a simple, pointed antigang message:

> G-A-N-G—*and that spells "gang."*
> *But that ain't for me*
> *Because I love my in-di-vi-du-a-li-ty.*

During the spring of 2008, Lopez dealt with junior high school kids between the ages of twelve and fourteen who told him, for the first time, "Hey, Papa Rap, you're disrespecting us because you say we're *not* in a gang."

That semester middle school students from Rogers and Springdale showed up at local parties and public dances in order to challenge each other, the kids from one school taunting and fighting the kids from the other. "And that is happening right now," he says. "The only reason I have not found this to be a threat is that we called the parents." Educating parents, he believes, is the most important way to keep children in line.

Lopez wants parents to be clued in regarding teen dress codes for school. "What, in fact, can a parent do with a junior high kid who's wearing gang clothes and feeling cool? The baggy pants, the bandanna, could all be from TV," he says. "Also, the kid needs to be able to tell his parents, 'Hey, a police officer today thought I was part of a gang.' If there is *not* more communication between parents and children, in ten years there will *really* be a gang problem here.

"And we're seeing too much emphasis on how the kid dresses. We need to say, 'I don't *care* how you dress as long as you're a good person.' If you're out there tagging, painting graffiti, fighting, and selling drugs, then that's a different story."

Parents may be the key to stopping their children's antisocial or criminal behavior, but Rogers has tried to reach out to them, says Lieutenant Johnson, with little success. "Many parents have been unresponsive," he says. "We can't seem to get them involved. I've done personal seminars with different groups, but not a lot of people want to get involved unless the organizations are well known and traditional parent-teacher organizations. These parents have busy lives. Sometimes they work long and different hours. Parents don't have dinner with their kids anymore; they're not as involved."

But Lopez doesn't buy these excuses. He regards local gang-prevention programs as woefully inadequate. "Now there's a window of opportunity, and the police departments could be helpful, but they are not," he says. "If I'm a police officer, why do I *not* have time to call a parent to see if he can help? But the police say they don't have time. They also seem to want to inflate the figures." Higher crime statistics, he points out, can potentially attract more federal funds.

"And how many neighborhood watches do they have in Hispanic communities?" he asks. "None. Two phone lines exist here in Rogers to report crime in Spanish, but they aren't being promoted in Spanish neighborhoods. And if you call 911, nobody knows about them either. So do authorities *really* want Latinos to report crime and support law and order?"

Meanwhile, Lopez says, tales abound of local police surfing MySpace, looking for videos of kids making gang signals with their hands. "One of them supposedly made a *W* to signal he was a member of the West Side Gang. It's like sign language. 'You'll know by my underwear what gang I belong to.' So I started to watch my hands. My hands are from the Papa Rap gang—they are signs of peace. I want kids to know I know about the signs. And how can I turn this gang into a 'good' gang? Can I find mentors for the kids? Can I turn this boy's thinking around to help him do something positive in the community?"

Not long ago a seven-year-old elementary school student in Lopez's school district, assigned to take a photo at home and then write about it, brought in the image of his elder brother, nine, making a gang signal with his hands. "And the teacher asked me if she should call the police," says Lopez. "No, I told her. 'Let the kid write his essay. Celebrate him and see what he knows. Then bring in the parents and the older child, and let them all talk about it.'"

For Lopez, the bottom line is that both schools and parents need to work together to help their children. "I tell parents, 'You need to ask questions and come to school and tell us if things are wrong. You need to help us be an agent of change,'" he says. "My job is to work for the future. If we embrace these children, they will be ours forever."

A Compassionate Counselor, a Cynical Eye

One man in the Hispanic community who is convinced that the gang issue is a nonissue is Carlos Amargós, the rangy young student relations coordinator and community liaison in the Rogers school district, who also happens to be Lopez's son-in-law. "I know what a gang is, and I haven't seen it in Rogers," he says with conviction. "Besides, a gang member is not going to come to school unless he is selling drugs."

Amargós believes that the police are creating unfounded fear in the community. "Yeah, it's their beans and rice, as we say in Puerto Rico," he says. "It's their food. They need to create problems so that they can get more money in federal funding. Three years ago I said it, and they got the funding. We need to start talking the truth. If we have three or five or ten people in a gang, I say, 'Let's get the Latino community leaders and go talk to them.' After all, [if gangs are here, and if you can find them] it doesn't just affect the Anglos; it affects everyone. Sure, there may be gang members in this area trying to recruit teenagers, but that doesn't mean we have a gang problem."

When I ask him about the 2006 gang initiation at Rogers High School, Amargós dismisses it out of hand, insisting that it was merely a parking-lot fight between two teenagers over a girl; the girl was eventually scratched up by another girl. "I know the people," he says adamantly.

So who is telling the truth? And who actually knows the truth?

For Amargós, the way in which community leaders approach young people is crucial to the teenagers' success, especially the most unruly ones. Schools must construct summer and afternoon programs, he says, to keep potential troublemakers busy and to give students a sense of community. During the spring 2008 semester, he organized a wide-ranging group of Latino kids to put together a campaign encouraging students to study for their literacy exams. The team created posters, T-shirts, and PSAs on local radio and television to encourage teenagers to do well. "It was awesome," he says. "We had some really tough kids there who felt part of that group. And you know what happened? The school's literacy scores went up."

Amargós says he manages to develop a rapport with the angriest and most disenfranchised students. "They basically say, 'Give me respect, and I'll do anything for you guys.' Sure, there are some who'll always do bad things, but instead of pointing fingers and making them feel like criminals, I say, 'Hey, I know you're not going on the right path. Come under my wing, and I'll guide you.'"

A Generation of Dead-End Kids

It is a fact that too many Hispanic students now find themselves dead-ended by the new 287(g) program penalizing those who are undocumented. One major problem, which few community leaders address, is the hopelessness that so many Hispanic kids feel. Right now only 10 percent of Latino teenagers in Roger go on to college, Amargós says, because if they were brought into the States illegally by their families at young ages, they are ineligible for most federal and nonfederal aid. So while they may dream of climbing out of the ghettos and becoming doctors or lawyers, astronauts or presidents, unless they can earn college degrees, their futures are limited to construction, housecleaning, or the poultry lines, just like their parents. "Most of these kids didn't have a say about whether or not they came across the border," says Amargós. "We're punishing them for something that's not their fault."

We are also making sure that they remain ghettoized. And without possibilities.

At this moment 90 percent of Hispanic teenagers in Northwest Arkansas who graduate from local high schools find their futures limited, no matter how bright they are or how good their grades were. They have, Amargós suggests, few choices between the extremes of either working at Burger King for $5.15 an hour or selling drugs for a gang for $2,000 a week. (A local law enforcement officer rebuts his information. "No street vendor makes that kind of money selling drugs in Northwest Arkansas," he says.)

"I love this country, but the immigration laws need to be fixed tomorrow," Amargós says. "These young people are the support of our great nation, and we are treating them like criminals."

When I ask him if he thinks cracking down on gangs, imagined or not, is yet another way for whites to persecute Hispanics, he laughs. "Let's put it this way. We're in the South. You know the story."

Is this not reverse racism? And wasn't the story about the whites and blacks? "Well, it's like they say," he explains, "the Latino is the new black. But it will change because the culture will change."

And at Rogers High School, how do the ethnic varieties mix? "We don't have the fights we saw ten years ago because you're white and I'm Latino," he says. Today kids band together according to interest and regardless of ethnicity—preppies hang with preppies; and athletes, smart kids, and nerds each band with like-minded friends. "And it will get even more integrated with the kids coming up," says Amargós. "After all, some of our elementary schools are 80 percent Latino."

What is so unusual is that even with their striking population explosion, the Hispanics of Northwest Arkansas are finding themselves, like the early American colonists, victims of taxation without representation. This may be partially self-imposed because, as of July 2009, few Latinos have even run for office, and none have won. Still, despite the large Latino population in the area and the fact that in both Rogers and Springdale, more than a third of the schoolchildren are Hispanic, not even one Hispanic has ever sat on the school boards of Rogers, Springdale, or Bentonville until 2008, when Eddie Cantu was appointed to fill a vacancy on Springdale's board. And not one Hispanic has sat on the city council of any of these towns. "We still don't have the kind of population that can win an election," Amargós explains. "A very small number of our people are able to vote and put somebody in a position of influence. We're not there yet."

Then he repeats what has become a Latino mantra: "But it will change; it will change."

The Outsider

Krist Bonilla, in the post-jump-in phase of his schooling, continued to feel stigmatized for a long while. The impossibly shy young man had been hanging out primarily with his younger brother, Eric, under their mother's watchful eyes. Yet the boys complained to their parents that even after returning to Bentonville High from the Regional Educational Alternative

Program (REAP), the resource officer, Steve Vera, continued to follow them around, sticking to them like gum to Krist's sneaker.

Worse, in the fall of 2007, not long after returning to school, Krist was inadvertently drawn into a second incident. This time an African American student whom he did not know jumped him from behind and slugged him in the eye. Perhaps it was asking too much of a sixteen-year-old to refrain from fighting back, and Krist did not; his eye bleeding, he jumped into the fray until a police officer pulled them apart. And the one unfortunate question he asked his opponent, the question that Vera later pounced on, was: "Are you a Crip or a Blood?"

Krist simply didn't think before he spoke, said his sister, who picked him up from school. "He was pretty beat up, and he was bleeding all over. And he was crying and totally upset. 'Now Mom's going to throw me out of the house,' he kept saying to me."

The school decided to suspend Krist for ten days because Vera, who came onto the scene of the fight well after it had begun, nevertheless insisted that the situation was gang related. Perhaps this is why he hammered away at Krist with his questions.

"He kept asking, 'Where are the other kids? Who are the others?'" says Sal. "Vera made such a big deal of it that Krist told him he had been a gang member in California." Worse, the officer had asked the boy so many times if he was a gang member that Krist—in youthful exasperation and without an adult advocating for him—replied, "Not yet!" When authorities later challenged him about why he would, in fact, say that, the frustrated young man exploded, "Because you keep asking the same thing."

His father had words with Vera as well. Boiling over with anger about this incident and the alleged jump-in, Sal warned the resource officer not to involve the other Hispanic kids who had been part of the first encounter; they had no play in this at all. He also ordered Vera to stop shadowing his sons. The warning, he later reported, seemed to have worked.

In the end, Krist was fortunate as well. A teacher and students had witnessed the attack, and when the incident went to the city court, they wrote letters explaining what they had seen and heard—that the other boy had hit Krist without provocation after mistaking him for someone else. Krist was vindicated.

"Everything eventually went fine," Sal reports, adding that after the court hearing he shook everybody's hand except Vera's. Small gestures sometimes satisfy in a big way.

As for the student who attacked Krist, school authorities told the Bonillas that the boy was eventually expelled and his family had moved from the state. Even though this incident brought up new questions about Krist's behavior and associations, there have been no subsequent incidents linking him to gangs or any other questionable activity.

Nevertheless, almost a year after this second pummeling, Krist's eye still seems slightly smaller and the eye socket more sunken in than it had been. These encounters had a cumulative emotional effect as well, deepening Krist's timidity and, for many months, compounding his isolation and discomfort at school.

"He feels so in danger there," his mother said. "He thinks they're looking to find something with him." He confided to her that he had wanted to ask a girl out on a date but was fearful because now he had a reputation as a "bad boy."

For the remainder of the school term, Krist pretty much kept to himself. After school he played football, basketball, and video games with his brother. Occasionally he mowed the Hoellers' lawn and walked their Chihuahua when they were out for long hours. And he loped about with the Bonillas' two dogs, Junior, a German shepherd, and Kikee, also a Chihuahua.

As much value as Krist found in REAP, it did not transform him into a motivated student. He pulled Bs and Cs in most of his classes, but with an F in geometry he was ineligible for the football or wrestling teams. Back at Bentonville High the following October, he began working with a math tutor, but Ruth, the worried mother hen, now kept him on a short leash, unwilling, even, to let him take an after-school job for fear that he would fall into bad company. Later she relented, and Krist found work at Taco Bell. But by summer he was again looking for a job and doing odd chores for the family's pastor and for neighbors. But he was never hired for the kind of sustained job that required him to show up every day.

In the end, the two incidents at Bentonville High and the semester-long banishment to REAP took a severe toll on Krist, making him feel like a permanent outsider at school. Psychologically, he never seemed to completely regain his footing, either socially or academically. I wonder what would have happened if he had not been suspended and sent away. Would he have tried out for the wrestling team, which the coach had been encouraging him to do? Would he have won a place on it, which might have given a boost to his self-esteem and provided the kind of built-in sports camaraderie from which multicultural friendships could have been born?

Instead, early in 2009, a semester short of graduation, he dropped out, permanently turning his back on the unconquerable mysteries of Pythagoras.

After hanging around the house for a few months, comforted only by his dogs and his loyal younger brother, Krist finally perked up. Rejecting the idea of cooking school, which his mother had been lobbying for, he pierced his ears and began spending every free moment with a pretty local high school girl. His parents bought him a car and helped him secure a job as a pressman at the *Morning News* in Springdale—his first serious full-time work. Despite their entreaties, however, Krist seemed indifferent to the idea of finishing school until his mother refused his repeated requests that she cosign a loan for newer, better wheels. After much back and forth, Ruth told him she would do it on one condition only: that he earn his GED. Nothing less than the prospect of a shiny new auto prompted Krist to enroll in a program at a local community college to get his high school equivalency diploma.

Granted, had the controversy over the alleged jump-in never happened, it is unlikely that Krist would have earned all As. Yet because it did happen, it created for the young man a terrible distraction and a sea of self-doubt and self-consciousness; it marked him in a way he was never able to overcome.

At least, not yet.

11

Springdale's Tough-as-Nails Lady Police Chief

....

There are some in Northwest Arkansas who would insist that Kathy O'Kelley eats spikes for breakfast, rivets for lunch, and number-nine roofing nails for dinner. *That's* how tough they say she is.

And clearly, she needs every bit of steel she possesses to deal with the chaotic growth of Springdale, the southernmost town in the Wal-Mart triad of Springdale, Bentonville, and Rogers that composes the greater part of Northwest Arkansas.

A statuesque and efficient-looking woman with short curly brown hair who runs a force of 117 officers, Chief O'Kelley calls to mind Jane Tennant, the hero of the PBS series *Prime Suspect*.

"Well, she *has* to be tough to be in the position she is in," says Ana Hart, the tactful executive director of Just Communities, a Springdale organization that advances diversity through education and training. "First of all, she's a leader. She takes action, she takes initiative, and she follows through. She's someone who's opening doors for everyone, and she's direct and passionate, which serves her well as chief."

O'Kelley retired from the North Little Rock Police Department in 2003 with the rank of captain after twenty-two years of service. Moving up to Fayetteville, she worked as an assistant director in the University of Arkansas Police Department for a year and a half before the Springdale Police Department hired her as its chief. It was December 2006, and O'Kelley, new to the area and its issues, at first seemed as if she would be able to smoothly bridge the hostility gap with the beleaguered Hispanic population and establish positive relationships, all the while enjoying a rosy honeymoon with potential detractors in the community.

Springdale has the largest number of immigrants in Northwest Arkansas, in part because Wal-Mart, Tyson Foods, and George's all offer plentiful employment for unskilled laborers. In addition, housing here is less expensive than in Bentonville.

"Our job is about law enforcement and crime suppression," O'Kelley, sleek in gray slacks, a navy turtleneck, and brown loafers, told me in April 2007 as we sat in her modest office with its muted forest-green walls and beige industrial carpeting. "And since most crime is local in nature, we need the help of our Hispanic population to solve it. And don't forget, Hispanics are being victimized as well."

Toward that end, O'Kelley initiated a Hispanic Advisory Group, with whom she meets when she needs assistance. From the beginning, however, it became evident that community harmony presupposed a delicate balance of understanding. Her intent, as the sociologist Robert D. Putnam might have put it, was to bridge social capital between the dominant whites and the new arrivals from nineteen Spanish-speaking cultures. The Hispanics, she explained, needed to become educated about United States laws—that is, about fundamental road and driving rules, about what is expected of community renters and owners, and about what an individual needs to do if stopped by a police officer. And Americans needed to become aware of Hispanic customs and to try to communicate with those who do not speak English.

"With the cooperation of the Jones Center, we received a grant and put together a video that we distributed at churches and social organizations," says O'Kelley. "We also instituted a mentoring program through the Hispanic Women's Association for bridging cultural gaps and learning survival skills in both languages. But we weren't very successful. One reason was that our Hispanic components were intimidated because they were working with law enforcement officers. Maybe if they hadn't had on uniforms, it might have been different from the onset. While I still think that type of arrangement could help both cultures, there's got to be a little trust."

O'Kelley, while looking to develop more crime-watch groups within various neighborhoods, underlines the barriers that have impeded their success. "In some of the areas that need us most," she says, "we're not going to have that trust. My communication with our Hispanic group is really about how they can help me get to the people who need our help."

Implementing 287(g)

During the late summer of 2007, Springdale, like Rogers, sent five police officers to train in the federal 287(g) program, whose chief purpose was to identify and deport criminals who were also illegal immigrants. But the Hispanics of Springdale were, back then, more receptive to O'Kelley's efforts.

"Probably one of the differences is that I have had an open dialogue with my Hispanic group, and they've known all along what I was doing and why," O'Kelley said confidently at the time. "So they may voice a little more support. We have a quid pro quo—they're trying to help us, and we're trying to help them."

All three towns chose to work with Immigration and Customs Enforcement (ICE) on what they call a task force model.

"This is the model we use with many organizations," says O'Kelley. "Here, we formed a task force in which our officers work under the supervision of ICE agents."

A year into the program, she reported, the task force had already built several cases and had one ready to go to trial. "Since this is the first time that ICE has used this approach," O'Kelley said, "we are still building protocols and procedures. Obviously there are growing pains about what works. Just getting our officers acclimated to the federal system has been a challenge." Not only is the law very complicated, but so, too, is its enforcement because so few officers are bilingual. Those who can speak Spanish get stuck doing most of the interviews, O'Kelley adds.

Two years later the chief continues to be vague and secretive about the program. Noting how, at the beginning, her task force was detaining an average of a hundred people a month, she refuses to give more recent figures, explaining that it is not her department's responsibility.

"ICE would release these figures because it's their program, not ours," she says, then quickly adds that the agency does not, as a rule, cooperate with the press.

A Love Affair Gone Sour

At the beginning Hispanic activists appreciated what they perceived as the new chief's openness. "From my point of view, she has an incredible knowledge of community building," says Ana Hart with her usual empathy. "She understands how she needs the community to work with her. She is a blessing."

By January 2008, however, many of O'Kelley's original supporters felt betrayed. They related stories of local police officers, in the name of 287(g), breaking down doors of apartments in search of undocumented workers, tales of cops making illegal searches and arresting brown-skinned people at traffic lights for no reason, anecdotes about mothers too scared to venture out of their apartments to take their kids to the park or to the mall for ice cream.

The usually agreeable activist Al "Papa Rap" Lopez is one who feels bitterness toward the chief and toward 287(g) as well. "It has turned out to be exactly what the Latino community feared it might become—a means of illegitimate harassment that has trampled on everyone's rights," he says. "I told the chief to her face that I was disappointed in her, and I was sorry I had supported her last year at a march of more than six thousand Hispanic people, where I interpreted for her and encouraged the Latino community here to support her, too."

What upset Lopez most was an initiative that O'Kelley proposed subsequent to 287(g), in which, within Springdale, a car could be towed if its driver did not have a valid license. "Hispanic people can live in Rogers and pray every day that they won't be caught by the police," says Lopez, referring back to 287(g), "but they *cannot* live in Springdale thinking that their car is going to be towed away. So I told the chief, 'Your timing is wrong.'"

Lopez sees 287(g) as the beginning of a plan to rid the area of Hispanics. "It's about white people here believing that there are too many people who speak Spanish and are taking over," he says.

Non-Hispanic outsiders such as Randy Capps of the Urban Institute support this interpretation. "My sense, having read what local officials and local police have said, is that one stated purpose of the 287(g) program was to cut down on violent crime, but another was to push undocumented immigrants out of the community," he says. "Most of these people were arrested for traffic violations or for using false Social Security numbers to get employment." Capps believes that between October 2007 and March 2008, three hundred people in Northwest Arkansas were arrested.

When I ask the chief why her former supporter, "Papa Rap" Lopez, and most of the Hispanic activist community are hostile to 287(g) and her initiative to engage them, she says, her voice visibly cool, "You're not going to get the full truth talking to them. Rather than being community advocates, they do more damage by what they put out." And here is the Catch-22 as she presents it: "They are too close to the situation. They are not dealing with the facts but with their own reality."

Yet, since this is a federal task force, O'Kelly says that she is not in a position to furnish the Hispanic community with all those facts. "So they deduce things based upon limited, and oftentimes erroneous, information."

It also vexes the chief that the Hispanic news reports only a part of the story. She does not seem to see the irony, frustration, or unfairness of a situation in which critical information is deliberately withheld from this community.

"If anybody is arrested on a traffic stop," she contends, "they're already a target of an investigation; it's *not* a random traffic stop."

O'Kelley claims that she knows of no doors that have been kicked in, unless the officers have a "knock" type of search warrant, wherein, if they hear movement after knocking, or see people inside a house, they can gain entrance. "Which is perfectly legal," she assures me. "My officers, who have the same protocols as any other agency, don't have *any* authority or power over immigration. Even if they know someone is undocumented, they cannot do anything about it. They are going to write that person a ticket and send him on his way. Only those officers assigned to the task force can exercise immigration authority."

For Springdale law enforcement, 287(g) is simply a tool with which to remove criminal elements from the city. "If I had the opportunity to remove a white person who was a criminal and send him to some other country where he would not be in my city to commit crime, I would also take advantage of that," O'Kelley says. "This tool just gives us the opportunity to remove an undocumented resident who is committing crimes so that he cannot commit them here in Springdale in the future."

The program's purpose, she reiterates, is *not* to nail undocumented residents simply because they do not have papers. "Now you won't hear that from the Hispanic community, but that is the truth," she says. "The target of our task force would have had to commit some kind of crime first, whether it is bringing in narcotics or identity theft."

Few people, O'Kelley claims, realize the far-reaching and often devastating effects of identity theft, wherein undocumented workers co-opt Social Security numbers that do not belong to them. "If you sit in my office and take calls from people who are victims of identity theft, you'll see the bigger picture," she says, and tells of one Miami mother of two who phoned, sobbing, because she had been turned down for a bank loan to buy a new home. The bank told her that she owned property in Springdale, Arkansas, which had, in fact, been bought by the person using her identification number illegally. A Los Angeles man was turned away by his bank for similar reasons. "By the way," says O'Kelley, "both of these callers [who complained to the police] about their stolen IDs are Hispanic. We are forgetting the living victims out there."

For all the chief's passion and vision, she is walking the edge of a razor blade, says Val Fernandez, adult program director for Just Communities. "Some people feel strongly towards her, some are against her, and then there are the immigrants," she says. "So she is in a delicate position as to how to best serve the community and keep the trust of both Latinos and the Old Guard. My take is that no matter what the chief does, she'll be criticized. Yet the woman is reaching out and talking to people. The important thing is that there are also many folks here who have taken an interest in forming relationships and getting to know each other's stories."

A New Kind of Chief

Her voice may turn frosty in seconds, and her glance can alternately wither and charm, but Kathy O'Kelley can also trot out a sense of humor at the appropriate moment if it so pleases her. When she first started, the chief says, she heard that jokes were going around in the police department about how the Springdale squad cars would get a makeover—mauve with pink stripes. "So at a mandatory meeting," she says, "I made a point of saying, 'The first thing that I would like to address is changing the colors of the cars, and I'm thinking about mauve.'

"But you know," she adds, "it's only normal for a male-dominated institution to be a little apprehensive when a female is coming on board. I came into this organization when it was on the tail end of a lot of controversy. There had been issues with a previous chief and some divisiveness in the department. Everyone was ready for a change, and we took a unique approach to it and have found some balance. I had a lot of work to do and tried to involve everybody in that process."

Brushing aside the notion that the men in her department might have trouble reporting to a female chief, O'Kelley says that she has not noticed any discontent among her officers. "That's not to say that they *don't* have trouble reporting to a woman and talk about it someplace else. But it has never been an overt situation," she acknowledges. "I think women have a much different approach to management than men, and I certainly rely on team involvement. My captains and I meet several times a week, we talk about issues, we plan together. I try to incorporate a participatory management style and teamwork, so that I'm not sitting here on my phone giving orders."

But becoming chief does carry new weight. O'Kelley left North Little Rock, where she had been a captain for thirteen years, because she wanted "to do something different." As a captain, she had sat in on disciplinary meetings or talked about issues, always firm about how the chief ought to handle them: "Why is he having a problem with this? I'd think. This is how *I'd* do it." Now the stakes are much bigger, she says with a small laugh. "It's always easy being second in command because you're not really the one holding the buck. When you're sitting in that [chief's] chair, it's different."

Cops on the Springdale beat willingly give O'Kelley points for her managerial and organizational skills. One officer commends her for bringing a professional's leadership style to the department. "Before her arrival, the policy book was very thin," he says. "O'Kelly has put intelligently crafted policies on the books with respect to things like pursuits, use of force, and all kinds of other cop stuff that is a little arcane for most people. And she does it in a way that makes sense. So she has really transformed the department from a disorganized amateur operation into something much more professional."

The chief seems, by nature, reserved about her work, but the walls of her office reveal some of her story. They include a variety of photographs and a diploma signed by former FBI director Louis Freeh certifying that she had gone through FBI training. Perhaps the centerpiece memento, however, is a framed, smiling caricature of her alongside a proclamation from the mayor of North Little Rock commemorating Kathy O'Kelley Day. A two-foot-high sculpture of a pair of gilt hands lifted in prayer sits on a coffee table; a black gym bag next to her desk seems austere and functional.

No surprise, then, that the chief also proves reticent about her private life. She says she is divorced but volunteers, "I have four children, and they all have four legs, long hair, and a tail." She is speaking, it turns out, about her cats, two of which are big males she rescued and had planned to find homes for. "That was a few years ago," she notes, "and they're still with me, so I might as well just say I have four cats." She lets them roam about her yard during the day, thanks to a product called Cat Fence-In.

But it is her frailest cat—a female who is deaf, clawless, and weighs only about three pounds—that rules the roost. "She has an attitude," says O'Kelley, a glint in her eye. "She just gives the others hell every day."

Gangs and the Business of Law Enforcement

The breadth of the issues that get brought to Chief O'Kelley's attention here in Springdale surprises her. "Many of them are really outside the general scope of law enforcement," she explains. "We're a community stakeholder and are seen as a problem solver. I have a lot of interest in building community bridges and need to do more about it."

She is acutely aware that the 287(g) program has impaired the police department's relationship with the Hispanic community. "It's hard to say to people, 'Trust us, we're here to protect you, *regardless* of your status,' when 287(g) is here," she explains. "Yet the truth is, when we are dealing with you as a victim, I don't care what your status is. In fact, there are visas available for undocumented people who are victims of crimes. For instance, if you're a witness in a drug investigation and cooperate with the police, you are eligible for a visa to remain in this country. Visas are also available to victims of domestic battery. It is important for people to know that a lot of domestic issues go unreported simply because undocumented victims fear going to the police. Usually Catholic Charities assists these people in making those visa applications."

Unfortunately, since 287(g), local Hispanic women have become even more fearful of reporting domestic abuse, especially if either they or their abusers have no papers; as a result, 2008 domestic abuse statistics have plummeted. Still, the Springdale Police Department, in collaboration with the Hispanic Women's Organization of Arkansas, Catholic Charities, and the women's shelters of Benton and Washington counties, has worked to inform the Latino community of this option. One problem, Margarita Solorzano, executive director of the Hispanic Women's Organization, points out, is that in order to get these visas, women must be courageous enough to cooperate with the police to prosecute their abusers. "It also takes some time, and it costs some money," she says. "It is not automatic."

Of particular pride to O'Kelley is her creation of a local SNAP team—an acronym for the Springdale Nuisance Abatement Partnership. This team addresses nuisance issues relating to quality of life and distressed neighborhoods—abandoned houses with overgrown lawns, rundown apartment buildings, or homes with too many cars piled on the lawns. "SNAP has eliminated the opportunities for crime to breed," she says, "and it has done quite a bit to clean up those areas of the community."

Still, with substantial Hispanic and Marshallese immigrant communities in the area, SNAP occasionally has to deal with serious social and legal situations. On November 10, 2008, a child wound up at a local hospital with mouse bites all over the head and legs. This led the Arkansas Department of Human Services to contact the Springdale Police Department.

"In what is believed to be the largest known case of overoccupancy in the city's history, police raided the house Oct. 29 with code officers and found piles of garbage, feces, faulty utilities, flammable materials stacked next to a water heater and mattresses in the bedrooms, living room and the garage," the article in *Arkansas Online* reported.[1] As it turned out, twenty-three Marshallese immigrants were living together in the crowded house. After the raid the residents dumped garbage and debris into the street before abandoning their makeshift living quarters.

When the newspaper contacted Carmen Chong Gum, the Marshallese outreach coordinator, she suggested that it was common in the Marshallese culture for needy friends and extended families to share the same room. "Maybe [the overoccupancy] was temporary and they were just taking care of relatives," she tried to explain. "It's hard to turn people away."[2]

Yet this news story irked at least one local middle-aged white man from the area. "This is why some of us in the community feel hostile toward immigrants," he said. "Whatever their nationality."

And then there are the gangs. Springdale, like its neighbors, seems to be on 24/7 gang alert. "Papa Rap would tell you that we don't have gangs," O'Kelley says, her voice dripping annoyance. "We *have* gangs. We have identified more than eighteen different gangs and have an active gang database. And we are seeing more recruiting in our middle schools."

When kids in the community commit burglaries, bypassing jewelry for guns, that is a sign that gangs are at the heart of the robberies, says O'Kelley. Recently, her department arrested a local middle school student responsible for forty-six burglaries; he had also been involved in a drive-by shooting. "But Papa Rap would say, 'Oh, we've misjudged this poor unfortunate young man,'" O'Kelley offers. "Papa Rap, to me, is an obstacle to being able to address things proactively because he wants to minimalize these kids' conduct [with the excuse that they are simply] emulating what they see on TV. We must have the cooperation of the Hispanic community, but we can't when one person is carrying this flag that we're overreacting. Papa Rap wants to reduce the issue to something ethnic—that we're attacking Hispanics. But that's *not* the case."

In 2007, Springdale introduced the Gang Resistance Education and Training program (GREAT) into the middle schools, but O'Kelley says that, even then, experts "felt we were too far behind the curve to have an impact." And so in the 2008–2009 school year, fourth and fifth graders went through the program, which intends to arm them with life skills to avoid the temptations of gangs. O'Kelley quickly points out that GREAT is directed not just at Hispanics but at white, black, Marshallese, and Asian children as well.

To make inroads in a community, most experts agree, gangs need to infiltrate a population of children who are vulnerable and needy. Almost all experts acknowledge the importance of parental programs and after-school components in combating the lure of gangs. Some programs, O'Kelley says, are currently being introduced; she is writing grants for others. "I don't necessarily see that those things are totally my responsibilities," she says. "We've got to engage in partnerships with schools and social service agencies. But I don't find that Papa Rap contributes in a positive way to those conversations and will probably not involve him in the future."

How, in the end, should we think about the fact that gang problems in Northwest Arkansas have escalated at the same time that its immigration problems have exploded?

"Gang issues are *not* related to undocumented residents," O'Kelley says with perhaps too much certainty. "These issues have come to us from Southern California as groups have relocated here."

On the other hand, O'Kelley concedes that the decade-long boom in Northwest Arkansas, combined with an influx of outsiders who have come here to work, has played a significant role. "When you have a rapid change in demographics, you have a change in perception," the chief admits. "And when you mix a lot of different people, you start to have conflict. That's what happened here. Rapid change creates problems."

Painting the Town Red—and Blue—and Green

In 2007 two Hispanic teens were convicted, in separate instances, of graffiti violations in Springdale. Oscar Martinez, a school dropout, returned to Springdale High School in March 2007 and went on a graffiti spree, defacing the building and various fences surrounding it. This was not his first offense; he had previously written the word *payaso*—Spanish for "clown"—which was, apparently, Martinez's nickname—in a park and carved it into a desk at the high school, according to court documents. After his second painting party at ten separate locations, Springdale police arrested the then-eighteen-year-old and sentenced him to a year and two months in jail, plus a fine of $361 in restitution and $225 in court costs.

Teenager Jose Vargas was also convicted of misdemeanor graffiti that March. Police said that he had painted the word *wizard* on a building and had been nabbed with blue paint on his hands. He, too, was sentenced to a year in jail and a $1,000 fine.

Never mind that back in 2002, a Hispanic graffiti felon had been convicted of painting graffiti at three locations in Springdale and had received only thirty days in jail for his crime. Addressing the steeper sentences, Springdale's city attorney Jeff Harper said he hoped that they would be a deterrent to other graffiti artists. "We're taking a stand on these graffiti cases," he said. "We're going to ask for the maximum every single time."

As with the student expulsions for the Bentonville "jump-in," this seemed like an unduly severe penalty for behavior that, while antisocial, was basically harmless.

By contrast, four white boys between the ages of fourteen and seventeen were arrested for vandalizing the Bentonville Cemetery on Southwest F Street one Saturday night in March 2007. During their defacement binge, they pushed over seventy headstones, cracking or breaking twenty-five of them.

Three of the teens, with no criminal records, pleaded not guilty to juvenile delinquency charges of felony first-degree criminal mischief and destruction of grave markers. One told the presiding Benton County circuit judge, Jay Finch, "We were walking to Wal-Mart and we cut through the cemetery. We just pushed them over. We weren't thinking . . . it just happened."

Original estimates of damage soared to $25,000, but after spending a mere $500 for materials to reglue broken headstones, a team of three parks employees worked for a reported 250 hours—estimated to be worth $4,000 in wages—and managed to make the repairs.

In the end, charges were dropped against the youngest vandal. The three other boys were sentenced to two years of probation and made responsible to repay the $4,000, to perform ninety-six hours of community service apiece, and to attend tours on cemetery history. The judge ordered the trio not to contact each other or do anything without their parents' permission. Two were ordered to wear home-monitoring devices.

Inconvenient, for sure. Annoying, perhaps. But certainly not the same as a year and two months in the slammer.

The activist Jim Miranda was among those who found the mildness of these sentences disturbing. "I thought, Boy, there is almost zero tolerance here in Springdale when a crime is committed by a minority, and especially a Hispanic. There seems to be a disparity between how Hispanic justice is carried out versus justice for non-Hispanic whites."

Yet in both these graffiti crimes, the boys were old enough to be tried as adults. Still, did the punishments really fit the crimes—or exceed them?

Since graffiti activity has, more and more, become associated with gangs, it remains a flashing neon "trouble" signal for Northwest Arkansas law enforcement. In fact, an urgent directive on the Springdale Police Department Web site cautions citizens: "It is imperative that graffiti be reported to the Springdale Police Department and removed immediately."

Springdale also felt the need to post online its 2007 graffiti statistics—454 incidents or reports, more than double the number of 220 for 2006, and 25 arrests. The clean-up costs to the city were $15,742.

The graffiti, usually found in open areas where people can easily see it, is really about gangs sending messages to each other, according to Corporal Craig Renfrow of the Rogers Crime Suppression Unit. "They're dissing each other. It's all about getting respect," he said in the *Morning News*, explaining that sometimes gangs mark over each other's graffiti—an act called cross-tagging, which is also considered a sign of major disrespect.

O'Kelley has seemed somewhat placatory about the area's graffiti problems. "You start labeling kids as gang members, and that's what they become," she said back in 2007. "Not all that activity is related to wannabe-gang activity. A lot of it is just street taggers displaying their art." As a result, she said, Springdale was planning to transform one of its parks into a skateboard park featuring a graffiti wall for would-be artists. (Luther George Park opened in summer 2009 at a cost of $800,000, but the budget did not allow for the construction of that graffiti wall.)

Meanwhile, perhaps out of shame for this rash of Hispanic-provoked graffiti, and perhaps to show community spirit, in July 2007 four members of the Northwest Arkansas Hispanic Council, along with the children of one member, chipped in to clean up the graffiti. Carrying a five-gallon bucket of white paint, paintbrushes, and rollers, they dipped, rolled, and covered almost a dozen instances of perceived disrespect. Raul Ruiz, chairman of the council, told reporters, "This is something we feel passionate about. We want to make sure [Northwest Arkansas] stays the way it's always been. We want people to know that Hispanics can get out there and beautify the area."

In return, the coordinator of the Springdale Nuisance Abatement Partnership, Sergeant Billy Turnbough, commended the council for its timely help. "You guys are bridging the gap for the general public," he said. "This is the kind of relationship we hope to develop in our cities."

A Female Warrior Forging Ahead

Since arriving in Springdale, O'Kelley has become aware that not just graffiti and gangs but also so many areas of law enforcement require better services. Yet she has neither the financial resources nor the workforce to address them sufficiently. The Springdale Police Department's payroll of 150, in a community where almost 40 percent of the residents are Hispanic, sorely lacks diversity. Whereas 67 percent of the chief's Hispanic Task Force officers are white, only 27 percent are Hispanic and few of them speak Spanish. As of April 2009, in fact, Springdale's 117 sworn police officers included only 7 Hispanics and one Marshallese, no African Americans, and, besides the chief herself, a mere 4 women. "I saw one blog in the newspaper saying I was dumbing down the department by hiring women," O'Kelley says, her eyes crinkling with amusement. But perhaps not enough.

Before applying to bring the 287(g) program to Springdale, O'Kelley analyzed crime demographics in Northwest Arkansas. Bentonville, she discovered, experienced eight property crimes per one thousand residents, whereas Springdale had about forty-three. That same year, 2007, the chief says, "We had two homicides, both Asian. One was an Asian from the West Coast who shot and killed his girlfriend; the other was a Marshall Islander who had raped and strangled a ten-year-old." Demographically, according to O'Kelley, 75 percent of those arrested in Springdale for drugs are white and 20 percent are Hispanic.

As the chief sits at one of her two wooden desks, the leafy treetops visible through the window behind her, I ask about the Asian symbol hanging on a silver chain around her neck, the only personal accessory punctuating her severe attire.

"It's supposed to bring me good luck," she says. "I don't know if it has yet or not. I suppose I got into a little feng shui stuff at some point, and this particular charm represents the three gods of longevity, wealth, and prosperity. I thought I couldn't go wrong."

But then she never thought she would be working in a law enforcement agency that was quite so underfinanced and understaffed. Or one that had both the usual assortment of issues and the newer, more complex ones spawned by the wave of unskilled and undocumented workers, by 287(g), and by gangs.

In fact, these relatively new social and economic issues confronting Springdale's police department and its schools can be regarded not as unique but as problems shared by almost all communities that experience the kind of swift and dramatic shift in demographics that has occurred in Northwest Arkansas, compounded by the current economic uncertainty. It is unrealistic to believe that any town, city, or county can be fully prepared for the newfound needs, responsibilities, and burdens of such tectonic change.

Acknowledging that her job has presented challenges, the chief says, almost with hope, "But a lot of the problem has just been a lack of communication."

She also estimates that her department is probably fifteen years behind where it should be in terms of staffing and equipment. Yet she was pleased that even in these dire times, the Springdale city council has been meeting most of her budget requests. "It may be that this department just didn't ask for anything before"—Kathy O'Kelley shrugs—"and simply accepted what was coming their way. I'm certainly not made like that.

"I will go to battle for what we need," she promises. "We have a lot to do."

12

A Chicken Plant Worker
Without Options

· · · · · · · · · ·

Friendly clutter marks Ahidee Noriega's tiny stone-and-wood ranch-style home, about a half mile down the road from the Rogers Cemetery. In the modest living room, too many sofa beds are draped with blankets; too many kids' shoes and boots are piled lamely outside a tiny closet; and in the kitchen, too many ceramic cows, all dappled black-and-white just like the trim on the cafe curtains, fill the shelves and window sill.

Most striking of all, however, is Noriega's army of angels—there are twenty-two in all—made of porcelain and wood, straw and paper, some perched on the living room fireplace and others dangling from its ceiling. One has even been brought to her as a gift all the way from Thailand. They are clearly her good-luck angels, and, as Noriega tells it, they are helping her hold dear to her faith.

When we first met in 2007, Noriega was already in the midst of her night-mare journey. A short, timid woman in an inexpensive ruffled rayon blouse the color of orange sherbet, she sat in an armchair in a local hotel, look-ing prim and uncomfortable as she told her Dickensian story. Occasionally, but rarely, she smiled from somewhere deep within her moon face; for the most part, she spoke in a small voice that seemed flat and without affect. "The day that I was fired," she said in an awkward combination of Spanish and halting English as she slowly sipped water, "everything changed."

With her short dark hair swept back from her brow and fastened by a child's barrette, Noriega, it struck me, looked more like a teenager than a thirty-something mother of three, including two teenage boys. A Mexican émigré and an American citizen, she had injured her knee in October 2005 while working on the line at Tyson Foods, separating chicken parts. For $9.45 an hour, she would sit all day at a table in a cold room, entering both the weight of the chicken part and the bag into the computer, then placing the chicken into the bag and reweighing it, and then repeating the task again and again.

Employed by Tyson for more than three years, Noriega had already complained to her supervisor that workers had from time to time caught their legs on an obstruction jutting out from the leg of the table. To protect herself as she worked her machine, Noriega turned her body. "And my knee just twisted," she told me.

Although she immediately complained to her supervisors, no one took her to the emergency room. Instead, she was sent to the nurse's station and then instructed to see her own doctor. In a complaint that Noriega made to the Northwest Arkansas Workers' Justice Center on February 27, 2006, she says that the Tyson nurse did not report the injury until Noriega had already been to see four physicians.

Despite her discomfort, Noriega returned to work, where, she claimed, the Tyson nurses continually harassed her. Among other things, they canceled her doctors' visits and also discouraged translators from accompanying her to medical appointments. Worse, at Tyson, Noriega was assigned a job standing in freezing temperatures; when she told her boss that it aggravated her knee problem, she was ignored. "In contrast," her complaint pointed out, "Mrs. Noriega has seen that [her supervisor] is accommodating and sympathetic to non-Spanish-speaking workers."

Noriega's luck plummeted even further in December when she found out she had uterine cancer, which required the removal of her uterus. This brought on a fierce depression. Then in early February doctors performed surgery on Noriega's knee, and the doctor told her that she could not return to work until February 16—and only with restrictions.

That morning, when Noriega phoned Tyson Foods, her supervisor abruptly fired her, explaining that she was being let go for not having come to work the previous week, beginning on February 9. Noriega, for her part, insists that nobody had told her to start on that date; moreover, she was simply following doctors' orders. Her Tyson supervisor remained unmoved.

If it seemed to Noriega that everything changed following her firing, the truth is that her home life had already begun to disintegrate. After she became ill, her husband, Joel, who earned $12 an hour on an assembly line at Superior Wheel, a Rogers company that makes rims for car tires, told her, "I don't love you. I never loved you."

But back then she was too sick and distraught to do anything but hope that he would have a change of heart.

Running Away

Noriega was born Maria Ahidee Ortiz Navarette in Ciudad de la Piedad Cavada, a small town in the state of Michoacán in west-central Mexico. She came here when she was fourteen, joining her parents and elder sister, who had already settled in Los Angeles. "I had a lot of dreams back then," she says in her soft, almost expressionless voice. "I went through the twelfth grade in Mexico, and then I tried going to school here. But my dad said no. He was a strict Catholic, and he felt that American schoolgirls were too fun-loving."

So instead he sent her to work. A Vietnamese woman paid her $4 an hour to sort merchandise for twelve hours a day at swap meets. "I started at seven in the morning and came back home at seven at night," she explains. There was nothing fun-loving about the meets. The work was dull, and since Noriega knew neither English nor Vietnamese, it was isolating as well.

Within the year, Joel Noriega, a young man who was from the same Mexican town as the Ortiz family, came to their home looking for help in bringing his brother to America. Joel was ten years older, he had a job, and he was an American citizen. Most important, their marriage eight months later enabled the shy teenager to get out from under her family's roof.

When I ask her why she married him, she gives a small shrug. "I'm crazy, maybe," she says. "You know, my mom and daddy were very strict. They would not let me go to movies or dancing."

Clearly, she hoped that life with this mature man who was willing to whisk her away from the stultifying atmosphere of her father's home would be easier. He would be her savior of sorts. But did she love him? "Maybe not," she tells me. "Because I was only fifteen."

Spiraling Downward

Fortunately, Joel's health insurance covered his wife's surgeries, because Tyson's did not. But Ahidee paid a price: she had not expected such total emotional disengagement from him—or such brutal treatment from her employer. "I became so depressed," she says, "and couldn't talk to my husband or sons after that." A doctor eventually prescribed medication for depression as well as for her diabetes.

Then Tyson refused to pay her for either her injury or her termination. So Noriega took her claim to Workers' Compensation. They set up a mediation, at which time Tyson gave her $600 and offered $250 in compensation. Incensed, Noriega filed a discrimination suit with the Northwest Arkansas Workers' Justice Center, accusing her Tyson supervisor of obstructing her medical attention, making derogatory remarks about her ethnicity, and not taking her injury seriously. "This is a slap in the face to me for my injury, for the time that I have been off, and for my family's suffering and my suffering," she told them. She committed to move forward with the case because she knew that the Tyson personnel expected she would simply give up.

Her mediator eventually delivered the bad news, telling her that Tyson only offered between $500 and $1,000 for similar injury lawsuits—less than most other companies—and was not planning to offer her a penny more. So she took her suit to one of the area's most prominent law firms, Kester Law, in Fayetteville. After a number of months, during which, she said, there was almost no communication from her attorney, Noriega claims she was told that the case had been decided against her and that Tyson owed her nothing. Dumbfounded, she to this day remains bitter about the decision—and the representation.

Charles Kester, whose law firm handled her case, has a different recollection altogether. "We had quite a bit of difficulty getting information from her," he says. "There was a documentation issue regarding a Wage and Hour 380 form for a Family and Medical Leave Act that protects her only if she provides the documentation that Tyson was required to give her under the statute. And she had to turn it in." Kester says that Noriega never responded to the firm's requests, and after asking her to provide the completed form a number of times, her attorney simply informed her that Kester Law was terminating her file and dropping the case.

Perhaps there were language issues, I suggest, since Noriega understood the situation so differently, but Kester says that everything had been explained to her in Spanish. More likely, Noriega was overwhelmed by her debilitating cancer surgery, its subsequent treatment, and a husband whom she describes as unfeeling. Perhaps, too, the situation was just too much. "I'm sorry she felt the way she did," says Kester. "I have no problem with looking at the paperwork today if she has got it. We really try to help the people who need our help." (Indeed, Kester represented, pro bono, Adriana Flores-Torres, the undocumented worker who in March of 2008 had been locked up in a cell at the Fayetteville courthouse and left, forgotten, for a weekend with no food or drink.)

....

Meanwhile, Noriega had to come to terms not only with her dire diagnosis, but with her failing marriage. For a long while, she says, her husband refused to pay the bills, but he also would not pack up and leave. Noriega stood by, powerless, as he moved his parents here from Mexico and installed them in her already-crowded home, totally relegating her to the role of an uncomfortable, and ailing, visitor. She says that he began to tell their three children, "I never loved your mom." It was one humiliation on top of another.

Noriega, however, still felt the need to defend Joel, insisting that, until her illness, he had never been this callous. "It's like having a new person in your house," she said in August 2007. "When I was diagnosed, I thought Joel would be more understanding and would protect me. I was caught totally by surprise when he said that he didn't love me. I never imagined he felt that way. And right now I don't know whether I love him."

Eventually, Joel moved out. With her health and lawsuit both in flux, a seriously depressed Noriega said wistfully, "I think I'd like to start a new life and change everything." By January 2008, she finally felt strong enough to work again, this time at George's, another chicken-processing plant in Springdale. But starting over was difficult. "I'm on the line—and on the floor again," she said back then, "and my knee hurts when I stand for a long time. The cold makes it stiff, and even though I put on bandages to compress it, it throbs after eight hours of standing."

But she is stuck—uneducated, unskilled, and, as she herself admits in Spanglish, "I didn't go to school, but I'm trying. I need to read better English. I need to learn to pronounce. I need conversation."

Noriega's story reflects that of thousands of immigrants across the nation who work on various assembly lines or in packing plants, suffer severe injuries, and are not compensated, yet whose educations are so meager that they can do little but soldier on, taking what menial paying tasks they can find. Her only triumph, she says, is her children, and Noriega speaks with pride and emotion about their achievements. Her eldest son, Noel, even while he attended Springdale High School, received a scholarship to an after-school program in engineering at the University of Arkansas, where he is now a scholarship undergraduate. And Edgar, soon on his way to college himself, represented Springdale High at a leadership contest in April 2009 in Hot Springs and has expressed interest in architectural drawing. "I always tell my kids to do their homework," she says. "I tell them, 'If you have school, you have everything.' This is the important thing."

. . . .

For a year, Noriega had fallen off my radar, and I had been unable to find her. Now I am pleased to be sitting opposite her in a booth at Abuelo's, the cavernous chain restaurant on Walton Boulevard that specializes in Mexican food. It is October 2008, and Noriega seems to be prevailing by dint of sheer will. Her cheeks are rosy. Dressed in a brown skirt and blouse and heels, her hair darker now and pulled back by a tortoiseshell band, and wearing a necklace that a friend gave her bearing the image of the Virgin Mary around her neck, she seems robust and well rid of her debilitating depression.

"You look good," I tell her.

She smiles and her eyes crinkle. "I was more depressed before."

But all is not quite as it seems. Her cancer has returned. "Doctors discovered an inoperable tumor behind my liver," she explains simply. "They said that if they took it out, I would die faster because the cancer would spread even more."

Instead, she has undergone radiation and five chemotherapy sessions, which, physicians told her, have controlled both the tumor and her diabetes. But the radiation creates a burning sensation in her belly that only eases with once-a-month injections, which target the pain.

As a result, Noriega no longer has the strength to labor on the line at any of the smaller poultry-processing plants in the area. She works when she is well enough and the tasks are not too demanding; currently, as a kitchen aide at the Innisfree Nursing Center in Rogers, she refills orange juice glasses, sets out snacks, and does other light work for $7.50 an hour.

And Joel has moved back into the house again, primarily to be near his sons. "Not like a couple, not like a marriage," she explains hesitantly. "And not exactly like friends because we don't share anything. The only thing we talk about is the children."

Does he help her when she is ill from her chemo? No, says Noriega, explaining that sixteen-year-old Edgar was the one who would take her to the bathroom after her treatments. Her boys, and one close friend from Tyson's, would feed her, clean for her, and provide support.

"It was the worst time of my life," Noriega admits, her eyes welling up with an uncharacteristic show of emotion. "I don't even know how to pay that friend back because she helped me so much. She advised my sons and my little girl, Dicia, who is just eight, talking to them so that they could understand what was going on with me."

That friend had also witnessed Noriega's injury at Tyson's, because they had worked together. "But she could not help with the lawyer," says Noriega. "She was scared that if she did, she would get fired."

. . . .

Valiantly steeling herself every day, Noriega attempts to live normally and care for her children. "I'm OK. I am still working at the nursing home," she says in the spring of 2009, sitting in a booth with Noel at their favorite Thai restaurant. "Sometimes I cannot sleep at night, my stomach burns so much." As though discussing the weather, she unemotionally notes that her doctor wants to put her in an experimental treatment "where they cover you with ice. There is a 50 percent chance you will get totally better, but a 50 percent chance you will die. I am too scared to try this, but the nurse keeps calling me up and saying, 'Are you ready for your therapy?' And I keep saying, 'No.'"

As for Noel, the lanky, low-key young college student, who happens to be at home for an overnight visit, admits that both his mother's illness and his parents' quarrels have proven to be difficult for him. Forced to be an adult while he was still a kid, he has often had to arbitrate between them. Sometimes I just want them to leave me out of it," he says.

His mother regards her son with a patient and adoring smile. "I think he is glad to be at school now," she observes calmly.

· · · · · · · · · ·

Noriega is convinced that her faith has brought with it courage. Catholicism has always been critical to her life, and no more so than at this moment. "My Father is everything," she tells me, a lone tear running down her cheek. "God has been the one who has lifted me up throughout this whole crisis. Without Him I would not be able to get up in the morning."

She also credits her husband's indifference with helping her. "I used to love him, but right now, no," she says. "I feel a lot of anger toward him because he was not there for me when I needed him the most. And I honestly think that is what has made me strong, very strong. It has made my two sons strong as well. I am proud of them. We will all survive."

Meanwhile, the angels are dancing in Noriega's living room. "They are a symbol for my kids. They are watching over me and watching over them," she says, "and making sure that everything goes really good."

13

A Once-Undocumented Housepainter Finds Money and God

. . . .

Shoot down Interstate 540, the artery connecting all of Northwest Arkansas, and just as you leave Rogers and head south toward Springdale, you can see a small, neat, unprepossessing white farmhouse sitting on a piece of rolling farmland, just behind a strange stone facade that looks like a cardboard castle. A handwrought sign in front of it, printed so casually that it might have been an afterthought, says simply CAESAR'S PAINTING.

Cesar Vargas bought the land and a small wooden house for $154,000 in 1995 after coming to the area from Peru as an undocumented immigrant and achieving some small success. Today, he says with satisfaction, it was appraised at more than $3.3 million, but Vargas, a small, slim man with a sweet, handsome face, has no intention of selling. Instead, he says, he wants to build a church here someday.

Of course, this is the buckle of America's Bible Belt, and so, unlike most northern highways—punctuated by sprawling factories, strip malls, motels, and little else—540 is already dotted with churches. There is St. Thomas Episcopalian and Grace Lutheran, among others. And at Exit 83, the Church at Pinnacle Hills's three gargantuan white crosses, the tallest being 165 feet high, dominate the horizon. Some call them majestic, while others whisper of their vulgarity.

On a balmy spring evening in 2007, Vargas sits in the wood-paneled study of one of three brick houses that he owns right next door to one another in the elite gated community of Pinnacle Hills in Rogers—a development that also features an upscale golf course and elegant tennis and country club. Vargas wears a charcoal fleece sweatshirt with yellow bands on it and a jaunty charcoal poor-boy cap. In front of him sits a Hewlett-Packard laptop, closed. Behind him a globe and a few pieces of Peruvian pottery exist as reminders, perhaps, of how far he has come, and a shelf full of books on faith suggest the work that still needs to be done. Some of the titles include *The Purpose-Driven Life* by Rick Warren, *Building Dynamic Faith* by the Reverend Jerry Falwell, and *Living the Extraordinary Life* by Charles Stanley, the senior pastor of megachurch the First Baptist Church Atlanta.

Vargas has just shown me around the largest of his homes, a ten-thousand-square-foot, turreted brick elephant that he designed himself. The place looks like a little boy's fantasy of wealth and comfort, with its imposing wrought-iron gate surrounding the property and decorated with British-style lion insignias that resemble royal family crests. Now empty of furniture, the mansion includes a prayer room, a projection room, a vaulted entranceway and triple-story hallway, garage space for five or six cars, and a series of interior apartments that might be nice for relatives or guests you hope never to see. Vargas; his wife, Esther; their son, Frank; daughter, Nataly; and an "adopted" son, Irish-born Andrew, who is Nataly's fiancé, lived here for a year, he said, but in fact, even he acknowledges, "It was much too big." So they bought two homes next door, which are both scaled for more intimate family life. And in the end, Vargas has recently discovered, that is what is most important.

Did he ever imagine, back when he was crossing rivers and tromping through fields, one of a pack of poor and hungry young Latinos determined to slip across the border and redefine the parameters of their lives, that he would enjoy such success? "All the time I knew in my heart that God has something big in store for me," Vargas says. "And now I am thinking it is not the money or power. It's that I can tell people to be a better person. I think money doesn't make you a better person. It doesn't make you happiness. I can get $5,000 cash in my pocket every week, but I don't care about it, because I make too much money."

Vargas is one undocumented worker who has defied the odds. In 1987, at the age of twenty and recently married, he left his hometown of Huaral, Peru, a city about forty miles north of Lima, to pursue the elusive American Dream. "We were very poor, and we didn't have a good life there," he says simply. So he journeyed through Central America to Mexico, crossing the border illegally and arriving in California with $20 in his pocket. Four months later, Esther and their infant son, Frank, followed. In the year that followed, Vargas helped bring out his mother, two brothers, and three sisters. During the next few years he supported perhaps twenty-five relatives and friends by helping them find work and shelter when they first arrived here.

Vargas may have been uneducated and relatively unskilled back then, but he possessed something else of value—a quiet, pleasing way and good energy. Moreover, he says, "I liked to work, even when I was ten years old." He had mowed the yard, taken out the trash, and washed cars in Huaral for his uncle, who eventually taught him how to paint and finish cabinets.

"And you know, sometimes I'd clean the cabinets four, five, or six times. I used a lot of material, but he really didn't care," Vargas says. "He said, 'It's OK, Cesar. Sometimes you're going to do a really bad job, but you're going to learn to do it better and better.'"

Vargas persisted until he did learn, all the while developing an enviable work ethic, which would be key to his success in Arkansas.

Migrating up to North Hollywood and hoping desperately for some opportunity to stay afloat, the young immigrant joined a group of similarly undocumented Peruvian day laborers who hung out on a certain street corner every morning, sitting and waiting, sometimes all day, for potential employers to drive by and choose them.

"Two weeks later a couple of guys show up, and one tells me he is looking for a painter," says Vargas, who admits in still-heavily-accented English that, at the beginning, his comprehension was so bad he wasn't quite sure what kind of job the man was trying to fill. "So I looked at him and just smiled and moved my head to say I was ready to work, and his friend, a very old man, says, 'Come,'" Vargas recalls. After fifteen minutes, one of the men, in Spanish, warned him that the other, an American, was looking for someone who could speak English. "And in Spanish, I said, 'I don't speak English, but I'm a hard worker.' And he looked at me and said, 'OK, let's go.' The real reason he took me is because he needed to paint a second-floor window, and he was too old to climb the extension ladder to the second floor." Vargas worked for him for a day, and his boss was so pleased, he said, "I want to pick you up tomorrow."

And so began Vargas's three-year relationship with this elderly man, a skilled painter who taught him the fine points of spray-painting houses. At first he earned $7 an hour, but, he says, it was OK because the man was teaching him how to use the spraying machines, none of which existed in Peru. And Vargas kept improving. "I don't know, I like to work," he says. "I mean, I love to work. I'm an alcoholic worker."

"You mean, a workaholic," I say.

"Yes," he replies, laughing. He not only learned fast—he learned everything. Three weeks later the old man raised his pay to $10 an hour and, six months later, to $15 an hour. Eventually Vargas set out on his own.

At the time Vargas was sharing an $800-a-month, one-bedroom apartment with thirteen other people. He, his wife, son, and eventually their daughter lived in the bedroom. And everyone else—his and Esther's brothers, sisters, and cousins, primarily—shared the living room and dining room.

"We didn't have beds. We used the carpet," he said. "And sometimes when we'd go to the bathroom, we'd be stepping over an arm, or a leg or a head. 'Ow, ow!' 'Oh, sorry, sorry,' we'd say. But we had only one bathroom and had to take turns."

Throughout those early years, while Vargas painted, Esther cleaned houses for $6 an hour. And they counted their pennies and dimes. Even McDonald's was too expensive. For a treat, he says, "I'd take Frank to Carl's Jr. in California, and I'd order salad and French fries, and put a crunch on top. And he still remembers it as a big treat."

As hard as he worked and as much as he scrimped, Vargas had trouble saving money. So after having lived in Southern California for six years, he decided to move his family somewhere with more opportunity. He called a friend who had settled in Northwest Arkansas, which was inexpensive, safe from gang violence, and on the verge of an economic boom.

"So I told Esther to go and see if she liked it," he said. "She came here with my sister, and she telephoned me and said, 'I love Arkansas.'"

Vargas rented a truck, packed up their children and their few possessions, and two weeks later he had completed his cross-country move.

Boom Town

Nothing is ever as easy as it looks, and Arkansas was as indifferent to the Vargases as it is to most unskilled laborers. Yet the family had intuited correctly that Northwest Arkansas was an area with a low cost of living and big economic possibilities. In fact, in 1993 it was just revving up: Wal-Mart was actively seeking experienced middle and upper management from the nation's big cities. The company was expanding its computer database and hiring from an international pool of computer-savvy Asians. And corporate vendors were beginning to send their sales and marketing people to live in the area. Bentonville and its sister communities were about to explode with growth.

When the Vargases arrived in town, Esther went to work at Wal-Mart, translating product labels into Spanish for the corporation's Latin American stores for $8 an hour. Vargas, deciding that he no longer wanted to paint houses, started working on the line, first at Daisy Manufacturing Company in Rogers, then at Tyson Foods, removing chicken bones. He lasted three weeks before quitting. Then another chicken-processing plant, George's, Inc., hired him. On his first morning there, he put on a uniform that the company provided—white pants and shirt, white boots, and a paper hat for his head—and then entered a room bathed in violet light. This time his job was to hang live chickens on the line.

"And I began to bring them in," he says. "And when I hung them up, they started to poop. They pooped all over my face. I worked three hours and said, 'This is not for me.'"

Painting houses suddenly took on new appeal. Vargas and his brother, Leo, who had also migrated east to Arkansas, began working with a company called Gill's Painting. But one day early on, he was assisting a team that was painting a bank, and when one of the men charged with spraying the doors was enjoying an extra-long lunch, Vargas decided to take a risk and finish the job for him. His boss was so impressed with the quality of his work that he hired Vargas for that job and paid him well.

Next, at a gig painting a Springdale hospital, Vargas became supervisor to six Spanish workers and eight Americans. Although he still barely spoke English, his boss told him, "If they don't listen to you, send them home." Vargas has a quiet, I'm-minding-my-own-business way about him, and, sure enough, early on a worker refused to obey his instructions. So Vargas sent him home.

"And the guy got really upset and said, 'OK, I'm going to do it,'" he recalls. "After that, everybody started to be friendly. They knew I was running the job."

With just the slightest bit of encouragement, both Vargas and his wife displayed entrepreneurial skills that belied their humble origins. When Uncle Sam sent them a $1,500 return on taxes they were paying into a Social Security number that they had made up, Esther suggested that they borrow $1,500 more from family members and put a down payment on their first house. They did so and bought it for $86,000. As good fortune would have it, across the street lived a young builder who had just put up twenty homes in a new development. Vargas offered to paint for him. When the builder seemed skeptical, Vargas quickly told him, "If you don't like my job, don't pay me."

Before long, Vargas had left Gill's Painting behind, and Esther said so long to Wal-Mart. Vargas was bringing in more subcontracting than the builder could handle, and with Esther alongside him doing bookkeeping, they put together their own small business.

"And I was hiring other subcontractors to do the jobs," he says. "I had three guys here, four there, and seven working in another place. And a lot of builders called me and recommended me. I'm one of the first Spanish people in this part of Arkansas. So we called ourselves Caesar's Painting. And I changed the spelling to C-A-E-S-A-R like in Little Caesar Pizza. It seemed less Spanish."

Vargas recalls the day he had enough money to trade in his old, beat-up car, bought for $300, for a brand-new pickup truck. He went to a dealer, who showed him the small models. But Vargas was going for something bigger, showier, shinier. "That's expensive," the salesman cautioned him.

"Then he writes down the number—something like $25,000—as if I don't understand him," says Vargas. "And I say, 'OK.' And he asks to see my income tax because he doesn't believe me."

Naive and yet yearning to possess the truck, a symbol of his arrival, Vargas obediently returned to the dealer with his tax forms. Today he says with amusement: "And the guy is surprised by all the numbers he sees. And he says, 'What do you do for a living?' I say, 'I'm a painter.' And he tells me, 'Man, I'm in the wrong job.'"

With the pickup truck, his first new car ever, came unexpected problems.

"Funny," he muses. "All the time I drove in old cars, I never got a speeding ticket because I kept the windows open and could feel the noise and the wind. But in this car, I didn't feel the speed. And I got five speeding tickets."

There was also the little matter of his lawn. For a while Vargas kept all his equipment at his new home and worked out of his garage. Trucks and trailers hogged the driveway, sprawled across the lawn, and crowded the backyard; irate neighbors sent Vargas a letter saying they would take him to court if he didn't remove them. "And so I talked with Mama—I call my wife 'Mama' all the time—and said I needed to do something," he says.

Esther asked her husband to describe his dream house, and Vargas imagined a small cottage that he could see from the freeway with a pond for fishing and perhaps cows, chickens, and dogs. "And two days later she calls me and says, 'Cesar, I have found your house.'" It had plenty of rolling acreage and lots of room for storage. "The owner said, 'Cesar, if you offer me $154,000, I'm going to sell it to you.' So we bought the house. Two weeks later, somebody wanted to pay me $50,000 more than what I paid. And I asked my wife and son what they thought. And Frank said, 'Dad, all the time you wanted a house like this. Why would you want to sell it?' Five months later, somebody offered me three times what I paid. And my wife and son said the same thing."

The family moved into the small house on the property, which also became the offices and storage facility of his new company. And eventually, Vargas discovered why the land was escalating in value. The town of Rogers was about to start building the Pinnacle Hills Promenade, the area's first upscale shopping center, across the highway. It was a matter of good luck, pure and simple, just as it had been good luck that the Vargases had arrived in Northwest Arkansas at the precise time that its economic boom was gathering force.

But for the rest, says Esther, a slender, soft-spoken woman who also happens to be highly organized, "Cesar is a very good businessman. And he has been, right from the beginning."

Trying to account for his savvy business sense, Vargas suggests that a good businessman needs to know how to talk to prospective clients and price jobs smartly with subcontractors. And he should not be too easygoing either. Recalling a friend and early business partner who had a construction company that went bankrupt, he says, "He trusts people too much."

Vargas, it seems, trusts them just enough. He also owns what, on the surface, seems to be a mellow personality. It is impossible to imagine him losing his temper, berating an employee, or chiseling a customer. It is easy to understand why both companies and individuals might gravitate toward working with him.

And they have. Unable to hide his pleasure at his own accomplishments, Vargas told me in 2007, "I have one company to do just brick, one company just for driving, one company just for painting. I have so many companies."

But he does not crow about his wealth; he uses it as a morality tale. Yes, he shows visitors around his pseudo-castle like a kid who might enjoy playing Richard the Lionhearted in a school play. Later on he gets serious and admits how his workaholic habits almost cost him his family.

"I was poor and thinking that to make my wife happy, I'd buy her a car," he says. "And my family was asking me to give them my time, but I was working so hard."

It was easier, Vargas admits, to give them "things." When he began making serious money, he bought a Corvette for himself, a Hummer for Esther, and new cars for his son and daughter.

Then came a small epiphany. "I remember, one day when Nataly was thirteen, she asked me for money, and I gave her a one-hundred-dollar bill," says Vargas. "She looked at me and said, 'Dad, I know you love me, but I'm only thirteen. At least, you need to ask me what I'm going to do with the money. I could be buying drugs.' And she was right. I never asked about stuff like that because I didn't really care about the money."

Soon, however, Vargas was swimming in it. At the same time his world began to implode. He was working longer hours, never taking time to eat. He developed an ulcer and rarely saw his wife and children. He and Esther began to argue—mostly about how he was becoming so remote. They even went so far as to consult a divorce lawyer. Vargas says that he had been ready to split up the property and business, giving her 70 percent of everything. The entire family was miserable. Remembering how he had suffered when he was fourteen and his own parents divorced, he knew he needed to do something.

One of his friends—the former partner who went bankrupt—had actually introduced Vargas to God. But at the beginning, he was impatient with such conversation. "All the time, it was God, God, God," he says. And just when it looked bleakest for his relationship with Esther and the children, he says, "I asked God, 'Please don't take my family away.' I knew if I didn't have family, I would have nothing. I had so much pain inside because I didn't want to lose my wife or my kids. And I started to cry, cry, cry. We all cried. And I started to change."

At the same time, God seemed to be everywhere. Vargas met a pastor who had just come here from El Salvador and was looking for work.

Vargas gave him a construction job. In return, this man of God talked to Vargas every day about religion. "I listened," he says. "And it began to make sense."

A former nonpracticing Catholic, Vargas says, "I used to go to church empty and leave empty. I didn't believe in God."

When the pastor/construction worker told Vargas he had been an accountant back home, Vargas hired him to do his paperwork.

"And we made this church on one side of my office," he says. "At first, we were maybe four or six guys who would go there to pray. Now maybe sixty of us come to church on Tuesday, Friday, Saturday, and Sunday."

The local men and their families crowd into the plain, tiny space, which is why Vargas dreams of one day building a bigger one. "It will also be right next to my office," he says.

Yet for a long time, the Vargases preferred to attend the sleek glass-and-steel Church at Pinnacle Hills as a family.

A Pinnacle-Hills Kind of Easter

On Easter Sunday, the Vargases go to services at the fancy Baptist ministry, the Church at Pinnacle Hills, the enormous 187,600-square-foot glass-and-concrete structure just off I-540 at Exit 83 in Rogers. They arrive in two cars, listen as the pastor, Reverend Ronnie Floyd, sermonizes about God and goodness, and wave to some friends. Vargas says he was initially ambivalent about this big, gaudy church, with its stark, modern sanctuary, which suggests a convention center more than a house of worship.

"At first, I drove by and thought, 'This is just for the rich people,' which is not good," he remembers. "But one day a guy invited me to the church, and I really loved it. My children do, too, because they feel more comfortable when the service is in English."

The entire family, he says, was baptized here in the baptism tanks high above the stage. Then, says Vargas, his brother and sister, seeing the positive changes that their newfound religiosity had wrought on the family dynamic, also converted.

No church in Northwest Arkansas is more stylish or spectacular than this new Baptist church, built at a cost of more than $26 million and which on Easter Sunday is mobbed, mainly with whites and Hispanics. Its three huge crosses stand guard just outside the building, glinting in the sun as they overlook the highway. A fancy new five-star Embassy Suites Hotel and the upscale Pinnacle Hills Promenade sit like a couple of insolent but jazzy relatives right down the road—all signs of the area's new prosperity.

Inside, the auditorium is just as spectacular, with seating for twenty-four hundred and a vast glass wall rising up from behind the stage, against which the entire service plays out. Two enormous video screens hang high up, one at each side of the stage; also way up, and bookending the stage, a pair of clear glass baptism tanks are suspended, filled with water. This Easter Sunday afternoon, the room is about three-quarters full. But the focus is on the stage, the giant screens, the busy tanks. For much of the service, the screens project fierce images of a pain-shattered Christ on the cross. Then, when a half dozen men, women, and children are baptized, women in white robes, men in blue, we see them in duplicate—both in the actual tubs and on the screens, which reflect the baths, larger than life. Later, while the large choir sings watered-down gospel, a blinking advertisement flashes across the screen, selling a one-day father-and-son religious camp for $15. Altogether, it is quite a show.

The lithe, middle-aged pastor, Reverend Ronnie Floyd, leads the service. On Sundays, he is perhaps the busiest man in town, shuttling back and forth between the Pinnacle and the equally huge First Baptist Church of Springdale, where, earlier this morning, he had led a service that was broadcast here, just as this one is now simultaneously being broadcast there. Today, as Floyd bounds to the stage, he hardly appears ruffled by the commute; in his expensive-looking, well-cut, gray suit, crisp white shirt, and ecru silk tie, he looks fresh and quite rakish. In fact, some in the Jewish community, put off by the towering crosses that dominate the intersection and disappointed that the pastor never responded to their invitation to attend the synagogue dedication, refer to him as "Ronnie Armani."

The reverend's Web site, with its "online library," which sells his books and DVDs of his sermons, attests to Floyd's ambition. He calls himself a "Biblical Life Coach" and has a blog entitled "Between Sundays"; a television program, "Winners," which can be seen on various religious networks; and an official Web site, on which he claims to have baptized nearly twelve thousand people in twenty years. Parishioners can also sign up to hear his sermons on iPods.

But Floyd has also set himself up as a polarizing figure whose flashy church and similarly flashy ministry have put off a number of local people, including ex-mayor Terry Coberly. "I think of it as a cult," she says. "Some of us call it Six Flags over Jesus."

Coberly is not alone. A MySpace site features sixty-five registered anti-Pinnacle members who call the church an "ostentatious monument" and describe the Pinnacle and its pastor as "a black eye on the face of humanity." The site invites readers: "Join this group if you think it is morally wrong to spend 32 million dollars on a church building instead of using that money to help those that are less fortunate. Join this group if you think it is morally wrong for a church pastor to use millions of dollars, that people think they are giving to God, to buy a luxurious mansion and expensive cars. Join this group if you find this church's gaudy 'look at me' attitude very offensive. . . ."

For different reasons, Vargas decided to leave the Church at Pinnacle Hills in June 2007. While Nataly and his son-in-law-to-be, Andrew, still go there for Sunday services held in English, Vargas say that he and Esther felt that they needed to support their own small church instead, with its Spanish service, by attending it regularly.

Of Faith and Marriage

In the more than three years since the religious epiphany that Vargas credits with saving his marriage, his life has taken on a profoundly different emphasis. "Everybody soon began to change," he says. "It used to be that when we started to eat, we would just eat—and that's it. Now, before we eat, we pray. Before we work, we pray. We go to church every Sunday, whether it's snowing or raining. Whatever is going to happen outside, we are going."

Vargas also now takes time to breakfast with his family. Try calling his construction company between noon and 1:00 P.M., and no one answers; they are all at lunch. On weekends, he and Esther sometimes nap together in the afternoon. Dinners have become leisurely two-hour affairs at which the entire family can share the events of the day.

And although in the past he only drank socially, Vargas now avoids liquor altogether. "If you have whiskey or tequila in your house, it's like you have a snake," he says from time to time. This story about the perils of drink is one he relishes and recounts often. "You want to pet that snake.

But one day that snake is going to bite you—or your daughter." And so, taking to heart his pastor's warning, Vargas and his family ceremonially poured all the liquor—"the whiskey, the tequila, a lot of good and expensive bottles"—down the sink. "And when they marry and have their own families one day, my kids don't want to have the snake in the house either," he adds.

As relaxed as he seems, Vargas takes on an evangelical intensity when he talks about God and religion—and, by extension, his family. "You know, if somebody asks me what I have, I say, 'My sons, my wife, my daughter.' They are my fortune. This is what I have," he says.

These days his family includes not only his birth children, but also his "adopted" son, Andrew Deeter, a tall, blond, fatherless young Irishman who could not look more different from the small, dark, wiry, and strikingly handsome Vargas clan if he tried. While still in high school, Deeter came to Arkansas for an aborted reunion with his birth mother. Although that did not work out in fairy-tale fashion, the real fairy tale was that the Vargases found—and informally adopted—him. In October 2005, on the day he turned eighteen, Deeter moved out of his mother's home and in with the family. Now he works in construction at Caesar's Painting and, according to Vargas, is a natural. (Vargas's birth son, Frank, studied business at a local college and worked at the Walton-owned Arvest Bank before striking out on his own and coming to New York City for a brief stint in February 2009, with dreams of writing for *Saturday Night Live*; when his money ran out a month later, he returned home and rejoined the family business, vowing to save money for another more permanent move to the city.)

Deeter and Nataly, Vargas's beautiful daughter, who graduated from Bentonville High School in 2007 and attends nearby Northwest Arkansas Community College, part-time, while working at Caesar's Painting, became officially engaged in December 2008; they plan to marry in March 2010. Nobody in the family seems uneasy about the fact that she is both Deeter's "sister" and his fiancée.

With religion the focal point of his life, next to work, of course, Vargas programs his iPod with faith-based lectures and self-help books. "I try to learn something new every day, something I don't know," he says. "We like to watch Joel Osteen [the Texas-based televangelist] and a lot of shows on the Christian Channel."

For a while Vargas took special pride in his radio show, which aired once a week on La Seta, a local Spanish radio station. Getting the gig was so meaningful to him that, according to "Papa Rap" Lopez, who introduced Vargas to the station's owner, Vargas agreed to do a construction project in return for airtime. As both host and producer, he conveniently broadcast from home, rhapsodizing and improvising for twenty-five minutes about the benefits of godliness and, sometimes along with Esther, taking calls from his listeners. "If God changed my life, I know that He can change more people's lives if they go to church," he says.

Vargas also gave out practical pointers. "I told my audiences, 'You know, if you come to this country to work, you can buy a house.' And I told them how. And people called to say, 'Thank you, Cesar, for talking about those things.'"

But then came the economic downturn and, with it, a nationwide construction crisis. Soon Vargas would take a long leave from radio and turn his attention elsewhere.

Relative Issues

On a steamy Sunday afternoon in August 2007, while the temperature soars to the mid-nineties, the Vargas family is sitting at a small table at El Rincon Peruano, his sister-in-law Ana Camacho's postage-stamp-sized restaurant in Springdale that she opened the previous month in a small building owned by Vargas's brother. Despite the heat and their own slender physiques, everyone in the family orders piles of hearty workmen's food—a beef dish, fried fish, rice, and beans, as well as a tender, light seviche.

Life has not been as lucky for Camacho as it has been for the Vargases, who were fortunate to eventually gain political asylum in the United States through a fluke—the Communist guerrillas known as the Shining Path had taken over Esther's family home in Peru, making it impossible for her to go back and enabling her to earn refugee status. Camacho; her daughter, Magda; and husband, Juan Carlos Sanchez, who is Esther's brother, do not have legal papers and are facing deportation. Their situation is especially critical because Sanchez has been sitting in the Bentonville jail since November 15, 2006, charged with using false identification and possessing two guns (which illegal aliens are not allowed to own), after an unidentified person reported him to authorities. Esther and Cesar have been paying for Sanchez's legal representation, and at the moment the family is tense about the outcome of his case.

More than anything, however, Camacho fears that Sanchez will be sent back to Peru, and then she will be forced to support her children on her meager earnings from the tiny Peruvian restaurant. "When the [authorities] came, they told her that they knew she didn't have papers but they were just going to take him," says Magda, a pretty teenager with bottle-blond hair and a smile that is a carbon copy of her mother's. Magda is here today to help Camacho with her English as we speak.

During her husband's incarceration, Camacho, a small, round woman with merry eyes that mask her troubles, greets me at the home that she, Sanchez, Magda, and their two sons, one a teenager and the other still a small boy, shared before the arrest. Located at the dead end of a street in Rogers, it is right off the highway, with its strip malls and fast-food franchises, but here the pavement suddenly gives way to a bumpy dirt road, which winds around and quickly becomes secluded and rural, populated by parched trees, splintering wood fences, barbed wire, spotted cows, and little more. The family's ranch house, with its porch, two living rooms, large kitchen, and three bedrooms, on a few acres of property, may once have been attractive, but since the police raid, Camacho and her family have removed the furniture and cars and, for all intents and purposes, deserted it, temporarily moving in with her seventy-one-year-old mother-in-law—Esther's mother—as a safety precaution. "We're scared that if we move back here, immigration will come again," says Magda.

Now what is left are debris-filled wastebaskets, flies, a forlorn bridge table, three chairs, and, on the wall, a poster of Machu Picchu—barely the detritus of a family's life.

The economic boom that began in the late 1990s in Northwest Arkansas attracted tens of thousands of immigrants, among them Camacho and Sanchez. The couple came to the United States from Peru in 1991, making their way up through seven different Central American countries with Magda, then an infant. Crossing into the United States without immigration papers, they settled in North Hollywood and, with the help of Esther and Cesar, supported themselves with menial jobs. Camacho made plastic dolls and dildos for adult sex shops, then cleaned houses while raising her three children; Sanchez, like his brother-in-law, painted houses.

Inspired by Vargas's success with his house-painting and construction companies, Camacho and Sanchez moved to Northwest Arkansas in 1998. And just as their relatives had assured them, there seemed to be plenty of construction jobs available for hard workers. With so many newcomers moving to the area, subdivisions were popping up everywhere, and contractors, it seemed, could not build the sprawling single-family homes fast enough.

At the beginning, Camacho and Sanchez both took jobs at Tyson Foods, using work permits that they bought for $50 apiece, including fake Social Security numbers. For two years Camacho worked on Tyson's assembly line, breading chickens, then doing sanitation duty on the night shift. The pay? $7.50 an hour. "For me, [sanitation] was better than breading the chickens," she says. "I worked four hours, and I was paid for eight."

Sanchez subsequently built and painted houses for Vargas, his brother-in-law. Eventually, he became skilled and learned enough English to go out on his own. People in the business knew him as "Joe." By the time he was arrested, he had become so successful that he was earning, according to his wife, around $200,000 a year—a comfortable salary anywhere, but especially in Arkansas. Among his clients were Jim Walton, Sam's billionaire son, and his wife, Lynne, who are considered royalty in this part of the world.

Life, for a while, seemed easy, happy, perfect. But Sanchez too often indulged his taste for what his wife describes as "things." He made money but spent it fast. "He wouldn't save any of it," says Magda. "He'd buy four-wheelers, motorcycles, cars. We had six cars when they took him."

"He wasn't thinking for the future, only for the moment," adds Camacho, shaking her head.

Sanchez himself had always wanted to open a restaurant, says his daughter. But, typically, he wanted it to be a luxurious restaurant. "So he wanted all the money in place beforehand," explains Magda. "But after he got locked up, we just had to do what we could."

The result was El Rincon Peruano, where Camacho works, full-time, with her daughter, mother-in-law, and, on weekends, her sons all pitching in. Although the tiny restaurant, with its eight tables, is always crowded, the monthly rent, before factoring in food costs, is a hefty $2,000. Camacho pays cash for everything, explaining, "I don't have credit. I don't want credit cards. It's too hard."

....

When Sanchez was finally released from jail that November on a bond posted by Vargas, Ana closed the restaurant; Cesar supported them, says Esther, "by giving them jobs so that they can survive." Still, Ana remained fearful that the Immigration and Customs Enforcement agency would show up and take her away. And she feared, as well, the ultimate consequences for "Joe" Sanchez.

The worst thing, her lawyers told her as Sanchez awaited trial, was for him to be convicted of a felony for having possessed those two guns without a license. That would have meant automatic deportation. If he spent more than a year in jail, that, too, would have meant automatic deportation. But if Sanchez was charged with a misdemeanor instead, then he had a chance, she told me, and the lawyers whom the Vargases had hired would fight for him. Eventually, through this legal representation, Sanchez was able to secure a work permit and is now slowly trying to rebuild his own construction business, little by little, in this rocky economy. He awaits his final trial, but Esther says cautiously, "Now, finally, things look good. We are optimistic."

Meanwhile, the family's complicated undocumented status affects Magda most immediately. She graduated from high school in June 2008 and expressed a longing to go to a school such as the Fashion Institute of Technology. But without the appropriate immigration papers, that ambition will, most likely, be squelched; she is fearful of getting local help that might be available to undocumented students because it could inadvertently flag her family's status. What's more, with Sanchez awaiting a verdict that could return him permanently to Peru, the family has, thus far, been unable to give her that opportunity. Instead, Magda spent much of the past year working part-time, for hourly wages, at a skateboard store at the Pinnacle Hills Promenade.

The rub, of course, is that while her two brothers, born in the United States, are citizens, Magda, like her parents, remains undocumented. Although she has no memory of a world beyond this country, she struggles with a legal status that is in limbo and a life that she was forced to live, for a while, at least, in the heat of a hot kitchen in Springdale and in the dark shadows of a failed American Dream.

Housing Tremors and Immigration Traumas

For all of Cesar Vargas's success, by the last weeks in October 2007, the downturn in the national housing market had begun to affect him and his business. To complicate matters even further, Mayor Womack's immigration initiatives had already started impacting the local economy. On September 27 the city had signed an agreement with ICE. With ICE computer equipment now installed at the Rogers Police Department, six local police officers, among nineteen in all from the area, began to utilize their ICE training to check the immigration status of suspected illegal immigrants during routine law-enforcement duties. Womack, who vowed that Rogers would no longer serve as a refuge for illegal immigrants, said, "Law enforcement has a tool available to it now, and we are going to use that tool to the best of our ability."

"So far the city has played to its anti-immigrant element. In doing that, Rogers and its mayor have scared a lot of other residents," wrote the columnist George Arnold in the *Arkansas Democrat-Gazette* on October 9, 2007. "But maybe that's the point."

In the wake of 287(g), the Vargas family has worried about neighbors and relatives who do not have papers and are targeted by ICE. One couple were recently taken into custody while their two teenage daughters were deposited, bewildered and hysterical, in the home of family friends. "We are helping them get a lawyer," says Vargas. "But if the family cannot make payments on their house, they lose it."

Fear quickly blanketed the Hispanic community. "A lot of Spanish are now leaving for other cities and states," says Vargas—just the response, some say, that authorities are looking for. "I know seven or eight myself. There are many homes for sale, and nobody is buying. And there are not as many workers to do the work."

. . . .

Ten months later, the family's situation, like the nation's, is even more precarious. Northwest Arkansas, the all-too-recent boom town, has been just as susceptible as the rest of the United States to the economic collapse. By fall 2008, Vargas admitted that new construction jobs have just about evaporated. He has managed to keep busy by doing remodeling work, but the ready cash of previous years does not currently exist.

Although nobody can predict the long-term effect on the economy at large, Vargas worries for his own business for the short term. He has taken a million-dollar mortgage loan on his land that sits next to the highway. "I have so much property," he says, "and I have to pay interest on it." What's more, he has not yet been able to unload either his turreted house in the gated Pinnacle community or one of the normal-sized homes next door to it, all of which he has been trying to sell for two years.

The family is dealing with another problem as well. Vargas had put all of their savings into real estate. In addition to their three elegant homes, side by side at Pinnacle Hills, they had invested in seven others in varying price ranges. Many are worth far less now, in 2009, than they were when he bought them. What's more, while he is anxious to sell them, in the thick of the mortgage crisis, there is no available money—and no takers.

In fact, the Vargases have left Pinnacle Hills altogether, and while their three houses sit empty, craving buyers, they have moved into another pretty, if more compact, home in a lovely but slightly less grand subdivision five minutes away. This home has a small garden and an outdoor fireplace. "I love it," says Esther, ensconced in a big red velvet armchair in the pretty, gold-toned living room, with her husband and children gathered around her on a brisk autumn evening. "It feels more like a home, and we spend a lot more time together here. In the house we built at Pinnacle, we had to scream all the time."

"Putting all our money in one basket was a business lesson for us," she acknowledges. "But the good thing is that we are learning from our mistakes, and we are going to be better. I tell my children that there are scary moments in life, but they should not worry. Material things don't matter. I want them to trust in God."

Quick to offer financial support to friends and family with immigration problems, the Vargases help poor children in Peru, sending them toys, through a local family, every Christmas. They are also currently supporting a Peruvian pastor in Springdale who has started a new church of his own. "It's important for us to help other people," says Esther.

Vargas's generosity to friends, family, and the Hispanic community is legend, says "Papa Rap" Lopez, himself a beneficiary of the contractor's kindness. After a worker who had been hired to paint Lopez's house accidentally knocked down his carport and then quoted an extra $700 to fix it, Lopez contacted Vargas, whom he knew only by reputation. "Cesar showed up, painted my house, and rebuilt my carport," he explains, "and when I said, 'How much do I owe you?' he said, 'Nothing, Papa Rap. You do so much for the community, and this is my way of thanking you.' Actually, I had to stop asking Cesar to help me because he *never* wanted to charge me. So I got him the radio gig at La Seta as thanks."

Signs of Hope

In early 2009 the Vargas family was relieved to discover that its business had visibly begun to pick up. Caesar's Painting contracted to do a number of small jobs and also a big one, the construction from the ground up of a Hispanic bakery in Springdale, which will have ovens, cooling racks, and warehouse facilities as well as an actual bake shop. By April, Esther noted cheerily, "We're almost halfway finished."

Vargas, perennially low-key and cheery, sits in a zebra-striped chair, a gray terrier perched on his lap, a small diamond glinting from his ear, and retells another of his favorite stories—about how, when he was a small boy, his mother cooked him a sumptuous birthday meal of mashed potato and beef and how he felt like a king on this, his most important day. He adored the way his friends congratulated him and how he was the center of attention, and he hated how depressed he was on the next day, his non-birthday. "So when I came to America," he says, leaning over and smiling broadly, as if someone has just set a cake before him, "I said, 'From now on every day is my birthday.' That is why, when I do something [good,] my son Andrew comes in and says, 'Happy Birthday, Dad!' And when he sees someone who's upset, he says, 'Why aren't you smiling? It's not your birthday today?' I like to treat every day like it is my birthday."

It is striking that the man never seems ruffled or depressed, convinced, as he is, that his faith will see him through the most sudden and extreme business vicissitudes. He manages to convey, too, a certainty that he can help others find similar comfort, and he would never entertain the notion that God may not exist, or that God might not be looking out for him—or anyone else, for that matter.

"You have no idea how much life can change if you just open your heart to God," he says. "Then you really start to change. That's what I said on the radio and to people I know. In the next few years there are going to be a lot of divorces because of the economy. But if families pray together, they will feel stronger and know that God has something good waiting for them."

Vargas may speak with more certitude than others, but the way he embraces his religion recalls the fervor shared within the Muslim, Hindu, Jewish, and Christian communities as well.

"I tell people always: 'You can enjoy this life. You can be happy,'" he says simply. "I know. God gave me so much happiness, and that's a lot for anybody."

Epilogue

··········

The recalcitrant buds on the trees are, it seems, obstinately refusing to bloom, even though spring is well under way—a stern response, perhaps, to the paralyzing ice storms of this past winter. Or to the downward-spiraling economy.

As I guide my small gray rental car along the twisty rural road leading from the Northwest Arkansas Regional Airport into Bentonville, I wonder, will Wal-Mart, the hometown behemoth, and the area itself, be immune to those vicissitudes?

The answer, I find, is yes—and no.

Rogers mayor Steve Womack puts it aptly when I visit him a few days later. "Traditionally, economic recessions don't affect us quite as much or as quickly as other areas of the country," he says. "I think Sam Walton was the first to joke, 'We know the economy is in recession, but we've chosen *not* to participate.' Companies that are here do well, especially in recessionary times."

Almost miraculously, Wal-Mart reported an increase in sales for February, March, and April 2009, with an upturn in customer traffic as well, results that were especially impressive because most major chains were reporting declines.[1] In addition, net sales for April 2009 had increased 2.4 percent over sales for April 2008.

The corporation seems to understand the challenges necessary to remain competitive in recessionary times and is prepared to meet them. As early as June 2008, Wal-Mart announced that it was redesigning its logo. Deleting its famed hyphen, drawn as a star atop more than thirty-six hundred stores across America and enacted as a "squiggly" during the weekly home-office cheer ("Give me a 'W'. . . ."), the company created sleek new signage, which now displays the dehyphenated WALMART in white letters on an orange, or sometimes sky-blue, background, with a small but shop-happy yellow starburst as punctuation.

"This logo update is simply a reflection of the refreshed image of our stores and our renewed sense of purpose of helping people save money so they can live better," a company spokesman said in a written statement. Yes, live better *in a downward spiral*, he might have added.

This sudden refurbishing of the corporate visual image coincides with the refurbishing of its leadership: after a nine-year tenure as CEO, Lee Scott stepped down on January 31, 2009, and Mike Duke, vice chairman of the international division and one of the company's lieutenants since 1995, stepped up. Wal-Mart's ongoing attempts to rebrand itself as a friendly, nurturing workplace have come in the wake of a decade of nightmarish publicity and news reports accusing the company of serious ethical and business decisions, among them shortchanging employees by forcing them to work for free after clocking out; locking associates in stores overnight; denying them prompt medical treatment; underpaying them; and discriminating against women and minorities.

In addition, numerous critics have attacked Wal-Mart's anti-Obama, antiunion position and its active efforts to undermine the passage of the Employee Free Choice Act, also known as "card check," which would enable company associates to unionize, should they so desire. The corporation, wrote David Nassar on the *Huffington Post*, "has consistently chosen to underpay its workers to the benefit of the richest family in America— the Waltons."[2] Card check would potentially change all that, expanding— or, some say, bloating—the company payroll with larger salaries for the most poorly paid associates and, according to analysts like controversial CNBC-TV guru Jim Cramer, sending its stock price plummeting.

But in these shaky times, Wal-Mart needed to answer its critics. While still taking an antiunion stance, it shifted into combat mode to repair its former bad-boy image, attempting to do more than simply present a peppier logo. Toward that end, the corporation has begun providing more and better medical coverage for employees. In addition, in 2008 it distributed almost $1.2 billion in bonuses and financial incentives to its hourly workers, as well as more than $636.4 million in bonuses based on store performance. Then in March 2009, as the elite of failing financial institutions were simultaneously grabbing government bail-out money and paying themselves multimillion-dollar bonuses, Wal-Mart announced that it was awarding approximately $2 billion more in bonuses and financial incentives, again to its hourly associates. "While economic challenges forced others to step back, we moved forward," CEO Duke noted in a memo to employees, sounding much like the virtuous child who has just brought the teacher a shiny apple.

Is the company that America loves to hate trying to become the company America cannot help loving? Or is it simply doing smart business?

Like an Olympic skier, Wal-Mart has brilliantly absorbed the bumps and blows that have been by-products of our tanking economy. In fact, one could argue that no business has been better prepared to deal with such a climate than Sam Walton's baby. While the CEOs of America's three ailing auto companies flew to Washington from Detroit on individual private jets in late 2008 to beg for bail-out money, and while the head of Citibank obstinately defended his need for a $10 million office makeover at the same time that his company's stock was hemorrhaging, Wal-Mart was conducting business in its usual parsimonious way. After all, this company already required associates traveling across the country to share motel rooms, and then sent those associates into the marketplace with Lilliputian-sized business cards, which at ¼" x 2⅜" seem more appropriate to Business Barbie than to flesh-and-blood adults. Yet Wal-Mart's expertise at going lean and mean has produced results: although its stock has fluctuated about 15 percent for the year, the company's total sales for the fiscal year ending January 31, 2009, rose 7.2 percent to $401.24 billion—especially positive growth considering that sales from almost all other companies fell precipitously.

· · · · · · · · · ·

Still, Wal-Mart, to stay smart, needed to act defensively. In February 2009, just a few days after Duke took the helm, it announced that it was going to streamline operations even more by cutting between 700 and 800 jobs, or about 5 percent of its workers, from the home office, jolting the entire Bentonville community. Most of these positions were in real estate, with others in marketing, support staff, as well as merchandising for Sam's Club.[3] Insiders explain it away as the natural process of weeding out dead weight, which the company attempts every five years or so; even so, hard times create dire consequences for workers who lose jobs.

The *New York Times*, in reporting the cuts, noted that thousands of jobs had recently been eliminated by a number of retailers, and said: "Wal-Mart's cuts are modest compared with those of other chains like Saks, which laid off 9 percent of its work force."[4]

In another ironic retrenchment and reversal, the company, which during the past decade required apparel manufacturers from New York's garment center to either make constant visits or have a permanent presence in Bentonville—one reason for its hearty growth—has decided that, to be more competitive, it would relocate its apparel buyers *from* Bentonville to New York. "That move leaves some 100 apparel vendors that have offices in Bentonville . . . with their pants down," observed *Retailer Daily* a few days later.[5]

The more important question, perhaps, is how—or if—this decision will affect the economy of Bentonville. Indeed, how many apparel buyers and vendors will be closing up their local offices and moving back to their hometown headquarters? And who, if anyone, will be moving here to replace them?

As Wal-Mart Goes, So Goes Bentonville

Driving through the area's subdivisions at random on a surprisingly balmy spring morning, I notice the plummy redbud trees finally beginning to bloom, their rosy clusters peering, like pink halos, through wooded thickets or peeking out from behind a stone cottage here, a clapboard split-level there. Side by side with the prosperity that everyone has come to expect of the area with its grand gated communities and well-landscaped minimansions that house four- and-five-car garages, an abundance of smaller developments tell a different story—the story of hard times. Here, half-built houses sit like half-dressed orphans. In some cases, construction has been abandoned; in others, "for sale" signs punctuate untidy, browned-out lawns—sometimes seven or eight in a development—and empty lots, devoid of foliage, wait, like wallflowers at the prom, to be transformed and beautified.

In Rogers, says Mayor Womack, "the construction industry has all but halted. An inventory of houses is on the market. Subdivisions can't sell lots or build homes because of this inventory. And with the value of these homes deflating, people can't sell them because they owe more than the homes are worth."

"There are still positive things happening here," insists Rich Davis, whose job at the Chamber of Commerce is to help the community view a situation like this through rose-colored glasses. For one, Bentonville has created a land swap deal with the Arkansas National Guard that will bring a one-hundred-thousand-square-foot regional training center to the city. Tentatively scheduled for completion in 2011, this $23 million facility, which will create construction jobs, will eventually house forty full-time employees and five hundred Army reserve units at any given time.

Davis also points to the Crystal Bridges Museum, whose construction continues to move forward, along with the addition of bike and walking paths, as well as the new Children's Museum of Northwest Arkansas, which will be built on the Crystal Bridges property with seed money from the Walton Family Foundation. In addition, there is the now-completed renovation of Bentonville Square and the city's $110 million investment in a street-and-road upgrade. "In that bond issue," he says, "we are building an interchange on the federal highway *without* federal highway assistance. Just that alone will provide jobs."

More good news, he says, is that although Arkansas, like the rest of the country, feels the pinch created by the subprime feeding frenzy, there is still a positive absorption of new vacant houses, at least in Bentonville. "According to the University of Arkansas's Walton School of Business, eighteen months ago we had a five-year surplus of new homes," he says. "That has shrunk down to two years. But I have been speaking to realtors during the past month, and they are seeing an uptick in sales."

Not Ida Fineberg, however. A residential real estate broker, she works with her husband Steve of Steve Fineberg Real Estate, which specializes in commercial properties. "The housing market here has not hit bottom yet. It still seems to be deteriorating," Ida tells me at the end of May. "But once it hits bottom, this area, because of the companies that make their headquarters here and the vendor community, will rebound faster than most. We were among the last to fall into this abyss of slowness." She says that in her own neighborhood in Northwest Arkansas, "We got a terrific deal on our house a year ago. But our neighbor to our right recently bought theirs for $100,000 less. And the neighbor on the left has been foreclosed. Some money is coming into the banks, but it is not coming in fast enough."

The March 2009 report from the Arkansas Realtors Association confirms Fineberg's observations, announcing that sales in Benton County were down 21 percent and in Washington County, home to Springdale and Rogers, a whopping 35 percent. The average home price dropped 10 percent from March 2008 to around $162,000. Kathy Deck, director of the University of Arkansas's Center for Business and Economic Research, noted that prices were back down to 2004 levels and concluded, "So we've seen those gains that were accumulated in the boom evaporating."[6]

Even so, Deck noted, "Anecdotally, we're seeing a number of economic indicators that, if not showing dramatic improvement, certainly are beginning to bottom out." She then added, "I think we're going to continue to see housing struggle, but moving in the right direction."[7]

Most important, Davis says, Bentonville harbors long-term plans for urbanization. "We've renovated the square and brought new businesses to it. And what makes these kinds of new urban settings work is a critical mass of population during the daytime to support these businesses."

That mass is not there yet. But toward that end, the town's planners are considering more multistory, multiple-dwelling buildings, which combine retail commercial space, commercial office space, and condos and lofts. As the baby boom generation continues to age, he suggests, "The boomers, people in my age group, are saying, 'The reason I need to own a home is for the tax benefit,' which is shrinking annually. So my ideal home would be an urban loft that's affordable."

Multicultural Magnets

There is no doubt that Bentonville and its sister communities, Rogers and Springdale, have enjoyed a growing dynamism and prosperity during the past two decades. Traffic is increasingly dense; hospitals are overflowing. And there is still so much demand for luxury services that, to meet requests, Mercy Medical Center, a two-hundred-bed facility in Rogers, which recently moved to a newer, larger campus, still needed to convert semiprivate rooms to private. But without Wal-Mart, Bentonville would most likely be a white, Christian, emphatically homogeneous Ozarks town of little distinction. The area owes its rich diversity primarily to the power of the companies that drive Northwest Arkansas—Wal-Mart, and to a lesser extent, Tyson Foods, J. B. Hunt Trucking, and the myriad construction and trucking companies and meat-packing plants that attract low-skilled workers.

In fact, the rule that seems to hold throughout America is this: corporations that move to small towns draw diversity, especially attracting those workers who are part of the latest immigration waves. And that includes both educated scientific, medical, and technology workers with computer and technical skills—as a number from India, Pakistan, Japan, and China have proven to be—and unskilled workers willing to take menial jobs that most Americans do not want to do. Many migrate from Central and South America, but in recent years political refugees from Somalia and Sudan have arrived on America's shores, and corporations have snapped them up, relieved that they do not have to deal with these workers' immigration status or documentation.

And certainly the greater Bentonville area is not the only cultural magnet or the only exurb that is being enlivened by an influx of ethnic minorities. This has also become true of towns across America. Nowadays unlikely places such as King, Washington; Collin, Texas; Grand Island, Nebraska; Barron, Wisconsin; Carpentersville, Illinois; Postville, Iowa; and Lewiston, Maine, are developing multicultural ghettos and pockets of immigrants from Central and South America, Asia, and Africa, just the way cities such as Chicago, Detroit, and Dallas have in the past. "Racial and ethnic minorities now make up 18.3 percent of nonmetro residents and are geographically dispersed throughout the Nation," noted a U.S. Census Report in February 2007. "Hispanics and Asians are the fastest growing minority groups in the United States as a whole and in nonmetro areas. Their higher growth rates partly result from changes in U.S. immigration laws in the mid-1960s that favored immigration from non-European countries and from a growing demand for low-skill labor."

The 2006 Carsey Institute Reports on Rural America also found a surprising growth and new diversity in our nation's small towns.[8] Noting that rural America suffered a population drain between 1920 and 1960, the study points to a resurgence between 1990 and 2000 that created a migration of more than three million people to America's rural areas. What is critical, and positive, about these new streams of residents is that while whites in their twenties may be leaving these areas, young foreigners and immigrants are moving in, raising families, and infusing their new communities with a welcome energy and dynamism.

The arrival of large numbers of these low-skill immigrants in small towns revamps political and social structures and brings new and often challenging issues to the community regarding language, education, and even, in some cases, public health. For instance, Sasha Chanoff of the International Organization for Migration told the *Atlanta Journal-Constitution* in 2003 that a group of Somali immigrants, who had arrived to work in the meat-packing plants, were so unfamiliar with the modern world that they did not understand basic hygiene concepts and, on first seeing a bathtub, thought it was some type of boat. "They really don't have any exposure to modern development," Chanoff explained as a way of explaining how difficult it had been for the Somalis to adapt and for the community to absorb them. Yet because, as political refugees, they were unencumbered by immigration problems, the Somalis were considered highly desirable workers.

The *Shelbyville Times-Gazette* columnist Brian Mosely, in fact, turned a negative eye on their arrival, observing, "Suddenly introducing a society that is literally hundreds of years behind the times in the ways of hygiene, mannerisms, culture and the treatment of women into twenty-first century America is a recipe for sociological disaster. It is a massive shock to the Somalis and doesn't do the local communities any favors either."[9]

Yet Tyson Foods, which owns a meat-packing plant in Shelbyville, where Somali Muslims now compose an estimated 20 percent of the population, has tried to accommodate them. To make working conditions more amenable and worship easier, Tyson has built an Islamic prayer room on the premises.

Much like Northwest Arkansas, Shelbyville has been working actively to help immigrant groups transition into the community and to protect their rights as well. In spring 2008 the Tennessee Immigrant and Refugee Rights Coalition (TIRRC), a statewide grassroots organization that had been formed in 2001, created a public relations campaign for Shelbyville called the Welcoming Tennessee Initiative. It primarily addressed the white community and its response to the much larger Latino influx. This campaign consisted of billboards strategically placed next to the town highway entrances, which featured smiling, pleasant-looking, and well-dressed members of Shelbyville's Hispanic community alongside the slogan "Like you, we work hard, we pay taxes, and we are people of faith."

The TIRRC has also been working with Somali refugees, many of whom do not speak English, trying to educate them about what police and local community members expect of them. "I think with the Welcoming

Tennessee initiative, our focus here is going to be a great way to really put Shelbyville in the national spotlight," said Catalina Nieto, TIRRC's public awareness coordinator, "and hopefully Shelbyville could become a model for other cities [as to] how our communities really work together to learn about each other and move forward."

The Politics of Fear

It would be reasonable to expect that in the current unstable economic environment, both crime and gang activity in Northwest Arkansas would be increasing, and that such a situation would create a potential tinderbox. Indeed, both Mayor Steve Womack and Police Chief Kathy O'Kelley would have their constituents believe that gangs continue to present a serious community threat. Perhaps they are simply being vigilant. But Frank Head, the director of Immigration Services and Refugee Resettlement for Catholic Charities in Springdale, is highly skeptical. "Talk to O'Kelley or Womack, and you'd think the Bloods and Crips were about to rumble in the streets," he observes, adding that that is not the case.

Al "Papa Rap" Lopez, the student relations coordinator at Springdale High School, has always insisted that the gang issue was primarily a way to harass local Hispanics, especially those who are undocumented. Now he suggests that Rogers disbanded its gang task force in 2008 because there was no need for it.

Rogers's brand-new police chief, Steve Hamilton—tall, slender, bespectacled, and almost totally bald—would seem to agree. At the very least, he appears much more relaxed on the subject than his mayor. "I come from Springfield, Missouri, where they have a *real* gang problem," he tells me as he sits behind his desk in an office so plush that many a bank CEO would covet it. "I was talking to a lieutenant detective from Springfield, and he says that in the last thirty days, they have had eighteen shootings, all gang related. Now *that* is a gang problem. So maybe it's in the definition of what a problem is."

Hamilton sees in Rogers what he calls "anecdotal evidence" about tagging and gang members passing through. "The average person on the street is not going to be victimized by gang violence," he adds. "I was much more concerned last Saturday when a motorcycle gang called the Sons of Silence rode into town for the weekend."

. . . .

A year ago Rogers and Springdale were feeling pressed when some among the Latino population, reacting to the job slowdown in construction and to the growing fear of deportation as a result of Immigration and Customs Enforcement's 287(g) program, simply fled the area, many abandoning homes and splintering families in the process. Their departure, and the initiatives of ICE, have affected local economies and, most especially, businesses such as construction and poultry, the latter which has begun to import low-skilled workers from Puerto Rico, where there are no immigration issues because it is an American territory.

One Puerto Rican, Alexis Quinones, was lured to Springdale by George's Poultry after noticing a recruiting announcement in a Labor Department office. He came here two years ago with twenty-one others from Lauco, which, he says, is known as the land of coffee. "George's gave me a ticket and one month in a motel," he says, and in return he committed to work there for six months, during which time he had to repay his airfare and motel bill. Quinones operated a deboning machine for $8.80 an hour, but after his six months were up, he moved over to Cargill Poultry, another local plant, where he now packs turkey breasts, earning $9.20 an hour. Since ICE has cracked down on the local poultry plants, he says, "Jobs are out there. A lot of Puerto Ricans know it, and they are moving up here to take advantage of the opportunities. As for me, I came here to stay—and that's just what I'm doing."

. . . .

Since 287(g) became operational in October 2007, it has become a lightning rod sparking dissent in the community. Once again, Police Chief O'Kelley and Mayor Womack feel convinced that the program succeeds in apprehending felons. While O'Kelley refuses to offer up any figures, Womack says, "We have deported hundreds of people—my guess is upwards of one thousand. We have a model program, which the ICE people say is doing exactly what it was designed to do. All the people who were deported had law enforcement issues—I'm talking about law enforcement encounters. Every one of them had due process and was under the supervision of ICE. It's not like the city of Rogers decided to make an effort against immigrants. Only actionable intelligence or law enforcement encounters give us proper cause to deal with them."

Advocates for the Latino community, however, reject as nonsense the notion that ICE only pursues felons. "The 287(g) program introduces ICE into the day-to-day working of the city," explains Head, who each week speaks with dozens of desperate undocumented workers on the verge of deportation. "Pairing local police officers with omnipotent ICE officers allows them to pretty much violate the Constitution, in my opinion. That is, they knock on a door, armed with a warrant and looking for a meth dealer, and they go fishing. The person says, 'No, I never heard of Juan Gonzales.' 'But what about *you?*' the policeman asks. 'Do *you* have papers?' If not, these innocent people are detained. It's illegal search-and-seizure. But with Immigration, *nothing* seems to be illegal."

Even the U-visa, a special visa available for victims of domestic abuse, no longer offers a guarantee. Head says, "Now ICE throws the women into jail. It has gotten uglier. The rules keep changing without any public outcry." ICE, he claims, answers to no one. "Ask them who they are arresting. What are the crimes or the conviction rates? Somehow 287(g) is exempt from all accountability," he steams. "ICE says they don't keep statistics. But being required to keep statistics is the law. Why aren't the newspapers screaming about this? It is unconstitutional."

In fact, relations between the police and local Latinos have so disintegrated since the implementation of 287(g) that law enforcement is being compromised. Steve Hamilton, like Kathy O'Kelley, believes his department needs to create more trust with this minority community. In 2008, he points out, thirty-five rapes were reported in Rogers—a disproportionately large number, he says, considering the city's general lack of crime. Still, he observes, "If we do a good job [at building confidence with the Latinos], our crime rate is going to explode. As it now stands, if you're a victim of a crime and are undocumented, you are probably too afraid to report it."

Head agrees that 287(g) has created a severe breach of faith: "No question, undocumented immigrants would have cooperated with the police regarding crime and domestic abuse," he says. "But the police ran away from it."

As if to prove the untrustworthiness of authorities, the local newspaper, one mid-April morning, reports a grisly story, sensationally entitled "Springdale Alien Roundup," as if the immigrants were cattle.[10] The gist of it is that Ana Hart, the immigrants' advocate, having heard about twenty-four undocumented workers whose construction bosses had not paid them for a month and who were living in squalor in two small Springdale houses, called authorities, including ICE. Out of a perhaps-naive humanitarian impulse, Hart had hoped to get help for the immigrants, who were sleeping on filthy mattresses provided by their bosses and had no blankets, heat, or food; nor had they committed any felonies. Instead, all the men, except four who were held as witnesses, were arrested and shipped to various holding jails in Washington County on their way to being deported back to Mexico.

Springdale's police chief refused, as usual, to comment about the case, as she does about all ICE-related activities, but did offer up her support of Hart to the *Arkansas Democrat-Gazette*. "I think those people are being used as slave labor," she said. "On a humanitarian level, we need to go in and help them."

The Hispanic activist Jim Miranda also weighed in publicly. "Something like this sends ripples through the community," he noted. "Those people living in the shadows—those people end up being silent and they don't speak out." [11]

A few days later, Head appears disgusted. He finds ICE's secrecy, compounded by what he sees as local police collaboration, frustrating. "It's a Gestapo system," he says bluntly.

. . . .

Common sense tells us that we need to urgently rethink the Bush-era immigration policies—both those regarding undocumented workers and, as columnists like Thomas Friedman have been pointing out since the publication of his book *The World Is Flat*, students on visas with high-level professional and technical backgrounds and prowess who train at top American universities and are then sent back home, primarily to Asia, to fulfill their promise. Because of our strict immigration laws, many of these young men and women who want to settle here are unable to; as a result, our economy and our businesses, as well as our medical and scientific professions, are unable to benefit from our investment in their brainpower. President Obama has vowed to sharply change America's immigration policies. Administration officials have noted that he plans to recognize millions of illegal immigrants who are already living and working here. Hopefully, he will have the courage, the political capital, and the opportunity to make substantial and meaningful changes. [12]

Meanwhile, the *New York Times*' March 2009 editorial "Who's Running Immigration?" slammed America's long-standing immigration policies, chastising sheriffs around the country who have abused their powers under 287(g)—and backed up the complaints and suspicions of Northwest Arkansas's Hispanic activists. "Americans who might applaud any crackdown on illegal immigrants, particularly in a recession, should know that scattershot raids and rampaging sheriffs are not the answer," the *Times* wrote. "The idea that enforcement alone will eliminate the underground economy is a great delusion. It runs up against the impossible arithmetic of mass expulsion—no conceivable regime of raids will wrench 12 million illegal immigrants from their jobs and homes. The system under which illegal immigrants labor, without hope of assimilation, is not any less broken. A new report from the Government Accountability Office shows that federal oversight of the 287(g) program has been sorely lacking."

The Latino community won a major victory in May 2009 when the Supreme Court ruled that a person who uses false documents cannot be convicted of the crime of "aggravated identity theft" unless it can be proven that he or she knew that the identification number belonged to someone else. Prosecutors have relied on the identity theft law as a tool to prosecute and deport undocumented men and women who have been working here illegally.

The Supreme Court's ruling will eventually target companies who knowingly hire illegal workers, rather than focusing on the workers themselves. Still, Chief O'Kelley sees quite a different set of problems down the line for the American-born children of undocumented parents, many of whom sell their offsprings' identities every day, not understanding the consequences. "But some day these kids are going to grow up and try to get a job and a loan. And they are going to find that their identity has been sold and is being used by somebody else," she says. "Therein is where you will see the true victims and what the situation has cost them."

Night Rider

I am traveling down desolate Central Avenue at midnight on a moonless night, my last in Bentonville. My little car is trying to avoid the shoulder of a poorly lit winding road that, in the process of being widened, has been dug up and narrowed; tonight it is also patchy with orange tape and safety cones. I slow down to negotiate this construction, distracted as well by whirling blue lights that suddenly explode into my rearview mirror. The police? *What and who are they looking for?* I wonder. A siren screams.

Eventually, but not immediately, I pull over to the side of the road. *Do I have a flat tire? A broken brake light?* The cop car, followed by a backup, moves in behind me. I begin to shake. *What have I done?* A young officer, small, with wire-rimmed glasses and skin as fuzzless and pink as a Spaulding rubber ball, peers at me through my open window. He looks no more than eighteen, but he means business. *What have I done?* He orders me to open my door. Why was I driving so slowly, he asks. And why didn't I stop when I saw the car's whirling light? I respond stupidly that I could not remotely imagine that he was signaling me. He regards me as though I were an alien—the kind who descended from outer space—and asks if I have been drinking. No, I reply. But I have just arrived from an alternate universe called New York City, where I do not have a car and do not drive and did not know such a pokey pace on an empty street might land me in the clink.

My heart races as the boy-cop looks through my pocketbook, perhaps for a kilo of marijuana or a fifth of moonshine. "Officer," I say, as calmly as I can muster. "I'm a stranger here. The road is dark and there are no street lights. There is construction to my left and to my right. I am just being cautious."

He is not buying it. He instructs me to get out of my car, to stand behind it on the empty roadside with feet together, and while his three colleagues look on, to follow his finger without moving my head. I do what he requests, my eyes following his finger as it moves three feet to the left of me and then three feet to the right and then to the left again. "You are moving your head," he barks.

Images flash through my mind. I see all the undocumented Latino men and women who have been pulled over to the side of a hundred roads for a hundred minor driving infractions, real or imagined—men and women who were taken into custody and then were never again seen by their families. I am a dark-haired woman, and it is no monumental stretch of the imagination to think that perhaps this officer mistook me for a Latina and wanted to check out *my* documentation.

My knees buckle. I am scared.

But I am also shameless. I may have nothing to worry about, save my snaillike driving, but I apologize sweetly and drop the names of the police chiefs of Bentonville and Rogers. The fuzzless young man and his bristlier companions seem unimpressed, but a moment later they hand me back my belongings and let me go.

As I maneuver my car toward the highway ramp, I think how fitting it is that this scenario, occurring here and now on this ink-black night in Northwest Arkansas, should dramatize so vividly to me how the simple things we take for granted—our documentation, our citizenship, our identity—are, like those famous fictional letters of transit with which Rick buys Ilsa's freedom in *Casablanca*, so unbearably priceless.

Still, what if I had been undocumented? Or if I had left my license at home? Would they have locked me up in a holding cell in a neighboring county? Would I have become one of America's disappeared? Or worse, what might the outcome have been if any of the area's vulnerable undocumented women or their teenage daughters had been stopped instead?

For them, a sordid new nightmare would just be unfolding.

Moving Toward Harmony and Acceptance

In the final analysis, the economy and deep-seated tensions between the area's growing Hispanic population and local law enforcement may be of secondary importance to the real story in Bentonville, which is not about difference or intolerance but about harmony and acceptance in a community that was once emblematic of white Christian uniformity and powerful racist sentiment and separation.

Clearly, the way Bentonville has handled its diversity issues and evolved into a more urban and urbane environment has critical resonance for the rest of small-town America and its growing pains. For its story is the story of revitalization through diversity, immigration, technology, and careful nurturing by the town itself. And Bentonville—*all* of Northwest Arkansas—is important because it has inadvertently become a model for other communities.

The nature of America's relationship with its immigrants has always been a part of our national conversation. In 1907 Mary Antin, a Jewish immigrant from Poland, wrote in her memoir, *The Promised Land*:

What if the creature with the untidy beard carries in his bosom his citizenship papers? What if the cross-legged tailor is supporting a boy in college who is one day going to mend your state constitution for you? What if the rag picker's daughters are hastening over the ocean to teach your children in the public schools? Think, every time you pass the greasy alien on the street, that he was born thousands of years before the oldest native American; and he may have something to communicate to you, when you two shall have learned a common language.[13]

Such thoughtful authors as Antin were not alone in appreciating the value of our immigrant populations. More than half a century ago, two years before he became president, John F. Kennedy pointed out the debt we owe them. "Every ethnic minority, in seeking its own freedom, helped strengthen the fabric of liberty in American life," he wrote in his 1958 essay "A Nation of Immigrants." "Similarly, every aspect of the American economy has profited from the contributions of immigrants."

And, of course, the multiculturalism that we see today in small towns across America was, most importantly, reflected in the stirring result of our 2008 presidential race. In Chicago's Grant Park on the evening of November 4, 2008, people of all backgrounds gathered with shared pride to celebrate that national milestone, the election of our first multicultural president—a man who is black, white, and a self-described "mutt." Barack Obama's win by nearly 200 electoral votes and more than 9 million popular votes offers simple statistical confirmation of the leap that our nation's people have made.

As America prepares to enter the second decade of the twenty-first century, the transformation of Bentonville, formerly the buckle of the Bible Belt, exists as a compelling chronicle, a significant American touchstone in an unlikely locale that carries with it profound hope for our future as a nation.

Although the various ethnic and religious groups of Northwest Arkansas, as predicted by the sociologist Robert Putnam, do not mix and mingle freely as though no differences or distinctions exist, they do, by and large, show each other deep respect and the kind of courteous curiosity that makes for good neighborliness. In this town, transplanted Hispanics and native Arkansans share the same church pews, and Hindus and Jews share the small synagogue, a tiny former Assemblies of God church, as a Sunday school and occasional lecture auditorium when the Hindu swami visits from Dallas.

In this town, when the organization Rebuilding Together in Northwest Arkansas decides to refurbish a local Bentonville home—one of eight in the area—more than seventy-five volunteers show up on a Saturday afternoon to help Carlos Cano, an El Salvadoran immigrant who has recently been disabled by a brain tumor. Thanks to their manpower and donations from Lowe's, which provided insulation, roofing, cabinets, fixtures, and flooring, more than $50,000 worth of improvements are made.

Here, while some Latino children have admittedly had more difficulty assimilating than others, a seventeen-year-old Hispanic-born high school girl can observe proudly, "I think everyone has infinitely more similarities than differences. People here are surprisingly accepting. I know Indians and Americans, Spanish and Chinese. My boyfriend is blond and blue-eyed, my best friend is Guatemalan, and everyone falls somewhere in between."

And here, too, the Hindus, Christians, and Muslims of Wal-Mart, Tyson, and other local companies can go out onto the makeshift cricket field of a local park, crack the bat, and kick up some dirt while playing friendly matches. (In fact, Wal-Mart's Muslim community is growing so steadily that in early 2009 the Bentonville Muslims moved their mosque from the tiny house they had been renting to another double its size. "We were starting to violate local fire codes," says Zakir Syed, adding that now sometimes sixty people show up for evening services.)

It is also a point of pride that the town square celebrates both Christmas and Hannukah without incident. When Bentonville first hung Hannukah lights in the form of an oversized menorah and six-pointed Star of David in front of the Bentonville courthouse during the 2004 holiday season, any white supremacist or garden-variety anti-Semite could have pulled them down, written lurid slogans on the facade, or even marched on the square, like the Ku Klux Klan a mere decade earlier. But no one did.

When the community instituted its first Multicultural Festival, with booths explaining Islam, Hinduism, and Judaism, unpleasant incidents or boycotts could have occurred, but there was nothing of the sort. Rather, families of all ethnicities and denominations crowded into the square to sample food, listen to music, and expose their children to new cultures.

Bentonville, and most of Northwest Arkansas, serves as an exemplary community model. And the stories of its immigrants who made good in either grand or modest ways should make America proud. They not only worked hard, they were also helped by the trust of other Americans, who enabled them to succeed. Fadil Bayyari, for instance, was encouraged by a wealthy Wal-Mart store manager; Cesar Vargas, by a seasoned house-painter who shared with him his exacting techniques.

When towns function well and long-time citizens help newcomers thrive, these newcomers feel good about where and how they live—and they give back. One may become a state senator, as Antin suggests, a governor (think California), a janitor, or a builder. In Bayyari's case, he felt that his community had treated him so well on his journey to prosperity that he built parks and schools, churches, mosques, and shuls. In the process, the people of Northwest Arkansas and, by extension, America itself, became the beneficiaries, not just of Bayyari's generosity but of his success.

"I'm a conservative person. I try to look at people by their actions and their hearts rather than what language they speak," says Springdale's mayor, Doug Sprouse, who admits to being suspicious of messages about strength in diversity. "That rubs me the wrong way," he says. "I think our strength is in our unity. When diverse people unite around a purpose and a cause, regardless of where we're from, that's a good thing and moves us in the right direction." For him, as for Bayyari, that cause, of course, is to make Springdale the best place it can be. "The need for unity transcends whether a community is defined as diverse or not," he observes.

One woman who grew up in Bentonville characterizes the influx of ethnicities and religions as a source of energy and vitality: "This town used to be like white bread—nice and comfortable, but terribly dull. Now there's a dynamism here that makes life better and more exciting."

In late April, a few days after I leave the area, the Multicultural Festival joins forces with the first Farmer's Market of the year, producing an event that takes place on Bentonville Square and spills out onto surrounding streets. "What impresses me is the amount of change in this area," observes Syed, who has lived here since 2004. "I love the idea of diversity. You learn so much from each other's culture. As an Indian, the reason for my success in life is what I found taking the best things from Indian culture *and* American culture. It's like a big buffet table—you can eat whatever you want."

It is precisely this celebration of individual cultures in harmonious concert with the values of American life that strengthens and enriches not just our communities but the entire fabric of our nation.

Acknowledgments

. . . .

First, I would like to express my heartfelt thanks to the people of Northwest Arkansas who welcomed me into their homes and lives, telling me their stories with openness and trust. I feel fortunate to have made their acquaintance and, in many cases, wonderful friendships as well.

The point of diversity is to assimilate and to break down racial and ethnic barriers. Still, I am grateful to people in the many Bentonville communities for sharing, with honesty, their views, their dreams, and their discomforts or feelings of separateness. In the African American community, Shirley and Coleman Peterson and their children, Rana Peterson and Collin Peterson offered up rich and thoughtful observations. So, too, did Perrion Hurd; Emerson and Melanie Goodwin; Jessie Bryant; Moses Cooper; Curtis Smith; and, especially, Leatrice Gloria Robinson Stewart, her son, Carl Stewart, and his son, Ron Stewart.

In the Hindu community, I am indebted to B.K. Vasan, former president of the Hindu Association of Bentonville, and Subhir Katke, his vice president, who were kind enough to make introductions to Ajaydev Nallur, his wife, Subha, and their bright and lively daughters, Saranya and Varenya; to Murthy Kolluru and Padmaja Voosa Kolluru; and to Balu and Nirmala Kulkarni and Nirmala's mother, Parvathi Dugganapalli.

I am obliged to my new friend Al "Papa Rap" Lopez, who tirelessly introduced me to members of the Hispanic community of Northwest Arkansas and let me tag along with him to various diversity events and celebrations. Also, my sincerest thanks to the extraordinary Cesar and Esther Vargas and their children, Nataly, Frank, and Andrew Deeter for sharing their stories with me, and to Ana and Magda Camacho, Ray Hernandez, Carlos Amargós, and Margarita Solorzano. Also, many thanks to the most articulate of activists, Jim Miranda; Alejandro Aviles, Hispanic outreach coordinator of Legal Aid of Arkansas; Ana Hart, executive director, and Val Gonzalez, associate director, of Just Communities; and Moses Cooper. Thanks to Gloria and Pasquale Caldera, to the gentle and brave Ahidee Noriega and her son Noel, to Alexis Quinones, and to Lucy Daniel and Jason Garcia. And to the wonderful Bonilla brood—Sal, Ruth, and their children, Krist, Daisy, and Eric.

An article in the *New York Times* by Michael Barbaro, "The Wal-Mart Jews," offered me my first inspiration for this book. I would like to thank Etz Chaim's past presidents, Betsy Rosen and David Hoodis, as well as David's wife, Winnie; current president, Tom Douglass and his wife, Robyn; and Rabbi Jack Zanerhaft and cantorial soloist Debbye Zanerhaft for welcoming me to my first Bentonville Hanukkah, and for including me in subsequent Passovers and Yom Kippurs. My gratitude also extends to Etz Chaim members Marcy and Scott Winchester and their son Andrew; Betty Goldstein, Audrey Levin, Steve and Ida Fineberg, Yoni and Bart Wakefield, Steve Friedman, and, most especially, Paul and Carol Stuckey—all who provided thoughtful observations that helped me immeasurably. In the Jewish community Rabbi Mendel Greisman and his wife, Dobie, welcomed me to their Shabbas table, and Lee Paull also gave of his time and opinions. I appreciate, too, the scholarly guidance of Stuart Rockoff of the Institute of Southern Jewish Life in Jackson, Mississippi, and Rabbi Debra Lee Kassoff, as well as the compassionate conversation of Ralph Nesson. Thanks to Sylvia Greif for her recollections of growing up in Helena and to Myron Brody of the University of Arkansas. And most special thanks to Sheldon and Nicole Hirsch—you know who you are—for your friendship and soul-searching honesty.

The local community of Northwest Arkansas has been accessible and tremendously accommodating. Thanks to Bentonville High School personnel for setting up a roundtable for me with a group of impressive young students. To Edith and Gary Harvey, Pastor Roger Joslin, Blake Clardy, and Kathy Deck of the University of Arkansas Business School, as well as Stephanie Medford and Amanda Echegoyen, community outreach coordinator of the Jones Center, and Donna Myers. In Bentonville, to the warm and welcoming Debbie Matteri of In Season dress shop. To Perry Stamps of Peter Pan Dry Cleaners, to Daniella Fusco Alcaro. And to John Swearingen, Harley Mosher, and Gary Townzen of Townzen Barber Shop in Rogers.

In the Marshallese community, I would, foremost, like to thank the inimitable and totally original Saimon Milne, a security guard at the Jones Center, and his daughter Selena. My gratitude also extends to Albious Latior, Carmen Chong Gum, the Marshallese outreach coordinator, and Maribel Childress, principal of Monitor Elementary School, for her insights about the Marshall Islands.

Chace Smith, Greg Justins, and Jan Saumweber represented the Mormon community with charm and intelligence. I only wish I had had the time to do them justice.

The Muslim community welcomed me warmly as well. My thanks, especially, and my admiration to Fadil Bayyari, who was unfailingly generous with his time, his thoughts about the immigrant experience, and his contacts; to his wife, Lori, for her frankness. To the lovely Mahfuza Akhtar for her graciousness and dynamic recollections. Also, thanks to Zakir Syed, Humera Khan, Bilques Khod, Mason Hiba, Teguh Sridjajamerta, and Issa Abboud for their confidences and stories.

Northwest Arkansas's elected officials and law enforcement folks not only made themselves available but also offered up interesting facts and points of view about their community. I am grateful to former Bentonville mayor Terry Coberly and her husband, Jody, and to Kathy O'Kelley, police chief of Springdale, and Steve Womack, mayor of Rogers, for being straight shooters, helpful with both information and contacts, and fearless in their own points of view. Also, Steve Hamilton, police chief of Rogers, and James Allen, police chief of Bentonville. Ed Clifford, president of the Bentonville/Bella Vista Chamber of Commerce, and Rich Davis, the chamber's impressively knowledgeable and patient vice president of economic development. To Bentonville's Mayor Bob McCaslin; Springdale's Mayor Doug Sprouse and city attorney Jeff Harper; Dr. Gary Compton, Bentonville's superintendent of schools; and Andy Lee, former Benton County sheriff. To Lieutenant Mike Johnson of the Rogers Police Department; Randy Capps of the Urban Institute; Charles Kester of the Kester Law Firm; and Scott Hardin of the Arkansas Economic Development Commission.

I hold dear the hospitality extended to me by Homer and Dorothy Smith, and I thank Homer for so generously inviting me to share his weekly coffee dates with the old-time Springdale truckers, Carroll Crisler, Bobby Eldridge, Floyd Collins, Roy Anderson, and Lenny Brobst, who all had amazing stories with which to regale me. Also, I extend my thanks to those glorious daughters of the Dust Bowl, Peggy Banks, Geneva Mason, Marie Buell, and Nadine Hitt, with whom I spoke at Carol Girth's Shear Beauty Salon, in the shopping center near the Bentonville Square.

My thanks, too, to Marie Demeroukas, the photo archivist at the Shiloh Museum of Ozark History; Dr. Gaye Bland at the Rogers Historical Museum; Geoffrey Stark at the University of Arkansas Special Collections; Kent Marts at the *Benton County Daily Record*; and Johnny Haney for dipping into his private photo archive for me. I appreciated the enthusiasm and help of Sue Ann Pekel at the Bentonville Public Library. And thanks to the Embassy Suites Hotel in Rogers for its kind support in providing me a home away from home during my many visits. And to Larry Ash, the first person I met in Bentonville, for his tour around town, his smart suggestions, and his photos.

Most especially, my deepest gratitude to Lucille Rhodes, my longtime friend, for reading through the entire manuscript and offering up timely and thoughtful advice; to Arline Bronzaft for her sharp and insightful comments at both the start and the end of this project; to Susie and Ted Hoeller, whose excellent suggestions, observations, and helpful little news packets from Northwest Arkansas made my job much easier; to Joy Gould Boyum for her perceptive reads and wise assessments, as always; and to Jan Rosenberg Siegel for her encouragement and guidance. Thanks, too, to Sarah Sumler for research assistance and to Jacqueline Goldenberg, Fred Siegel, Ron Arias, Richard Aborn, and Judith Adler Hellman for their support; and to Ron Reed, whom I had the good fortune to meet at the 2006 Mid-Atlantic Popular American Culture Association Conference and who helped point me on my road to Bentonville.

And, of course, to Ryan Fischer-Harbage, my agent, for his unflagging belief in this project.

Finally, I would like to recognize the City University of New York for granting me a PSC-CUNY 39 Research Award and to thank Lehman College for a 2008 George N. Shuster Fellowship and two Faculty Development Research Grants to allow me time and travel to work on this project. All were much needed and appreciated.

Notes

· · · · · · · · · ·

INTRODUCTION

1. When *Fortune* magazine published the rankings of America's largest corporations on April 19, 2009, Exxon Mobil, with revenues of $442 billion in 2008, replaced Wal-Mart as number one. Wal-Mart, which had been at the top of the rankings for six consecutive years, had revenues of $405 billion. While Exxon Mobil profited from the recent spike in oil prices, Wal-Mart suffered from the recession, although to a lesser degree than most retailers. CNNMoney.com, "Fortune 500 2009," May 4, 2009, http://money.cnn.com/magazines/fortune/fortune500/2009/full_list/.
2. Sam Walton with John Huey, *Sam Walton: Made in America* (New York: Doubleday, 1992), 32.
3. Doris and William Lewis are pseudonyms for a Fayetteville couple.

1. A BLACK MAN REDEFINES A WHITE COMPANY

1. Don Soderquist, *The Wal-Mart Way* (Nashville: T. Nelson, 2005), 45, quoted in Nelson Lichtenstein, "Geography and Gender: The Origins and Reproduction of Wal-Mart's Managerial Culture" (speech, Yale Law School, New Haven, CT, February 6, 2006).

2. Nelson Lichtenstein, "Wal-Mart: A Template for Twenty-First-Century Capitalism," in *Wal-Mart: The Face of Twenty-First-Century Capitalism*, ed. Nelson Lichtenstein (New York: New Press, 2006), 18.

3. Liza Featherstone, *Selling Women Short: The Landmark Battle for Workers' Rights at Wal-Mart"* (New York: Basic Books, 2005), 100–101.

4. According to the 1990 U.S. Census, Bentonville had a total population of 10,975, only 27 of whom were black. In comparison, the black population of the state was 373,912, out of a total state population of 2,350,725, with the densest populations of African Americans on the eastern and southern borders and in the Little Rock area.

5. John F. Bradbury Jr. and Richard W. Hatcher III, "Civil War in the Ozarks," *OzarksWatch* 4, no. 4 (Spring 1991); 5, no. 1 (Summer 1991), http://thelibrary.springfield.missouri.org/lochist/periodicals/ozarkswatch/ow404e.htm; James A. Holmes, *A History of Ozark County 1841–1991* (Gainesville, MO: Ozark County Genealogical and Historical Society, 1991).

6. James W. Loewen, *Sundown Towns: A Hidden Dimension of American Racism* (New York: New Press, 2005), 95.

7. Information obtained from the 1890 U.S. Census.

8. *The Encyclopedia of Arkansas History and Culture*, s.v. "Sundown Towns" (by James Loewen), www.encyclopediaofarkansas.net/encyclopedia/entry-detail.aspx?search=1&entryID=3658 (accessed July 6, 2009).

9. Pseudonym given by the author.

2. A MUSLIM PHILANTHROPIST CHAMPIONS THE JEWS

1. Sam Walton with John Huey, *Sam Walton: Made in America* (New York: Doubleday, 1992), 32.

2. Ibid, 36.

3. Ibid.

4. Pew Research Center, *Muslim Americans: Middle Class and Mostly Mainstream*, May 22, 2007, http://people-press.org/report/?reportid=329.

5. Ibid.

3. A SHUL IS BORN

1. The family has asked to remain pseudonymous.

2. John Henley Jr., "Rogers Officials Ask for Services to Stop," *Morning News* (Fayetteville, AR), October 21, 2007.

3. Carolyn Gray LeMaster, *A Corner of the Tapestry: A History of the Jewish Experience in Arkansas, 1820s–1990s* (Fayetteville: University of Arkansas Press, 1994), 34.

4. Ibid, 100.

5. Samantha Friedman, "Jewish Camp Scholarships Are Offered," *Arkansas Democrat-Gazette*, April 18, 2009.

4. A HINDU FAMILY'S DELICATE BALANCE

1. Dan Hurley, "Divorce Rate: It's Not as High as You Think," *New York Times*, April 19, 2005.

5. A MARSHALLESE SECURITY GUARD "TALKS STORY"

1. Eleanor Evans, "Minority Enrollment Figures Increase at NWACC," *Benton County Daily Record* (Fayetteville, AR), October 14, 2008.

2. John Lloyd, "Study Paints Bleak Picture of Diversity," *Financial Times* (London), October 8, 2006.

3. Ron Wood, "Marshallese Gather to Celebrate," *Morning News*, May 24, 2008.

6. OF BUYERS AND SELLERS

1. Nelson Lichtenstein, "Wal-Mart: A Template for Twenty-First-Century Capitalism," in *Wal-Mart: The Face of Twenty-First-Century Capitalism*, ed. Nelson Lichtenstein (New York: New Press, 2006), 17.

2. Ibid.

3. Ibid.

4. Ibid, 18.

5. Jeff M. Sellers, "Deliver Us from Wal-Mart?" *Christianity Today*, April 22, 2005.

6. Paul Davis, "Why Christian Retail Book Market Self-Help Books Get Attention of Wal-Mart, Target & Grocery Stores," EzineArticles, June 13, 2008, www.ezinearticles.com/?Why-Christian-Retail-Book-Market-Self-Help-Books-Get-Attention-of-Wal-Mart,-Target-and-Grocery-Stores&id=1247852.

7. Hollywood, Florida, resident Jay Richitelli filed suit against Wal-Mart on July 6, 2008, accusing the company of negligence and failure to warn in light of multiple snake attacks in its Florida garden centers.

Wal-Mart, while unwilling to discuss the suit, said through a spokes-woman, "The safety of our customers is always the top priority." Jon Burstein, "Snakebite Sparks Lawsuit Against Wal-Mart," *Miami Herald*, February 16, 2009. The family of Jdimytai Damour, a guard who was trampled to death by a bargain-hunting crowd at the Wal-Mart in Valley Stream, Long Island, on Black Friday, November 28, 2008, accused the company of providing inadequate security at the front entrance during the store's opening moments and filed a wrongful-death lawsuit. In May 2009 Wal-Mart—while refusing to admit any wrongdoing—agreed to increase its future post-Thanksgiving crowd-control efforts in its ninety-two New York stores, to donate $1.5 million to Nassau County social service programs, and to hire local high school students. In addition, the company established a $400,000 compensation fund to help repay the expenses of those who were injured in the stampede. The guard's family, through an attorney, announced that it would nevertheless proceed with its lawsuit.

8. A pseudonym for an ex-Wal-Mart vendor who requested anonymity.
9. Nelson Lichtenstein, interview in "Is Wal-Mart Good for America?" *Frontline*, PBS, November 16, 2004.
10. A pseudonym for an ex-Wal-Mart vendor who requested anonymity.

7. BENTONVILLE'S EX-MAYOR, THE BOOM TOWN, AND THE DAUGHTERS OF THE DUST BOWL

1. J. Dickson Black, *History of Benton County* (Little Rock, AR: Black, 1975), 265.
2. Downtown Bentonville, Inc., "Economic Development and Planning," www.downtownbentonville.org/planning.
3. Paul L. Caron, "Median U.S. Gross Income: $61,500," TaxProf Blog, February 29, 2008, http://taxprof.typepad.com/taxprof_blog/2008/02/median-us-gross.html.
4. Arkansas Realtors Association, "Summary of January 2008 Housing Market Report," March 2008.
5. Kim Souza, "Northwest Arkansas Building Slowdown Continues," *Morning News*, June 11, 2008.
6. Stacey Roberts, "Economy's Low Point Looming, Construction Conference Hears," *Arkansas Democrat-Gazette*, February 18, 2009.
7. Kim Souza, "Home Prices Sink Lower," *Morning News*, April 1, 2009.

8. David Smith, "Severity of Drop in Home Sales Ebbs," *Arkansas Democrat-Gazette*, November 14, 2008.
9. Ibid.
10. Amanda O'Toole, "Crystal Bridges Case Sheds Light on Contributions," *Arkansas Democrat-Gazette*, August 27, 2008.

8. A TRUCKER IN "CHICKENDALE"

1. Gary Rivlin, "Seeing Google with the Eyes of Forest Gump," *New York Times*, August 10, 2004.
2. Tyson Foods Web site, www.tyson.com.
3. Ibid.
4. David Barboza, "Tyson Foods Indicted in Plan to Smuggle Illegal Workers," *New York Times*, December 20, 2001.
5. Peter Rousmaniere, "The Tyson Foods Illegal Immigrant Case: Past and Present," Working Immigrants blog, July 3, 2009, www.workingimmigrants.com/2006/04/the_tyson_foods_illegal_immigr.html.
6. Michael Wines, "Russia's Latest Export: Bad Jokes About U.S. Chickens," *New York Times*, March 2, 2002.
7. United Food and Commercial Workers International Union, "Injury and Injustice—America's Poultry Industry," www.ufcw.org/press_room/fact_sheets_and_backgrounder/poultryindustry_.cfm.
8. David Barboza, "Tyson Foods Indicted in Plan to Smuggle Illegal Workers," *New York Times*, December 20, 2001.
9. Joseph Rosenbloom, "Victims in the Heartland: How Immigration Policy Affects Us All," *American Prospect*, June 30, 2003, www.prospect.org/cs/articles?article=victims_in_the_heartland.
10. Melinda Ammann, "Breast Men," *Reason*, July 2002, www.reason.com/news/show/28480.html.

9. THE MAYOR OF ROGERS TAKES ON UNDOCUMENTED WORKERS

1. "Between 1990 and 2000, the native-born population grew 12 percent; between 2000 and 2005, it did not grow at all. From 1990 to 2000, the number of native workers in manufacturing fell by 9,000, while the number of immigrants rose by 12,000. Manufacturing, especially poultry and other food processing, employed the most immi-

grants—42 percent in 2000." Winthrop Rockefeller Foundation, news release, April 3, 2007.

2. Erica L. Green, "Partnership with ICE a Hot Ticket for Local Law Enforcement," Medill Reports Washington, December 11, 2008.

3. Dr. Gaye Bland (director, Rogers Historical Museum), in conversation with author.

10. INCIDENT AT BENTONVILLE HIGH

1. The Bentonville High School Handbook, in its section on antigang policy, defines a gang as "any group of two or more persons whose purposes include the commission of illegal acts, or acts in violation of disciplinary rules of the school district." The policy goes on to describe "gang related or gang-like activity" as including not only violence but also wearing clothing or symbols "showing membership or affiliation with any gang." Such behavior also extends to graffiti-painting and gestures or handshakes that might suggest gang affiliation.

2. Robert D. Putnam, *Bowling Alone: The Collapse and Revival of American Community* (New York: Simon & Schuster, 2000), 312.

3. Michelle Bradford, "Rogers: Gangs Under Scrutiny," *Arkansas Democrat-Gazette*, March 31, 2008.

4. Robin Mero, "Attorney: Witness in 'Strange but Fortunate' Situation," *Morning News*, July 6, 2008.

5. Robin Mero, "Prosecutor Drops Charges Against Hernandez," *Morning News*, July 15, 2008.

6. Robin Mero, "Criminal Gangs Influence Locals," *Morning News*, March 29, 2008.

7. Section 5-74-103 of the Arkansas Penal Code defines a gang as: "Any group of three (3) or more individuals who commit a continuing series of two (2) or more predicate criminal offenses undertaken in concert with each other."

8. Robin Mero, "Officers Combat Gang Growth," *Morning News*, March 29, 2008.

11. SPRINGDALE'S TOUGH-AS-NAILS LADY POLICE CHIEF

1. Richard Massey, "Filthy House Leads to Charges for 9," *Arkansas Democrat-Gazette*, November 10, 2008.

2. Ibid.

EPILOGUE

1. Stephanie Rosenbloom, "Sales Fall Sharply for Retailers Not Named Wal-Mart," *New York Times*, February 6, 2009; Stephanie Rosenbloom "Retailers Report Another Drop in March," *New York Times*, April 10, 2009.

2. David Nassar, "Will Mike Duke Help Wal-Mart Workers Live Better?" *Huffington Post*, February 4, 2009, www.huffingtonpost.com/david-nassar/will-mike-duke-help-wal-m_b_163919.html.

3. In March 2009, the corporation closed an optical lab in Ohio, leaving approximately 650 more workers unemployed.

4. Stephanie Rosenbloom, "Wal-Mart to Cut 700 to 800 Jobs at Headquarters," *New York Times*, February 11, 2009.

5. "Wal-Mart's Apparel Operations Move to New York," *Retailer Daily*, February 12, 2009, www.retailerdaily.com/entry/11396/wal-marts-apparel-operations-move-to-new-york/.

6. David Smith, "March Home Sales in State Down 20%," *Arkansas Democrat-Gazette*, May 8, 2009.

7. Ibid.

8. The study was funded by the Annie E. Carsey Foundation and the W. K. Kellogg Foundation.

9. Brian Mosely, "Opinion: Somalians Respond Poorly to Local Hospitality," *Shelbyville Times-Gazette*, December 29, 2007.

10. Adam Wallworth, "Springdale Alien Roundup Raises Questions," *Arkansas Democrat-Gazette*, April 13, 2009.

11. Ibid.

12. Julia Preston, "Obama to Push Immigration Bill as One Priority," *New York Times*, April 9, 2009.

13. Mary Antin, *The Promised Land* (New York: Houghton Mifflin Company, 1912).

Bibliography

··········

Black, J. Dickson. *History of Benton County: 1836–1936*. Little Rock, AR: Black, 1975.

Bloom, Stephen G. *Postville: A Clash of Cultures in Heartland America*. New York: Harcourt, 2000.

Collins, Marilyn H. *Rogers: The Town the Frisco Built*. Rogers, AR: Rogers Historical Museum, 2002.

Dicker, John. *The United States of Wal-Mart*. New York: Jeremy P. Tarcher/ Penguin Books, 2005.

Doob, Christopher Bates. *Race, Ethnicity, and the American Urban Mainstream*. Boston: Allyn & Bacon, 2005.

Ehrenreich, Barbara. *Nickel and Dimed: On (Not) Getting By in America*. New York: Henry Holt, 2008.

Evans, Eli N. *The Lonely Days Were Sundays: Relfections of a Jewish Southerner*. Jackson: University Press of Mississippi, 1993.

Evans, Eli N. *The Provincials: A Personal History of Jews in the South*. Rev. ed. New York: Free Press, 1997.

Featherstone, Liza. *Selling Women Short: The Landmark Battle for Workers' Rights at Wal-Mart*. New York: Basic Books, 2005.

Fishman, Charles. *The Wal-Mart Effect: How the World's Most Powerful Company Really Works—and How It's Transforming the American Economy*. New York: Penguin, 2006.

Hellman, Judith Adler. *The World of Mexican Migrants: The Rock and the Hard Place*. New York: New Press, 2008.

Hoeller, Susie L. *Impasse: Border Walls or Welcome the Stranger*. Bentonville, AR: Hoeller/Booklocker.com, 2008.

Kidder, Tracy. *Home Town*. New York: Washington Square Press/Pocket Books, 1999.

Kugelmass, Jack. *The Miracle at Intervale Avenue: The Story of a Jewish Congregation in the South Bronx*. New York: Columbia University Press, 1996.

LeBlanc. Adrian Nicole. *Random Family: Love, Drugs, Trouble and Coming of Age in the Bronx*. New York: Scribner, 2003.

LeMaster, Carolyn Gray. *A Corner of the Tapestry: A History of the Jewish Experience in Arkansas, 1820s–1990s*. Fayetteville: University of Arkansas Press, 1994.

Lichtenstein, Nelson, ed. *Wal-Mart: The Face of Twenty-First Century Capitalism*. New York: New Press, 2006.

Loewen, James W. *Sundown Towns: A Hidden Dimension of American Racism*. New York: New Press, 2005.

Lynd, Robert S., and Helen Merrell Lynd. *Middletown: A Study in Modern American Culture*. New York: Harcourt Brace Jovanovich, 1957.

Millard, Ann V., and Jorge Chapa. *Apple Pie and Enchiladas: Latino Newcomers in the Rural Midwest*. Austin: University of Texas Press, 2004.

Myerhoff, Barbara. *Number Our Days*. New York: Touchstone Books/Simon & Shuster, 1978.

Putnam, Robert D. *Bowling Alone: The Collapse and Revival of American Community*. New York: Simon & Schuster, 2000.

Putnam, Robert D., and Lewis M. Feldstein, with Don Cohen. *Better Together: Restoring the American Community*. New York: Simon & Schuster, 2003.

Salamon, Sonya. *Newcomers to Old Towns: Suburbanization of the Heartland*. Chicago: University of Chicago Press. 2003.

Schlosser, Eric. *Fast Food Nation: The Dark Side of the All-American Meal*. New York: Harper Perennial, 2004.

Soderquist, Don. *The Wal-Mart Way: The Inside Story of the Success of the World's Largest Company*. Nashville: T. Nelson, 2005.

Walton, Sam, with John Huey. *Sam Walton, Made in America: My Story*. New York: Doubleday, 1992.

Index

· · · · · · · · · ·